# STATUTORY SUPPLEMENT TO
# LABOR LAW IN THE CONTEMPORARY WORKPLACE
## Second Edition

■ ■ ■

by

### Kenneth G. Dau-Schmidt
*Willard and Margaret Carr Professor of Labor and Employment Law*
*Indiana University–Bloomington, School of Law*

### Martin H. Malin
*Professor of Law and Director of the Institute for Law and the Workplace*
*Chicago-Kent College of Law, Illinois Institute of Technology*

### Roberto L. Corrada
*Professor of Law and Mulligan Burleson Chair in Modern Learning*
*University of Denver, Sturm College of Law*

### Christopher David Ruiz Cameron
*Professor of Law*
*Southwestern Law School/Los Angeles*

### Catherine L. Fisk
*Chancellor's Professor of Law*
*University of California, Irvine, School of Law*

for
**THE LABOR LAW GROUP**

**AMERICAN CASEBOOK SERIES®**

WEST
ACADEMIC
PUBLISHING

Mat #41497214

*American Casebook Series* is a trademark registered in the U.S. Patent and Trademark Office.

© 2009 By THE LABOR LAW GROUP
© 2014 By THE LABOR LAW GROUP
    444 Cedar Street, Suite 700
    St. Paul, MN 55101
    1-877-888-1330

West, West Academic Publishing, and West Academic are trademarks of West Publishing Corporation, used under license.

Printed in the United States of America

**ISBN:** 978-0-314-28938-4

# FOREWORD

## THE LABOR LAW GROUP

The Labor Law Group had its origins in the desire of scholars to produce quality casebooks for instruction in labor and employment law. Over the course of its existence, the hallmarks of the Group have been collaborative efforts among scholars, informed by skilled practitioners, under a cooperative nonprofit trust in which royalties from past work finance future meetings and projects.

At the 1946 meeting of the Association of American Law Schools, Professor W. Willard Wirtz delivered a compelling paper criticizing the labor law coursebooks then available. His remarks so impressed those present that the Labor Law Roundtable of the Association organized a general conference on the teaching of labor law to be held in Ann Arbor in 1947. The late Professor Robert E. Mathews served as coordinator for the Ann Arbor meeting, and several conferees agreed to exchange proposals for sections of a new coursebook that would facilitate training exemplary practitioners of labor law. Beginning in 1948, a preliminary mimeographed version was used in seventeen schools; each user supplied comments and suggestions for change. In 1953, a hardcover version was published under the title *Labor Relations and the Law*. The thirty-one "cooperating editors" were so convinced of the value of multicampus collaboration that they gave up any individual claims to royalties. Instead, those royalties were paid to a trust fund to be used to develop and "provide the best possible materials" for training students in labor law and labor relations. The Declaration of Trust memorializing this agreement was executed November 4, 1953, and remains the Group's charter.

The founding committee's hope that the initial collaboration would bear fruit has been fulfilled. Under Professor Mathews's continuing leadership, the Group's members produced *Readings on Labor Law* in 1955 and *The Employment Relation and the Law* in 1957, edited by Robert Mathews and Benjamin Aaron. Charles A. Reynard followed Professor Mathews and briefly served as chair of the Group until his death in 1959. A second edition of *Labor Relations and the Law* appeared in 1960, with Benjamin Aaron and Donald H. Wollett as coeditors of the book and cochairs of the Group, and a third edition was published in 1965, with Jerre S. Williams as Group chair and editor. (Williams was later a judge of the United States Court of Appeals for the Fifth Circuit and the first chairman of the Administrative Conference of the United States.)

In June 1969 the Group, now chaired by William P. Murphy, sponsored a conference to reexamine the labor law curriculum. Practitioners and full-time teachers, including nonmembers as well as members of the Group, attended the meeting, held at the University of Colorado. In meetings that followed the conference, the Group decided to reshape its work substantially. It restructured itself into ten task forces, each assigned a unit of no more than two hundred pages on a discrete topic such as employment discrimination or union-member relations. An individual teacher could then choose two or three of these units as the material around which to build a particular course. This multiunit approach dominated the Group's work throughout much of the 1970s under Professor Murphy and his successor as chair, Herbert L. Sherman, Jr.

As the 1970s progressed and teachers refined their views about what topics to include and how to address them, some units were dropped from the series while others increased in scope and length. Under Professor Sherman's leadership, the Group planned a new series of six enlarged books to cover the full range of topics taught by labor and employment law teachers. Professor James E. Jones, Jr., was elected chair in 1978, and he shepherded to completion the promised set of six full-size, independent casebooks. The Group continued to reevaluate its work and eventually decided that it was time to convene another conference of law teachers.

In 1984 the Group, now chaired by Robert Covington, sponsored another general conference to discuss developments in the substance and teaching of labor and employment law, this time in Park City, Utah. Those discussions and a subsequent working session led to the conclusion that the Group should devote principal attention to three new conventional length coursebooks, one devoted to employment discrimination, one to union-management relations, and one to the individual employment relationship. In addition, work was planned on more abbreviated coursebooks to serve as successors to the Group's earlier works covering public employment bargaining and labor arbitration.

In 1989, with Alvin Goldman as chair, the Group met in Breckenridge, Colorado, to assess its most recent efforts and develop plans for the future. In addition to outlining new coursebook projects, the Group discussed ways to assist teachers of labor and employment law in their efforts to expand conceptual horizons and perspectives. In pursuit of the latter goals it cosponsored, in 1992, a conference held at the University of Toronto, Faculty of Law, at which legal and nonlegal specialists examined alternative models of corporate governance and their impact on workers.

When Robert J. Rabin became chair in 1996, the Group and a number of invited guests met in Tucson, Arizona, to celebrate the imminent fiftieth anniversary of the Group. The topics of discussion included the impact of the global economy and of changing forms of representation on the teaching of labor and employment law, and the impact of new technologies of electronic publishing on the preparation of teaching materials. The Group honored three of its members who had been present at the creation of the Group, Willard Wirtz, Ben Aaron, and Clyde Summers. The Group next met in Scottsdale, Arizona, in December 1999, to discuss the production of materials that would more effectively bring emerging issues of labor and employment law into the classroom. Among the issues discussed were integration of international and comparative materials into the labor and employment curriculum and the pedagogical uses of the World Wide Web.

Laura J. Cooper became chair of the Group in July 2001. In June 2003, the Group met in Alton, Ontario, Canada. The focus there was on "labor law on the edge"—looking at doctrinal synergies between workplace law and other legal and social-science disciplines—and "workers on the edge"—exploring the legal issues of highly compensated technology workers, vulnerable immigrant employees, and unionized manufacturing employees threatened by foreign competition. The Group also heard a report from its study of the status of the teaching of labor and employment law in the nation's law schools and discussed the implications of the study for the Group's future projects. Members of the Group began work on the casebook on international labor law at this meeting. During Professor Cooper's term, the Group also finished its popular reader *Labor Law Stories*, which examines the stories behind many of the most important American labor law cases.

In July 2005, Kenneth G. Dau-Schmidt became the chair of the Labor Law Group. Shortly after his election, the Group held a meeting in Chicago with nationally recognized practitioners to discuss how best to teach students about the practice of labor law in the new global economy of the information age. The outline that resulted from this meeting served as the basis for *Labor Law in the Contemporary Workplace*. Following the Chicago meeting, the Group met several times to work on new editions of its books and develop new projects: June 2006 in Saratoga Springs, New York; June 2007 in St. Charles, Illinois; and June 2010 in Arrowhead, California. Group projects that grew out of or benefited from these meetings include *International Labor Law: Cases and Materials on Workers' Rights in the Global Economy* and *A Concise Hornbook on Employment Law*. The Group, in partnership with the American Bar Association Section of Labor and Employment Law, created instructional materials for the Capstone Course in Labor and Employment Law, a simulation integrating disparate substantive areas with practice skills and professional responsibility. The Group also hosted: a November 2007 symposium on the problems of low-wage workers, the proceedings of which were published in the *Minnesota Law Review*; a February 2009 symposium on the American Law Institute's Proposed Restatement of Employment Law, the proceedings of which were published in the *Employee Rights and Employment Policy Journal*; and a November 2010 symposium on labor and employment law policies under the Obama administration, the proceedings of which were published in the *Indiana Law Journal*.

Marion Crain became chair of the Group at the beginning of 2011. That same year, the Group sponsored a one-day conference on the crisis confronting public-sector employment, the proceedings of which were published in the *ABA Journal of Labor & Employment Law*. In 2011 the Group also hosted a meeting of experts in Chicago to consider the ongoing Restatement of Employment Law project. In June 2012, the Group met in Asheville, North Carolina, and approved the formation of an editorial policy committee charged with establishing policies to ensure that the Group's products continue to reflect its tradition of close collaboration and high standards. The Asheville meeting served as the genesis for a labor arbitrator training workshop for academics in Chicago in December 2012. In February 2013, the Group cosponsored a symposium at the University of California–Irvine School of Law on alternatives to the Wagner Act and employment law models of workplace protection. The proceedings of the conference, called "Re-imagining Labor Law: Building Worker Collectivities After the NLRA," will be published in the *UC Irvine Law Review*. Under Professor Crain's leadership, the Group also has continued to release new editions of its casebooks.

At any one time, roughly twenty-five to thirty members are actively engaged in the Group's work; this has proven to be a practical size, given the challenges of communication and logistics. Coordination and editorial review of the projects are the responsibility of the executive committee, whose members are the successor trustees of the Group. Governance is by consensus; votes are taken only to elect trustees and to determine whom to invite to join the Group. Since 1953, more than eighty persons have worked on Group projects; in keeping with the original agreement, none has ever received anything more than reimbursement of expenses.

The Labor Law Group currently has eight books in print. In addition to this volume, West has published *Public Sector Employment: Cases and Materials* (Second Edition) by Martin H. Malin, Ann C. Hodges, and Joseph E. Slater; *Principles of Employment Law* by Peggie R. Smith, Ann C. Hodges, Susan J. Stabile, and Rafael Gely; *International Labor Law: Cases and Materials on Workers' Rights in the Global Economy* by James

Atleson, Lance Compa, Kerry Rittich, Calvin William Sharpe, and Marley S. Weiss; *Employment Discrimination Law: Cases and Materials on Equality in the Workplace* (Eighth Edition) by Dianne Avery, Maria L. Ontiveros, Roberto L. Corrada, Michael L. Selmi, and Melissa Hart; *ADR in the Workplace* (Third Edition) by Laura J. Cooper, Dennis R. Nolan, Richard A. Bales, and Stephen F. Befort; and *Legal Protection for the Individual Employee* (Fourth Edition) by Kenneth G. Dau-Schmidt, Robert N. Covington, and Matthew W. Finkin. Foundation Press has published the Group's eighth book, *Labor Law Stories*, edited by Laura J. Cooper and Catherine L. Fisk.

This is the second edition of *Labor Law in the Contemporary Workplace*. The first edition, by Kenneth G. Dau-Schmidt, Martin H. Malin, Roberto L. Corrada, Christopher David Ruiz Cameron, and Catherine L. Fisk, was published by West in 2009.

THE EXECUTIVE COMMITTEE

RICHARD A. BALES (TREASURER)
STEPHEN BEFORT
MARION G. CRAIN (CHAIR)
CYNTHIA ESTLUND
MELISSA HART
KERRY RITTICH
PEGGIE R. SMITH (SECRETARY)

# THE LABOR LAW GROUP

## EXECUTIVE COMMITTEE

**Marion G. Crain**
*Chair*
*Washington University–St. Louis*

**Richard A. Bales**
*Ohio Northern University*

**Stephen Befort**
*University of Minnesota*

**Cynthia Estlund**
*New York University*

**Melissa Hart**
*University of Colorado–Boulder*

**Kerry Rittich**
*University of Toronto*

**Peggie R. Smith**
*Washington University–St. Louis*

# THE LABOR LAW GROUP

---

## EDITORIAL POLICY COMMITTEE

**Ruben Garcia**
*University of Nevada–Las Vegas*

**Rafael Gely**
*University of Missouri*

**Julius G. Getman**
*University of Texas (Emeritus)*

**Alvin L. Goldman**
*University of Kentucky (Emeritus)*

**Joseph R. Grodin**
*University of California–Hastings (Emeritus)*

**Melissa Hart**
*University of Colorado–Boulder*

**Ann C. Hodges**
*University of Richmond*

**Alan Hyde**
*Rutgers University–Newark*

**James E. Jones, Jr.**
*University of Wisconsin–Madison (Emeritus)*

**Pauline T. Kim**
*Washington University–St. Louis*

**Tom Kohler**
*Boston College*

**Brian A. Langille**
*University of Toronto*

**Orly Lobel**
*University of San Diego*

**Deborah Malamud**
*New York University*

**Martin H. Malin**
*Illinois Institute of Technology, Chicago–Kent College of Law*

# TABLE OF CONTENTS

Title I—National Labor Relations Act (49 Stat. 449 (1935))

Title II—Conciliation of Labor Disputes in Industries Affecting
Commerce; National Emergencies

# STATUTORY SUPPLEMENT TO
# LABOR LAW IN THE CONTEMPORARY WORKPLACE

## Second Edition

# SHERMAN ACT

■ ■ ■

26 Stat. 209 (1890), *as amended*, 15 U.S.C. §§ 1 et seq.

## § 1. Trusts, etc., in Restraint of Trade Illegal; Penalty

Every contract, combination in the form of trust or otherwise, or conspiracy, in restraint of trade or commerce among the several States, or with foreign nations, is declared to be illegal. Every person who shall make any contract or engage in any combination or conspiracy hereby declared to be illegal shall be deemed guilty of a felony, and, on conviction thereof, shall be punished by fine not exceeding $100,000,000 if a corporation, or, if any other person, $1,000,000, or by imprisonment not exceeding 10 years, or by both said punishments, in the discretion of the court.

(July 2, 1890, c. 647, § 1, 26 Stat. 209; Aug. 17, 1937, c. 690, Title VIII, 50 Stat. 693; July 7, 1955, c. 281, 69 Stat. 282; Dec. 21, 1974, Pub. L. No. 93–528, § 3, 88 Stat. 1708; Dec. 12, 1975, Pub. L. No. 94–145, § 2, 89 Stat. 801; Nov. 16, 1990, Pub. L. No. 101–588, § 4(a), 104 Stat. 2880; June 22, 2004, Pub. L. No. 108–237, Title II, § 215(a), 118 Stat. 668.)

## § 2. Monopolizing Trade a Felony; Penalty

Every person who shall monopolize, or attempt to monopolize, or combine or conspire with any other person or persons, to monopolize any part of the trade or commerce among the several States, or with foreign nations, shall be deemed guilty of a felony, and, on conviction thereof, shall be punished by fine not exceeding $100,000,000 if a corporation, or, if any other person, $1,000,000, or by imprisonment not exceeding 10 years, or by both said punishments, in the discretion of the court.

(July 2, 1890, c. 647, § 2, 26 Stat. 209; July 7, 1955, c. 281, 69 Stat. 282; Dec. 21, 1974, Pub. L. No. 93–528, § 3, 88 Stat. 1708; Nov. 16, 1990, Pub. L. No. 101–588, § 4(b), 104 Stat. 2880; June 22, 2004, Pub. L. No. 108–237, Title II, § 215(b), 118 Stat. 668.)

(Sections 3 through 10 omitted)

# THE CLAYTON ACT

■ ■ ■

38 Stat. 730 (1914), *as amended*, 15 U.S.C. §§ 12 et seq.

## § 1 (§ 12). Definitions; Short Title

(a) "Antitrust laws," as used herein, includes the Act entitled "An Act to protect trade and commerce against unlawful restraints and monopolies," approved July second, eighteen hundred and ninety; sections seventy-three to seventy-six, inclusive, of an Act entitled "An Act to reduce taxation, to provide revenue for the Government, and for other purposes," of August twenty-seventh, eighteen hundred and ninety-four; an Act entitled "An Act to amend sections seventy-three and seventy-six of the Act of August twenty-seventh, eighteen hundred and ninety-four, entitled 'An Act to reduce taxation, to provide revenue for the Government, and for other purposes,'" approved February twelfth, nineteen hundred and thirteen; and also this Act.

"Commerce," as used herein, means trade or commerce among the several States and with foreign nations, or between the District of Columbia or any Territory of the United States and any State, Territory, or foreign nation, or between any insular possessions or other places under the jurisdiction of the United States, or between any such possession or place and any State or Territory of the United States or the District of Columbia or any foreign nation, or within the District of Columbia or any Territory or any insular possession or other place under the jurisdiction of the United States: Provided, That nothing in this Act contained shall apply to the Philippine Islands.

The word "person" or "persons" wherever used in this Act shall be deemed to include corporations and associations existing under or authorized by the laws of either the United States, the laws of any of the Territories, the laws of any State, or the laws of any foreign country.

## § 4 (§ 15). Suits by Persons Injured

Any person who shall be injured in his business or property by reason of anything forbidden in the antitrust laws may sue therefor in any district court of the United States in the district in which the defendant resides or is found or has an agent, without respect to the amount in controversy, and shall recover threefold the damages by him sustained, and the cost of suit, including a reasonable attorney's fee.

## § 6 (§ 17). Antitrust Laws Not Applicable to Labor Organizations

The labor of a human being is not a commodity or article of commerce. Nothing contained in the antitrust laws shall be construed to forbid the existence and operation of labor, agricultural, or horticultural organizations, instituted for the purposes of mutual help, and not having capital stock or conducted for profit, or to forbid or restrain individual members of such organizations from lawfully carrying out the legitimate objects thereof; nor shall such organizations, or the members thereof, be held or construed to be illegal combinations or conspiracies in restraint of trade, under the antitrust laws.

## § 16 (§ 26). Injunctive Relief for Private Parties; Exception; Costs

Any person, firm, corporation, or association shall be entitled to sue for and have injunctive relief, in any court of the United States having jurisdiction over the parties, against threatened loss or damage by a violation of the antitrust laws, including sections 13, 14, 18, and 19 of this title, when and under the same conditions and principles as injunctive relief against threatened conduct that will cause loss or damage is granted by courts of equity, under the rules governing such proceedings, and upon the execution of proper bond against damages for an injunction improvidently granted and a showing that the danger of irreparable loss or damage is immediate, a preliminary injunction may issue: Provided, That nothing herein contained shall be construed to entitle any person, firm, corporation, or association, except the United States, to bring suit for injunctive relief against any common carrier subject to the jurisdiction of the Surface Transportation Board under subtitle IV of Title 49. In any action under this section in which the plaintiff substantially prevails, the court shall award the cost of suit, including a reasonable attorney's fee, to such plaintiff.

## § 20 (29 U.S.C. § 52). Statutory Restriction of Injunctive Relief

No restraining order or injunction shall be granted by any court of the United States, or a judge or the judges thereof, in any case between an employer and employees, or between employers and employees, or between employees, or between persons employed and persons seeking employment, involving, or growing out of, a dispute concerning terms or conditions of employment, unless necessary to prevent irreparable injury to property, or to a property right, of the party making the application, for which injury there is no adequate remedy at law, and such property or property right must be described with particularity in the application, which must be in writing and sworn to by the applicant or by his agent or attorney.

And no such restraining order or injunction shall prohibit any person or persons, whether singly or in concert, from terminating any relation of employment, or from ceasing to perform any work or labor, or from recommending, advising, or persuading others by peaceful means so to do; or from attending at any place where any such person or persons may lawfully be, for the purpose of peacefully obtaining or communicating information, or from peacefully persuading any person to work or to abstain from working; or from ceasing to patronize or to employ any party to such dispute, or from recommending, advising, or persuading others by peaceful and lawful means so to do; or from paying or giving to, or withholding from, any person engaged in such dispute, any strike benefits or other moneys or things of value; or from peaceably assembling in a lawful manner, and for lawful purposes; or from doing any act or thing which might lawfully be done in the absence of such dispute by any party thereto; nor shall any of the acts specified in this paragraph be considered or held to be violations of any law of the United States.

# THE RAILWAY LABOR ACT OF 1926

■ ■ ■

44 Stat. 577 (1926), *as amended*, 45 U.S.C. §§ 151–188

## SUBCHAPTER I. GENERAL PROVISIONS

### § 1 (§ 151). Definitions; Short Title

When used in this chapter and for the purposes of this chapter—

First. The term "carrier" includes any railroad subject to the jurisdiction of the Surface Transportation Board, any express company that would have been subject to subtitle IV of Title 49, as of December 31, 1995, and any company which is directly or indirectly owned or controlled by or under common control with any carrier by railroad and which operates any equipment or facilities or performs any service (other than trucking service) in connection with the transportation, receipt, delivery, elevation, transfer in transit, refrigeration or icing, storage, and handling of property transported by railroad, and any receiver, trustee, or other individual or body, judicial or otherwise, when in the possession of the business of any such "carrier": *Provided, however*, That the term "carrier" shall not include any street, interurban, or suburban electric railway, unless such railway is operating as a part of a general steam-railroad system of transportation, but shall not exclude any part of the general steam-railroad system of transportation now or hereafter operated by any other motive power. The Surface Transportation Board is authorized and directed upon request of the Mediation Board or upon complaint of any party interested to determine after hearing whether any line operated by electric power falls within the terms of this proviso. The term "carrier" shall not include any company by reason of its being engaged in the mining of coal, the supplying of coal to a carrier where delivery is not beyond the mine tipple, and the operation of equipment or facilities therefor, or in any of such activities.

Second. The term "Adjustment Board" means the National Railroad Adjustment Board created by this chapter.

Third. The term "Mediation Board" means the National Mediation Board created by this chapter.

Fourth. The term "commerce" means commerce among the several States or between any State, Territory, or the District of Columbia and any foreign nation, or between any Territory or the District of Columbia and any State, or between any Territory and any other Territory, or between any Territory and the District of Columbia, or within any Territory or the District of Columbia, or between points in the same State but through any other State or any Territory or the District of Columbia or any foreign nation.

Fifth. The term "employee" as used herein includes every person in the service of a carrier (subject to its continuing authority to supervise and direct the manner of rendition of his service) who performs any work defined as that of an employee or subordinate official in the orders of the Surface Transportation Board now in effect, and as the same may be amended or interpreted by orders hereafter entered by the Board pursuant to the authority which is conferred upon it to enter orders amending or interpreting such existing orders: *Provided, however*, That no occupational classification made by order of the Surface Transportation Board shall be construed to define the crafts according to which railway employees may be organized by their voluntary action, nor shall the jurisdiction or powers of such employee organizations be regarded as in any way limited or defined by the provisions of this chapter or by the orders of the Board.

The term "employee" shall not include any individual while such individual is engaged in the physical operations consisting of the mining of coal, the preparation of coal, the handling (other than movement by rail with standard railroad locomotives) of coal not beyond the mine tipple, or the loading of coal at the tipple.

Sixth. The term "representative" means any person or persons, labor union, organization, or corporation designated either by a carrier or group of carriers or by its or their employees, to act for it or them.

Seventh. The term "district court" includes the United States District Court for the District of Columbia; and the term "court of appeals" includes the United States Court of Appeals for the District of Columbia.

This chapter may be cited as the "Railway Labor Act."

## § 2 (§ 151a).    General Purposes

The purposes of the chapter are: (1) To avoid any interruption to commerce or to the operation of any carrier engaged therein; (2) to forbid any limitation upon freedom of association among employees or any denial, as a condition of employment or otherwise, of the right of employees to join a labor organization; (3) to provide for the complete independence of carriers and of employees in the matter of self-organization to carry out the purposes of this chapter; (4) to provide for the prompt and orderly settlement of all disputes concerning rates of pay, rules, or working conditions; (5) to provide for the prompt and orderly settlement of all disputes growing out of grievances or out of the interpretation or application of agreements covering rates of pay, rules, or working conditions.

## § 2  (§ 152).  General Duties

### First. Duty of carriers and employees to settle disputes

It shall be the duty of all carriers, their officers, agents, and employees to exert every reasonable effort to make and maintain agreements concerning rates of pay, rules, and working conditions, and to settle all disputes, whether arising out of the application of such agreements or otherwise, in order to avoid any interruption to commerce or to the operation of any carrier growing out of any dispute between the carrier and the employees thereof.

### Second. Consideration of disputes by representatives

All disputes between a carrier or carriers and its or their employees shall be considered, and, if possible, decided, with all expedition, in conference between representatives designated and authorized so to confer, respectively, by the carrier or carriers and by the employees thereof interested in the dispute.

### Third. Designation of representatives

Representatives, for the purposes of this chapter, shall be designated by the respective parties without interference, influence, or coercion by either party over the designation of representatives by the other; and neither party shall in any way interfere with, influence, or coerce the other in its choice of representatives. Representatives of employees for the purposes of this chapter need not be persons in the employ of the carrier, and no carrier shall, by interference, influence, or coercion seek in any manner to prevent the designation by its employees as their representatives of those who or which are not employees of the carrier.

### Fourth. Organization and collective bargaining; freedom from interference by carrier; assistance in organizing or maintaining organization by carrier forbidden; deduction of dues from wages forbidden

Employees shall have the right to organize and bargain collectively through representatives of their own choosing. The majority of any craft or class of employees shall have the right to determine who shall be the representative of the craft or class for the purposes of this chapter. No carrier, its officers, or agents shall deny or in any way question the right of its employees to join, organize, or assist in organizing the labor organization of their choice, and it shall be unlawful for any carrier to interfere in any way with the organization of its employees, or to use the funds of the carrier in maintaining or assisting or contributing to any labor organization, labor representative, or other agency of collective bargaining, or in performing any work therefor, or to influence or coerce employees in an effort to induce them to join or remain or not to join or remain members of any labor organization, or to deduct from the wages of employees any dues, fees, assessments, or other contributions payable to labor organizations, or to collect or to assist in the collection of any such dues, fees, assessments, or other contributions: *Provided*, That nothing in this chapter shall be construed to prohibit a carrier from permitting an employee, individually, or local representatives of employees from conferring with management during working hours without loss of time, or to prohibit a carrier from furnishing free transportation to its employees while engaged in the business of a labor organization.

### Fifth. Agreements to join or not to join labor organizations forbidden

No carrier, its officers, or agents shall require any person seeking employment to sign any contract or agreement promising to join or not to join a labor organization; and if any such contract has been enforced prior to the effective date of this chapter, then such carrier shall notify the employees by an appropriate order that such contract has been discarded and is no longer binding on them in any way.

### Sixth. Conference of representatives; time; place; private agreements

In case of a dispute between a carrier or carriers and its or their employees, arising out of grievances or out of the interpretation or application of agreements concerning rates of pay, rules, or working conditions, it shall be the duty of the designated representative or representatives of such carrier or carriers and of such employees, within ten days after the receipt of notice of a desire on the part of either party to confer in respect to such dispute, to specify a time and place at which such conference shall be held: *Provided*, (1) That the place so specified shall be situated upon the line of the carrier involved or as otherwise mutually agreed upon; and (2) that the time so specified shall allow the designated conferees reasonable opportunity to reach such place of conference, but shall not exceed twenty days from the receipt of such notice: And *provided further*, That nothing in this chapter shall be construed to supersede the provisions of any agreement (as to conferences) then in effect between the parties.

### Seventh. Change in pay, rules, or working conditions contrary to agreement or to section 156 forbidden

No carrier, its officers, or agents shall change the rates of pay, rules, or working conditions of its employees, as a class, as embodied in agreements except in the manner prescribed in such agreements or in section 156 of this title.

### Eighth. Notices of manner of settlement of disputes; posting

Every carrier shall notify its employees by printed notices in such form and posted at such times and places as shall be specified by the Mediation Board that all disputes between the carrier and its employees will be handled in accordance with the requirements of this chapter, and in such notices there shall be printed verbatim, in large type, the third, fourth, and fifth paragraphs of this section. The provisions of said paragraphs are made a part of the contract of employment between the carrier and each employee, and shall be held binding upon the parties, regardless of any other express or implied agreements between them.

### Ninth. Disputes as to identity of representatives; designation by Mediation Board; secret elections

If any dispute shall arise among a carrier's employees as to who are the representatives of such employees designated and authorized in accordance with the requirements of this chapter, it shall be the duty of the Mediation Board, upon request of either party to the dispute, to investigate such dispute and to certify to both parties, in writing, within thirty days after the receipt of the invocation of its services, the name or names of the individuals or organizations that have been designated and authorized to represent the employees involved in the dispute, and certify the same to the carrier. Upon receipt of such certification the carrier shall treat with the representative so certified as the representative of the craft or class for the purposes of this chapter. In such an investigation, the Mediation Board shall be authorized to take a secret ballot of the employees involved, or to utilize any other appropriate method of ascertaining the names of their duly designated and authorized representatives in such manner as shall insure the choice of representatives by the employees without interference, influence, or coercion exercised by the carrier. In the conduct of any election for the purposes herein indicated the Board shall designate who may participate in the election and establish the rules to govern the election, or may appoint a committee of three neutral persons who after hearing shall within ten days designate the employees who may participate in the election. The Board shall have access to and have power to make copies of the books and records of the carriers to obtain and utilize such information as may be deemed necessary by it to carry out the purposes and provisions of this paragraph.

### Tenth. Violations; prosecution and penalties

The willful failure or refusal of any carrier, its officers or agents, to comply with the terms of the third, fourth, fifth, seventh, or eighth paragraph of this section shall be a misdemeanor, and upon conviction thereof the carrier, officer, or agent offending shall be subject to a fine of not less than $1,000, nor more than $20,000 or imprisonment for not more than six months, or both fine and imprisonment, for each offense, and each day during which such carrier, officer, or agent shall willfully fail or refuse to comply with the terms of the said paragraphs of this section shall constitute a separate offense. It shall be the duty of any United States attorney to whom any duly designated representative of a carrier's employees may apply to institute in the proper court and to prosecute under the direction of the Attorney General of the United States, all necessary proceedings for the enforcement of the provisions of this section, and for the punishment of all violations thereof and the costs and expenses of such prosecution shall be paid out of the appropriation for the expenses of the courts of the United States: *Provided,* That nothing in this chapter shall be construed to require an individual employee to render labor or service without his consent, nor shall anything in this chapter be construed to make the quitting of his labor by an individual employee an illegal act; nor shall any court issue any process to compel the performance by an individual employee of such labor or service, without his consent.

### Eleventh. Union security agreements; check-off

Notwithstanding any other provisions of this chapter, or of any other statute or law of the United States, or Territory thereof, or of any State, any carrier or carriers as defined in this chapter and a labor organization or labor organizations duly designated and authorized to represent employees in accordance with the requirements of this chapter shall be permitted—

(a) to make agreements, requiring, as a condition of continued employment, that within sixty days following the beginning of such employment, or the effective date of such agreements, whichever is the later, all employees shall become members of the labor organization representing their craft or class: *Provided,* That no such agreement shall require such condition of employment with respect to employees to whom membership is not available upon the same terms and conditions as are generally applicable to any other member or with respect to employees to whom membership was denied or terminated for any reason other than the failure of the employee to tender the periodic dues, initiation fees, and assessments (not including fines and penalties) uniformly required as a condition of acquiring or retaining membership.

(b) to make agreements providing for the deduction by such carrier or carriers from the wages of its or their employees in a craft or class and payment to the labor organization representing the craft or class of such employees, of any periodic dues, initiation fees, and assessments (not including fines and penalties) uniformly required as a condition of acquiring or retaining membership: *Provided,* That no such agreement shall be effective with respect to any individual employee until he shall have furnished the employer with a written assignment to the labor organization of such membership dues, initiation fees, and assessments, which shall be revocable in writing after the expiration of one year or upon the termination date of the applicable collective agreement, whichever occurs sooner.

(c) The requirement of membership in a labor organization in an agreement made pursuant to subparagraph (a) of this paragraph shall be satisfied, as to both a present or future employee in engine, train, yard, or hostling service, that is, an employee engaged in any of the services or capacities covered in the First division of paragraph (h) of section 153 of this title defining the jurisdictional scope of the First Division of the National Railroad Adjustment Board, if said employee shall hold or acquire membership in any one of the labor organizations, national in scope, organized in accordance with this chapter and admitting to membership employees of a craft or class in any of said services; and no agreement made pursuant to subparagraph (b) of this paragraph shall provide for deductions from his wages for periodic dues, initiation fees, or assessments payable to any labor organization other than that in which he holds membership: *Provided, however*, That as to an employee in any of said services on a particular carrier at the effective date of any such agreement on a carrier, who is not a member of any one of the labor organizations, national in scope, organized in accordance with this chapter and admitting to membership employees of a craft or class in any of said services, such employee, as a condition of continuing his employment, may be required to become a member of the organization representing the craft in which he is employed on the effective date of the first agreement applicable to him: *Provided, further*, That nothing herein or in any such agreement or agreements shall prevent an employee from changing membership from one organization to another organization admitting to membership employees of a craft or class in any of said services.

(d) Any provisions in paragraphs Fourth and Fifth of this section in conflict herewith are to the extent of such conflict amended.

## § 3 (§ 153). National Railroad Adjustment Board

### First. Establishment; composition; powers and duties; divisions; hearings and awards; judicial review

There is established a Board, to be known as the "National Railroad Adjustment Board", the members of which shall be selected within thirty days after June 21, 1934, and it is provided—

(a) That the said Adjustment Board shall consist of thirty-four members, seventeen of whom shall be selected by the carriers and seventeen by such labor organizations of the employees, national in scope, as have been or may be organized in accordance with the provisions of sections 151a and 152 of this title.

(b) The carriers, acting each through its board of directors or its receiver or receivers, trustee or trustees, or through an officer or officers designated for that purpose by such board, trustee or trustees, or receiver or receivers, shall prescribe the rules under which its representatives shall be selected and shall select the representatives of the carriers on the Adjustment Board and designate the division on which each such representative shall serve, but no carrier or system of carriers shall have more than one voting representative on any division of the Board.

(c) Except as provided in the second paragraph of subsection (h) of this section, the national labor organizations, as defined in paragraph (a) of this section, acting each through the chief executive or other medium designated by the organization or association thereof, shall prescribe the rules under which the labor members of the Adjustment Board shall be selected and shall select such members and designate the division on which each member shall serve; but no labor organization shall have more than one voting representative on any division of the Board.

(d) In case of a permanent or temporary vacancy on the Adjustment Board, the vacancy shall be filled by selection in the same manner as in the original selection.

(e) If either the carriers or the labor organizations of the employees fail to select and designate representatives to the Adjustment Board, as provided in paragraphs (b) and (c) of this section, respectively, within sixty days after June 21, 1934, in case of any original appointment to office of a member of the Adjustment Board, or in case of a vacancy in any such office within thirty days after such vacancy occurs, the Mediation Board shall thereupon directly make the appointment and shall select an individual associated in interest with the carriers or the group of labor organizations of employees, whichever he is to represent.

(f) In the event a dispute arises as to the right of any national labor organization to participate as per paragraph (c) of this section in the selection and designation of the labor members of the Adjustment Board, the Secretary of Labor shall investigate the claim of such labor organization to participate, and if such claim in the judgment of the Secretary of Labor has merit, the Secretary shall notify the Mediation Board accordingly, and within ten days after receipt of such advice the Mediation Board shall request those national labor organizations duly qualified as per paragraph (c) of this section to participate in the selection and designation of the labor members of the Adjustment Board to select a representative. Such representative, together with a representative likewise designated by the claimant, and a third or neutral party designated by the Mediation Board, constituting a board of three, shall within thirty days after the appointment of the neutral member, investigate the claims of the labor organization desiring participation and decide whether or not it was organized in accordance with sections 151a and 152 of this title and is otherwise properly qualified to participate in the selection of the labor members of the Adjustment Board, and the findings of such boards of three shall be final and binding.

(g) Each member of the Adjustment Board shall be compensated by the party or parties he is to represent. Each third or neutral party selected under the provisions of paragraph (f) of this section shall receive from the Mediation Board such compensation as the Mediation Board may fix, together with his necessary traveling expenses and expenses actually incurred for subsistence, or per diem allowance in lieu thereof, subject to the provisions of law applicable thereto, while serving as such third or neutral party.

(h) The said Adjustment Board shall be composed of four divisions, whose proceedings shall be independent of one another, and the said divisions as well as the number of their members shall be as follows:

First division: To have jurisdiction over disputes involving train-and yard-service employees of carriers; that is, engineers, firemen, hostlers, and outside hostler helpers, conductors, trainmen, and yard-service employees. This division shall consist of eight members, four of whom shall be selected and designated by the carriers and four of whom shall be selected and designated by the labor organizations, national in scope and organized in accordance with sections 151a and 152 of this title and which represent employees in engine, train, yard, or hostling service: *Provided, however*, That each labor organization shall select and designate two members on the First Division and that no labor organization shall have more than one vote in any proceedings of the First Division or in the adoption of any award with respect to any dispute submitted to the First Division: *Provided further*, however, That the carrier members of the First Division shall cast no more than two votes in any proceedings of the division or in the adoption of any award with respect to any dispute submitted to the First Division.

Second division: To have jurisdiction over disputes involving machinists, boilermakers, blacksmiths, sheet-metal workers, electrical workers, carmen, the helpers and apprentices of all the foregoing, coach cleaners, power-house employees, and railroad-shop laborers. This division shall consist of ten members, five of whom shall be selected by the carriers and five by the national labor organizations of the employees.

Third division: To have jurisdiction over disputes involving station, tower, and telegraph employees, train dispatchers, maintenance-of-way men, clerical employees, freight handlers, express, station, and store employees, signal men, sleeping-car conductors, sleeping-car porters, and maids and dining-car employees. This division shall consist of ten members, five of whom shall be selected by the carriers and five by the national labor organizations of employees.

Fourth division: To have jurisdiction over disputes involving employees of carriers directly or indirectly engaged in transportation of passengers or property by water, and all other employees of carriers over which jurisdiction is not given to the first, second, and third divisions. This division shall consist of six members, three of whom shall be selected by the carriers and three by the national labor organizations of the employees.

(i) The disputes between an employee or group of employees and a carrier or carriers growing out of grievances or out of the interpretation or application of agreements concerning rates of pay, rules, or working conditions, including cases pending and unadjusted on June 21, 1934, shall be handled in the usual manner up to and including the chief operating officer of the carrier designated to handle such disputes; but, failing to reach an adjustment in this manner, the disputes may be referred by petition of the parties or by either party to the appropriate division of the Adjustment Board with a full statement of the facts and all supporting data bearing upon the disputes.

(j) Parties may be heard either in person, by counsel, or by other representatives, as they may respectively elect, and the several divisions of the Adjustment Board shall give due notice of all hearings to the employee or employees and the carrier or carriers involved in any disputes submitted to them.

(k) Any division of the Adjustment Board shall have authority to empower two or more of its members to conduct hearings and make findings upon disputes, when properly submitted, at any place designated by the division: *Provided, however*, That except as provided in paragraph (h) of this section, final awards as to any such dispute must be made by the entire division as hereinafter provided.

(l) Upon failure of any division to agree upon an award because of a deadlock or inability to secure a majority vote of the division members, as provided in paragraph (n) of this section, then such division shall forthwith agree upon and select a neutral person, to be known as "referee", to sit with the division as a member thereof, and make an award. Should the division fail to agree upon and select a referee within ten days of the date of the deadlock or inability to secure a majority vote, then the division, or any member thereof, or the parties or either party to the dispute may certify that fact to the Mediation Board, which Board shall, within ten days from the date of receiving such certificate, select and name the referee to sit with the division as a member thereof and make an award. The Mediation Board shall be bound by the same provisions in the appointment of these neutral referees as are provided elsewhere in this chapter for the appointment of arbitrators and shall fix and pay the compensation of such referees.

(m) The awards of the several divisions of the Adjustment Board shall be stated in writing. A copy of the awards shall be furnished to the respective parties to the controversy, and the awards shall be final and binding upon both parties to the dispute. In case a dispute arises involving an interpretation of the award, the division of the Board upon request of either party shall interpret the award in the light of the dispute.

(n) A majority vote of all members of the division of the Adjustment Board eligible to vote shall be competent to make an award with respect to any dispute submitted to it.

(o) In case of an award by any division of the Adjustment Board in favor of petitioner, the division of the Board shall make an order, directed to the carrier, to make the award effective and, if the award includes a requirement for the payment of money, to pay to the employee the sum to which he is entitled under the award on or before a day named. In the event any division determines that an award favorable to the petitioner should not be made in any dispute referred to it, the division shall make an order to the petitioner stating such determination.

(p) If a carrier does not comply with an order of a division of the Adjustment Board within the time limit in such order, the petitioner, or any person for whose benefit such order was made, may file in the District Court of the United States for the district in which he resides or in which is located the principal operating office of the carrier, or through which the carrier operates, a petition setting forth briefly the causes for which he claims relief, and the order of the division of the Adjustment Board in the premises. Such suit in the District Court of the United States shall proceed in all respects as other civil suits, except that on the trial of such suit the findings and order of the division of the Adjustment Board shall be conclusive on the parties, and except that the petitioner shall not be liable for costs in the district court nor for costs at any subsequent stage of the proceedings, unless they accrue upon his appeal, and such costs shall be paid out of the appropriation for the expenses of the courts of the United States. If the petitioner shall finally prevail he shall be allowed a reasonable attorney's fee, to be taxed and collected as a part of the costs of the suit. The district courts are empowered, under the rules of the court governing actions at law, to make such order and enter such judgment, by writ of mandamus or otherwise, as may be appropriate to enforce or set aside the order of the division of the Adjustment Board: *Provided, however,* That such order may not be set aside except for failure of the division to comply with the requirements of this chapter, for failure of the order to conform, or confine itself, to matters within the scope of the division's jurisdiction, or for fraud or corruption by a member of the division making the order.

(q) If any employee or group of employees, or any carrier, is aggrieved by the failure of any division of the Adjustment Board to make an award in a dispute referred to it, or is aggrieved by any of the terms of an award or by the failure of the division to include certain terms in such award, then such employee or group of employees or carrier may file in any United States district court in which a petition under paragraph (p) could be filed, a petition for review of the division's order. A copy of the petition shall be forthwith transmitted by the clerk of the court to the Adjustment Board. The Adjustment Board shall file in the court the record of the proceedings on which it based its action. The court shall have jurisdiction to affirm the order of the division, or to set it aside, in whole or in part, or it may remand the proceedings to the division for such further action as it may direct. On such review, the findings and order of the division shall be conclusive on the parties, except that the order of the division may be set aside, in whole or in part, or remanded to the division, for failure of the division to comply with the requirements of this chapter, for failure of the order to conform, or confine itself, to matters within the scope of the division's jurisdiction, or for fraud or corruption by a member of the division making the order. The judgment of the court shall be subject to review as provided in sections 1291 and 1254 of Title 28.

(r) All actions at law based upon the provisions of this section shall be begun within two years from the time the cause of action accrues under the award of the division of the Adjustment Board, and not after.

(s) The several divisions of the Adjustment Board shall maintain headquarters in Chicago, Illinois, meet regularly, and continue in session so long as there is pending before the division any matter within its jurisdiction which has been submitted for its consideration and which has not been disposed of.

(t) Whenever practicable, the several divisions or subdivisions of the Adjustment Board shall be supplied with suitable quarters in any Federal building located at its place of meeting.

(u) The Adjustment Board may, subject to the approval of the Mediation Board, employ and fix the compensations of such assistants as it deems necessary in carrying on its proceedings. The compensation of such employees shall be paid by the Mediation Board.

(v) The Adjustment Board shall meet within forty days after June 21, 1934, and adopt such rules as it deems necessary to control proceedings before the respective divisions and not in conflict with the provisions of this section. Immediately following the meeting of the entire Board and the adoption of such rules, the respective divisions shall meet and organize by the selection of a chairman, a vice chairman, and a secretary. Thereafter each division shall annually designate one of its members to act as chairman and one of its members to act as vice chairman: *Provided, however,* That the chairmanship and vice-chairmanship of any division shall alternate as between the groups, so that both the chairmanship and vice-chairmanship shall be held alternately by a representative of the carriers and a representative of the employees. In case of a vacancy, such vacancy shall be filled for the unexpired term by the selection of a successor from the same group.

(w) Each division of the Adjustment Board shall annually prepare and submit a report of its activities to the Mediation Board, and the substance of such report shall be included in the annual report of the Mediation Board to the Congress of the United States. The reports of each division of the Adjustment Board and the annual report of the Mediation Board shall state in detail all cases heard, all actions taken, the names, salaries, and duties of all agencies, employees, and officers receiving compensation from the United States under the authority of this chapter, and an account of all moneys appropriated by Congress pursuant to the authority conferred by this chapter and disbursed by such agencies, employees, and officers.

(x) Any division of the Adjustment Board shall have authority, in its discretion, to establish regional adjustment boards to act in its place and stead for such limited period as such division may determine to be necessary. Carrier members of such regional boards shall be designated in keeping with rules devised for this purpose by the carrier members of the Adjustment Board and the labor members shall be designated in keeping with rules devised for this purpose by the labor members of the Adjustment Board. Any such regional board shall, during the time for which it is appointed, have the same authority to conduct hearings, make findings upon disputes and adopt the same procedure as the division of the Adjustment Board appointing it, and its decisions shall be enforceable to the same extent and under the same processes. A neutral person, as referee, shall be appointed for service in connection with any such regional adjustment board in the same circumstances and manner as provided in paragraph (l) of this section, with respect to a division of the Adjustment Board.

### Second. System, group, or regional boards: establishment by voluntary agreement; special adjustment boards: establishment, composition, designation of representatives by Mediation Board, neutral member, compensation, quorum, finality and enforcement of awards

Nothing in this section shall be construed to prevent any individual carrier, system, or group of carriers and any class or classes of its or their employees, all acting through their representatives, selected in accordance with the provisions of this chapter, from mutually agreeing to the establishment of system, group, or regional boards of adjustment for the purpose of adjusting and deciding disputes of the character specified in this section. In the event that either party to such a system, group, or regional board of adjustment is dissatisfied with such arrangement, it may upon ninety days' notice to the other party elect to come under the jurisdiction of the Adjustment Board.

If written request is made upon any individual carrier by the representative of any craft or class of employees of such carrier for the establishment of a special board of adjustment to resolve disputes otherwise referable to the Adjustment Board, or any dispute which has been pending before the Adjustment Board for twelve months from the date the dispute (claim) is received by the Board, or if any carrier makes such a request upon any such representative, the carrier or the representative upon whom such request is made shall join in an agreement establishing such a board within thirty days from the date such request is made. The cases which may be considered by such board shall be defined in the agreement establishing it. Such board shall consist of one person designated by the carrier and one person designated by the representative of the employees. If such carrier or such representative fails to agree upon the establishment of such a board as provided herein, or to exercise its rights to designate a member of the board, the carrier or representative making the request for the establishment of the special board may request the Mediation Board to designate a member of the special board on behalf of the carrier or representative upon whom such request was made. Upon receipt of a request for such designation the Mediation Board shall promptly make such designation and shall select an individual associated in interest with the carrier or representative he is to represent, who, with the member appointed by the carrier or representative requesting the establishment of the special board, shall constitute the board. Each member of the board shall be compensated by the party he is to represent. The members of the board so designated shall determine all matters not previously agreed upon by the carrier and the representative of the employees with respect to the establishment and jurisdiction of the board. If they are unable to agree such matters shall be determined by a neutral member of the board selected or appointed and compensated in the same manner as is hereinafter provided with respect to situations where the members of the board are unable to agree upon an award. Such neutral member shall cease to be a member of the board when he has determined such matters. If with respect to any dispute or group of disputes the members of the board designated by the carrier and the representative are unable to agree upon an award disposing of the dispute or group of disputes they shall by mutual agreement select a neutral person to be a member of the board for the consideration and disposition of such dispute or group of disputes. In the event the members of the board designated by the parties are unable, within ten days after their failure to agree upon an award, to agree upon the selection of such neutral person, either member of the board may request the Mediation Board to appoint such neutral person and upon receipt of such request the Mediation Board shall promptly make such appointment. The neutral person so selected or appointed shall be compensated and reimbursed for expenses by the Mediation Board. Any two members of the board shall be competent to render an award. Such awards shall be final and binding upon both parties to the dispute and if in favor of the petitioner, shall direct the other party to comply therewith on or before the day named. Compliance with such awards shall be enforceable by proceedings in the United States district courts in the same manner and subject to the same provisions that apply to proceedings for enforcement of compliance with awards of the Adjustment Board.

## § 4  (§ 154). National Mediation Board

### First. Board of Mediation abolished; National Mediation Board established; composition; term of office; qualifications; salaries; removal

The Board of Mediation is abolished, effective thirty days from June 21, 1934, and the members, secretary, officers, assistants, employees, and agents thereof, in office upon June 21, 1934, shall continue to function and receive their salaries for a period of thirty days from such date in the same manner as though this chapter had not been passed. There is established, as an independent agency in the executive branch of the Government, a board to be known as the "National Mediation Board", to be composed of three members appointed by the President, by and with the advice and consent of the Senate, not more than two of whom shall be of the same political party. Each member of the Mediation Board in office on January 1, 1965, shall be deemed to have been appointed for a term of office which shall expire on July 1 of the year his term would have otherwise expired. The terms of office of all successors shall expire three years after the expiration of the terms for which their predecessors were appointed; but any member appointed to fill a vacancy occurring prior to the expiration of the term for which his predecessor was appointed shall be appointed only for the unexpired term of his predecessor. Vacancies in the Board shall not impair the powers nor affect the duties of the Board nor of the remaining members of the Board. Two of the members in office shall constitute a quorum for the transaction of the business of the Board. Each member of the Board shall receive necessary traveling and subsistence expenses, or per diem allowance in lieu thereof, subject to the provisions of law applicable thereto, while away from the principal office of the Board on business required by this chapter. No person in the employment of or who is pecuniarily or otherwise interested in any organization of employees or any carrier shall enter upon the duties of or continue to be a member of the Board. Upon the expiration of his term of office a member shall continue to serve until his successor is appointed and shall have qualified.

All cases referred to the Board of Mediation and unsettled on June 21, 1934, shall be handled to conclusion by the Mediation Board.

A member of the Board may be removed by the President for inefficiency, neglect of duty, malfeasance in office, or ineligibility, but for no other cause.

### Second. Chairman; principal office; delegation of powers; oaths; seal; report

The Mediation Board shall annually designate a member to act as chairman. The Board shall maintain its principal office in the District of Columbia, but it may meet at any other place whenever it deems it necessary so to do. The Board may designate one or more of its members to exercise the functions of the Board in mediation proceedings. Each member of the Board shall have power to administer oaths and affirmations. The Board shall have a seal which shall be judicially noticed. The Board shall make an annual report to Congress.

### Third. Appointment of experts and other employees; salaries of employees; expenditures

The Mediation Board may (1) subject to the provisions of the civil service laws, appoint such experts and assistants to act in a confidential capacity and such other officers and employees as are essential to the effective transaction of the work of the Board; (2) in accordance with chapter 51 and subchapter III of chapter 53 of Title 5, fix the salaries of such experts, assistants, officers, and employees; and (3) make such expenditures (including expenditures for rent and personal services at the seat of government and elsewhere, for law books, periodicals, and books of reference, and for printing and binding, and including expenditures for salaries and compensation, necessary traveling expenses and expenses actually incurred for subsistence, and other necessary expenses of the Mediation Board, Adjustment Board, Regional Adjustment Boards established under paragraph (w) of section 153 of this title, and boards of arbitration, in accordance with the provisions of this section and sections 153 and 157 of this title, respectively), as may be necessary for the execution of the functions vested in the Board, in the Adjustment Board and in the boards of arbitration, and as may be provided for by the Congress from time to time. All expenditures of the Board shall be allowed and paid on the presentation of itemized vouchers therefor approved by the chairman.

## Fourth. Delegation of powers and duties

The Mediation Board is authorized by its order to assign, or refer, any portion of its work, business, or functions arising under this chapter or any other Act of Congress, or referred to it by Congress or either branch thereof, to an individual member of the Board or to an employee or employees of the Board to be designated by such order for action thereon, and by its order at any time to amend, modify, supplement, or rescind any such assignment or reference. All such orders shall take effect forthwith and remain in effect until otherwise ordered by the Board. In conformity with and subject to the order or orders of the Mediation Board in the premises, [and] such individual member of the Board or employee designated shall have power and authority to act as to any of said work, business, or functions so assigned or referred to him for action by the Board.

## Fifth. Transfer of officers and employees of Board of Mediation; transfer of appropriation

All officers and employees of the Board of Mediation (except the members thereof, whose offices are abolished) whose services in the judgment of the Mediation Board are necessary to the efficient operation of the Board are transferred to the Board, without change in classification or compensation; except that the Board may provide for the adjustment of such classification or compensation to conform to the duties to which such officers and employees may be assigned.

All unexpended appropriations for the operation of the Board of Mediation that are available at the time of the abolition of the Board of Mediation shall be transferred to the Mediation Board and shall be available for its use for salaries and other authorized expenditures.

## § 5 (§ 155). Functions of Mediation Board

### First. Disputes within jurisdiction of Mediation Board

The parties, or either party, to a dispute between an employee or group of employees and a carrier may invoke the services of the Mediation Board in any of the following cases:

(a) A dispute concerning changes in rates of pay, rules, or working conditions not adjusted by the parties in conference.

(b) Any other dispute not referable to the National Railroad Adjustment Board and not adjusted in conference between the parties or where conferences are refused.

The Mediation Board may proffer its services in case any labor emergency is found by it to exist at any time.

In either event the said Board shall promptly put itself in communication with the parties to such controversy, and shall use its best efforts, by mediation, to bring them to agreement. If such efforts to bring about an amicable settlement through mediation shall be unsuccessful, the said Board shall at once endeavor as its final required action (except as provided in paragraph third of this section and in section 160 of this title) to induce the parties to submit their controversy to arbitration, in accordance with the provisions of this chapter.

If arbitration at the request of the Board shall be refused by one or both parties, the Board shall at once notify both parties in writing that its mediatory efforts have failed and for thirty days thereafter, unless in the intervening period the parties agree to arbitration, or an emergency board shall be created under section 160 of this title, no change shall be made in the rates of pay, rules, or working conditions or established practices in effect prior to the time the dispute arose.

### Second. Interpretation of agreement

In any case in which a controversy arises over the meaning or the application of any agreement reached through mediation under the provisions of this chapter, either party to the said agreement, or both, may apply to the Mediation Board for an interpretation of the meaning or application of such agreement. The said Board shall upon receipt of such request notify the parties to the controversy, and after a hearing of both sides give its interpretation within thirty days.

### Third. Duties of Board with respect to arbitration of disputes; arbitrators; acknowledgment of agreement; notice to arbitrators; reconvening of arbitrators; filing contracts with Board; custody of records and documents

The Mediation Board shall have the following duties with respect to the arbitration of disputes under section 157 of this title:

(a) On failure of the arbitrators named by the parties to agree on the remaining arbitrator or arbitrators within the time set by section 157 of this title, it shall be the duty of the Mediation Board to name such remaining arbitrator or arbitrators. It shall be the duty of the Board in naming such arbitrator or arbitrators to appoint only those whom the Board shall deem wholly disinterested in the controversy to be arbitrated and impartial and without bias as between the parties to such arbitration. Should, however, the Board name an arbitrator or arbitrators not so disinterested and impartial, then, upon proper investigation and presentation of the facts, the Board shall promptly remove such arbitrator.

If an arbitrator named by the Mediation Board, in accordance with the provisions of this chapter, shall be removed by such Board as provided by this chapter, or if such an arbitrator refuses or is unable to serve, it shall be the duty of the Mediation Board, promptly, to select another arbitrator, in the same manner as provided in this chapter for an original appointment by the Mediation Board.

(b) Any member of the Mediation Board is authorized to take the acknowledgement of an agreement to arbitrate under this chapter. When so acknowledged, or when acknowledged by the parties before a notary public or the clerk of a district court or a court of appeals of the United States, such agreement to arbitrate shall be delivered to a member of said Board or transmitted to said Board, to be filed in its office.

(c) When an agreement to arbitrate has been filed with the Mediation Board, or with one of its members, as provided by this section, and when the said Board has been furnished the names of the arbitrators chosen by the parties to the controversy it shall be the duty of the Board to cause a notice in writing to be served upon said arbitrators, notifying them of their appointment, requesting them to meet promptly to name the remaining arbitrator or arbitrators necessary to complete the Board of Arbitration, and advising them of the period within which, as provided by the agreement to arbitrate, they are empowered to name such arbitrator or arbitrators.

(d) Either party to an arbitration desiring the reconvening of a board of arbitration to pass upon any controversy arising over the meaning or application of an award may so notify the Mediation Board in writing, stating in such notice the question or questions to be submitted to such reconvened Board. The Mediation Board shall thereupon promptly communicate with the members of the Board of Arbitration, or a subcommittee of such Board appointed for such purpose pursuant to a provision in the agreement to arbitrate, and arrange for the reconvening of said Board of Arbitration or subcommittee, and shall notify the respective parties to the controversy of the time and place at which the Board, or the subcommittee, will meet for hearings upon the matters in controversy to be submitted to it. No evidence other than that contained in the record filed with the original award shall be received or considered by such reconvened Board or subcommittee, except such evidence as may be necessary to illustrate the interpretations suggested by the parties. If any member of the original Board is unable or unwilling to serve on such reconvened Board or subcommittee thereof, another arbitrator shall be named in the same manner and with the same powers and duties as such original arbitrator.

(e) Within sixty days after June 21, 1934, every carrier shall file with the Mediation Board a copy of each contract with its employees in effect on the 1st day of April 1934, covering rates of pay, rules, and working conditions. If no contract with any craft or class of its employees has been entered into, the carrier shall file with the Mediation Board a statement of that fact, including also a statement of the rates of pay, rules, and working conditions applicable in dealing with such craft or class. When any new contract is executed or change is made in an existing contract with any class or craft of its employees covering rates of pay, rules, or working conditions, or in those rates of pay, rules, and working conditions of employees not covered by contract, the carrier shall file the same with the Mediation Board within thirty days after such new contract or change in existing contract has been executed or rates of pay, rules, and working conditions have been made effective.

(f) The Mediation Board shall be the custodian of all papers and documents heretofore filed with or transferred to the Board of Mediation bearing upon the settlement, adjustment, or determination of disputes between carriers and their employees or upon mediation or arbitration proceedings held under or pursuant to the provisions of any Act of Congress in respect thereto; and the President is authorized to designate a custodian of the records and property of the Board of Mediation until the transfer and delivery of such records to the Mediation Board and to require the transfer and delivery to the Mediation Board of any and all such papers and documents filed with it or in its possession.

## § 6 (§ 156). Procedure in Changing Rates of Pay, Rules, and Working Conditions

Carriers and representatives of the employees shall give at least thirty days' written notice of an intended change in agreements affecting rates of pay, rules, or working conditions, and the time and place for the beginning of conference between the representatives of the parties interested in such intended changes shall be agreed upon within ten days after the receipt of said notice, and said time shall be within the thirty days provided in the notice. In every case where such notice of intended change has been given, or conferences are being held with reference thereto, or the services of the Mediation Board have been requested by either party, or said Board has proffered its services, rates of pay, rules, or working conditions shall not be altered by the carrier until the controversy has been finally acted upon, as required by section 155 of this title, by the Mediation Board, unless a period of ten days has elapsed after termination of conferences without request for or proffer of the services of the Mediation Board.

## § 7 (§ 157). Arbitration

### First. Submission of controversy to arbitration

Whenever a controversy shall arise between a carrier or carriers and its or their employees which is not settled either in conference between representatives of the parties or by the appropriate adjustment board or through mediation, in the manner provided in sections 151–156 of this title such controversy may, by agreement of the parties to such controversy, be submitted to the arbitration of a board of three (or, if the parties to the controversy so stipulate, of six) persons: *Provided, however,* That the failure or refusal of either party to submit a controversy to arbitration shall not be construed as a violation of any legal obligation imposed upon such party by the terms of this chapter or otherwise.

## Second. Manner of selecting board of arbitration

Such board of arbitration shall be chosen in the following manner:

(a) In the case of a board of three the carrier or carriers and the representatives of the employees, parties respectively to the agreement to arbitrate, shall each name one arbitrator; the two arbitrators thus chosen shall select a third arbitrator. If the arbitrators chosen by the parties shall fail to name the third arbitrator within five days after their first meeting, such third arbitrator shall be named by the Mediation Board.

(b) In the case of a board of six the carrier or carriers and the representatives of the employees, parties respectively to the agreement to arbitrate, shall each name two arbitrators; the four arbitrators thus chosen shall, by a majority vote, select the remaining two arbitrators. If the arbitrators chosen by the parties shall fail to name the two arbitrators within fifteen days after their first meeting, the said two arbitrators, or as many of them as have not been named, shall be named by the Mediation Board.

## Third. Board of arbitration; organization; compensation; procedure

### (a) Notice of selection or failure to select arbitrators

When the arbitrators selected by the respective parties have agreed upon the remaining arbitrator or arbitrators, they shall notify the Mediation Board; and, in the event of their failure to agree upon any or upon all of the necessary arbitrators within the period fixed by this chapter, they shall, at the expiration of such period, notify the Mediation Board of the arbitrators selected, if any, or of their failure to make or to complete such selection.

### (b) Organization of board; procedure

The board of arbitration shall organize and select its own chairman and make all necessary rules for conducting its hearings: *Provided, however,* That the board of arbitration shall be bound to give the parties to the controversy a full and fair hearing, which shall include an opportunity to present evidence in support of their claims, and an opportunity to present their case in person, by counsel, or by other representative as they may respectively elect.

*(c) Duty to reconvene; questions considered*

Upon notice from the Mediation Board that the parties, or either party, to an arbitration desire the reconvening of the board of arbitration (or a subcommittee of such board of arbitration appointed for such purpose pursuant to the agreement to arbitrate) to pass upon any controversy over the meaning or application of their award, the board, or its subcommittee, shall at once reconvene. No question other than, or in addition to, the questions relating to the meaning or application of the award, submitted by the party or parties in writing, shall be considered by the reconvened board of arbitration or its subcommittee.

Such rulings shall be acknowledged by such board or subcommittee thereof in the same manner, and filed in the same district court clerk's office, as the original award and become a part thereof.

*(d) Competency of arbitrators*

No arbitrator, except those chosen by the Mediation Board, shall be incompetent to act as an arbitrator because of his interest in the controversy to be arbitrated, or because of his connection with or partiality to either of the parties to the arbitration.

*(e) Compensation and expenses*

Each member of any board of arbitration created under the provisions of this chapter named by either party to the arbitration shall be compensated by the party naming him. Each arbitrator selected by the arbitrators or named by the Mediation Board shall receive from the Mediation Board such compensation as the Mediation Board may fix, together with his necessary traveling expenses and expenses actually incurred for subsistence, while serving as an arbitrator.

*(f) Award; disposition of original and copies*

The board of arbitration shall furnish a certified copy of its award to the respective parties to the controversy, and shall transmit the original, together with the papers and proceedings and a transcript of the evidence taken at the hearings, certified under the hands of at least a majority of the arbitrators, to the clerk of the district court of the United States for the district wherein the controversy arose or the arbitration is entered into, to be filed in said clerk's office as hereinafter provided. The said board shall also furnish a certified copy of its award, and the papers and proceedings, including testimony relating thereto, to the Mediation Board to be filed in its office; and in addition a certified copy of its award shall be filed in the office of the Interstate Commerce Commission: *Provided, however*, That such award shall not be construed to diminish or extinguish any of the powers or duties of the Interstate Commerce Commission, under subtitle IV of Title 49.

*(g) Compensation of assistants to board of arbitration; expenses; quarters*

A board of arbitration may, subject to the approval of the Mediation Board, employ and fix the compensation of such assistants as it deems necessary in carrying on the arbitration proceedings. The compensation of such employees, together with their necessary traveling expenses and expenses actually incurred for subsistence, while so employed, and the necessary expenses of boards of arbitration, shall be paid by the Mediation Board.

Whenever practicable, the board shall be supplied with suitable quarters in any Federal building located at its place of meeting or at any place where the board may conduct its proceedings or deliberations.

*(h) Testimony before board; oaths; attendance of witnesses; production of documents; subpoenas; fees*

All testimony before said board shall be given under oath or affirmation, and any member of the board shall have the power to administer oaths or affirmations. The board of arbitration, or any member thereof, shall have the power to require the attendance of witnesses and the production of such books, papers, contracts, agreements, and documents as may be deemed by the board of arbitration material to a just determination of the matters submitted to its arbitration, and may for that purpose request the clerk of the district court of the United States for the district wherein said arbitration is being conducted to issue the necessary subpoenas, and upon such request the said clerk or his duly authorized deputy shall be, and he is, authorized, and it shall be his duty, to issue such subpoenas.

Any witness appearing before a board of arbitration shall receive the same fees and mileage as witnesses in courts of the United States, to be paid by the party securing the subpoena.

## § 8 (§ 158). Agreement to Arbitrate; Form and Contents; Signatures and Acknowledgment; Revocation

The agreement to arbitrate—

(a) Shall be in writing;

(b) Shall stipulate that the arbitration is had under the provisions of this chapter;

(c) Shall state whether the board of arbitration is to consist of three or of six members;

(d) Shall be signed by the duly accredited representatives of the carrier or carriers and the employees, parties respectively to the agreement to arbitrate, and shall be acknowledged by said parties before a notary public, the clerk of a district court or court of appeals of the United

States, or before a member of the Mediation Board, and, when so acknowledged, shall be filed in the office of the Mediation Board;

(e) Shall state specifically the questions to be submitted to the said board for decision; and that, in its award or awards, the said board shall confine itself strictly to decisions as to the questions so specifically submitted to it;

(f) Shall provide that the questions, or any one or more of them, submitted by the parties to the board of arbitration may be withdrawn from arbitration on notice to that effect signed by the duly accredited representatives of all the parties and served on the board of arbitration;

(g) Shall stipulate that the signatures of a majority of said board of arbitration affixed to their award shall be competent to constitute a valid and binding award;

(h) Shall fix a period from the date of the appointment of the arbitrator or arbitrators necessary to complete the board (as provided for in the agreement) within which the said board shall commence its hearings;

(i) Shall fix a period from the beginning of the hearings within which the said board shall make and file its award: *Provided*, That the parties may agree at any time upon an extension of this period;

(j) Shall provide for the date from which the award shall become effective and shall fix the period during which the award shall continue in force;

(k) Shall provide that the award of the board of arbitration and the evidence of the proceedings before the board relating thereto, when certified under the hands of at least a majority of the arbitrators, shall be filed in the clerk's office of the district court of the United States for the district wherein the controversy arose or the arbitration was entered into, which district shall be designated in the agreement; and, when so filed, such award and proceedings shall constitute the full and complete record of the arbitration;

(l) Shall provide that the award, when so filed, shall be final and conclusive upon the parties as to the facts determined by said award and as to the merits of the controversy decided;

(m) Shall provide that any difference arising as to the meaning, or the application of the provisions, of an award made by a board of arbitration shall be referred back for a ruling to the same board, or, by agreement, to a subcommittee of such board; and that such ruling, when acknowledged in the same manner, and filed in the same district court clerk's office, as the original award, shall be a part of and shall have the same force and effect as such original award; and

(n) Shall provide that the respective parties to the award will each faithfully execute the same.

The said agreement to arbitrate, when properly signed and acknowledged as herein provided, shall not be revoked by a party to such agreement: *Provided, however*, That such agreement to arbitrate may at any time be revoked and canceled by the written agreement of both parties, signed by their duly accredited representatives, and (if no board of arbitration has yet been constituted under the agreement) delivered to the Mediation Board or any member thereof; or, if the board of arbitration has been constituted as provided by this chapter, delivered to such board of arbitration.

### § 9 (§ 159). Award and Judgment Thereon; Effect of Chapter on Individual Employee

#### First. Filing of award

The award of a board of arbitration, having been acknowledged as herein provided, shall be filed in the clerk's office of the district court designated in the agreement to arbitrate.

#### Second. Conclusiveness of award; judgment

An award acknowledged and filed as herein provided shall be conclusive on the parties as to the merits and facts of the controversy submitted to arbitration, and unless, within ten days after the filing of the award, a petition to impeach the award, on the grounds hereinafter set forth, shall be filed in the clerk's office of the court in which the award has been filed, the court shall enter judgment on the award, which judgment shall be final and conclusive on the parties.

#### Third. Impeachment of award; grounds

Such petition for the impeachment or contesting of any award so filed shall be entertained by the court only on one or more of the following grounds:

(a) That the award plainly does not conform to the substantive requirements laid down by this chapter for such awards, or that the proceedings were not substantially in conformity with this chapter;

(b) That the award does not conform, nor confine itself, to the stipulations of the agreement to arbitrate; or

(c) That a member of the board of arbitration rendering the award was guilty of fraud or corruption; or that a party to the arbitration practiced fraud or corruption which fraud or corruption affected the result of the arbitration: *Provided, however*, That no court shall entertain any such petition on the ground that an award is invalid for uncertainty; in such case the proper remedy shall be a submission of such award to a reconvened board, or subcommittee thereof, for interpretation, as provided by this chapter: *Provided further*, That an award contested as herein provided shall be construed liberally by the court, with a view to favoring its validity, and that no award shall be set aside for trivial irregularity or clerical error, going only to form and not to substance.

### Fourth. Effect of partial invalidity of award

If the court shall determine that a part of the award is invalid on some ground or grounds designated in this section as a ground of invalidity, but shall determine that a part of the award is valid, the court shall set aside the entire award: *Provided, however*, That, if the parties shall agree thereto, and if such valid and invalid parts are separable, the court shall set aside the invalid part, and order judgment to stand as to the valid part.

### Fifth. Appeal; record

At the expiration of 10 days from the decision of the district court upon the petition filed as aforesaid, final judgment shall be entered in accordance with said decision, unless during said 10 days either party shall appeal therefrom to the court of appeals. In such case only such portion of the record shall be transmitted to the appellate court as is necessary to the proper understanding and consideration of the questions of law presented by said petition and to be decided.

### Sixth. Finality of decision of court of appeals

The determination of said court of appeals upon said questions shall be final, and, being certified by the clerk thereof to said district court, judgment pursuant thereto shall thereupon be entered by said district court.

### Seventh. Judgment where petitioner's contentions are sustained

If the petitioner's contentions are finally sustained, judgment shall be entered setting aside the award in whole or, if the parties so agree, in part; but in such case the parties may agree upon a judgment to be entered disposing of the subject matter of the controversy, which judgment when entered shall have the same force and effect as judgment entered upon an award.

### Eighth. Duty of employee to render service without consent; right to quit

Nothing in this chapter shall be construed to require an individual employee to render labor or service without his consent, nor shall anything in this chapter be construed to make the quitting of his labor or service by an individual employee an illegal act; nor shall any court issue any process to compel the performance by an individual employee of such labor or service, without his consent.

## § 9A (§ 159a).    Special Procedure for Commuter Service

*(a) Applicability of provisions*

Except as provided in section 590(h) of this title, the provisions of this section shall apply to any dispute subject to this chapter between a publicly funded and publicly operated carrier providing rail commuter service (including the Amtrak Commuter Services Corporation) and its employees.

*(b) Request for establishment of emergency board*

If a dispute between the parties described in subsection (a) of this section is not adjusted under the foregoing provisions of this chapter and the President does not, under section 160 of this title, create an emergency board to investigate and report on such dispute, then any party to the dispute or the Governor of any State through which the service that is the subject of the dispute is operated may request the President to establish such an emergency board.

*(c) Establishment of emergency board*

(1) Upon the request of a party or a Governor under subsection (b) of this section, the President shall create an emergency board to investigate and report on the dispute in accordance with section 160 of this title. For purposes of this subsection, the period during which no change, except by agreement, shall be made by the parties in the conditions out of which the dispute arose shall be 120 days from the day of the creation of such emergency board.

(2) If the President, in his discretion, creates a board to investigate and report on a dispute between the parties described in subsection (a) of this section, the provisions of this section shall apply to the same extent as if such board had been created pursuant to paragraph (1) of this subsection.

*(d) Public hearing by National Mediation Board upon failure of emergency board to effectuate settlement of dispute*

Within 60 days after the creation of an emergency board under this section, if there has been no settlement between the parties, the National Mediation Board shall conduct a public hearing on the dispute at which each party shall appear and provide testimony setting forth the reasons it has not accepted the recommendations of the emergency board for settlement of the dispute.

*(e) Establishment of second emergency board*

If no settlement in the dispute is reached at the end of the 120-day period beginning on the date of the creation of the emergency board, any party to the dispute or the Governor of any State through which the service that is the subject of the dispute is operated may request the President to establish another emergency board, in which case the President shall establish such emergency board.

*(f) Submission of final offers to second emergency board by parties*

Within 30 days after creation of a board under subsection (e) of this section, the parties to the dispute shall submit to the board final offers for settlement of the dispute.

*(g) Report of second emergency board*

Within 30 days after the submission of final offers under subsection (f) of this section, the emergency board shall submit a report to the President setting forth its selection of the most reasonable offer.

*(h) Maintenance of status quo during dispute period*

From the time a request to establish a board is made under subsection (e) of this section until 60 days after such board makes its report under subsection (g) of this section, no change, except by agreement, shall be made by the parties in the conditions out of which the dispute arose.

*(i) Work stoppages by employees subsequent to carrier offer selected; eligibility of employees for benefits*

If the emergency board selects the final offer submitted by the carrier and, after the expiration of the 60-day period described in subsection (h) of this section, the employees of such carrier engage in any work stoppage arising out of the dispute, such employees shall not be eligible during the period of such work stoppage for benefits under the Railroad Unemployment Insurance Act [45 U.S.C.A. § 351 et seq.].

*(j) Work stoppages by employees subsequent to employees offer selected; eligibility of employer for benefits*

If the emergency board selects the final offer submitted by the employees and, after the expiration of the 60-day period described in subsection (h) of this section, the carrier refuses to accept the final offer submitted by the employees and the employees of such carrier engage in any work stoppage arising out of the dispute, the carrier shall not participate in any benefits of any agreement between carriers which is designed to provide benefits to such carriers during a work stoppage.

## § 10 (§ 160).   Emergency Board

If a dispute between a carrier and its employees be not adjusted under the foregoing provisions of this chapter and should, in the judgment of the Mediation Board, threaten substantially to interrupt interstate commerce to a degree such as to deprive any section of the country of essential transportation service, the Mediation Board shall notify the President, who may thereupon, in his discretion, create a board to investigate and report respecting such dispute. Such board shall be composed of such number of persons as to the President may seem desirable: *Provided, however,* That no member appointed shall be pecuniarily or otherwise interested in any organization of employees or any carrier. The compensation of the members of any such board shall be fixed by the President. Such board shall be created separately in each instance and it shall investigate promptly the facts as to the dispute and make a report thereon to the President within thirty days from the date of its creation.

There is authorized to be appropriated such sums as may be necessary for the expenses of such board, including the compensation and the necessary traveling expenses and expenses actually incurred for subsistence, of the members of the board. All expenditures of the board shall be allowed and paid on the presentation of itemized vouchers therefor approved by the chairman.

After the creation of such board and for thirty days after such board has made its report to the President, no change, except by agreement, shall be made by the parties to the controversy in the conditions out of which the dispute arose.

## § 11 (§ 161).     Effect of Partial Invalidity of Chapter

If any provision of this chapter, or the application thereof to any person or circumstance, is held invalid, the remainder of the chapter, and the application of such provision to other persons or circumstances, shall not be affected thereby.

## § 12 (§ 162).     Authorization of Appropriations

There is authorized to be appropriated such sums as may be necessary for expenditure by the Mediation Board in carrying out the provisions of this chapter.

## § 14 (§ 163).     Repeal of Prior Legislation; Exception

Chapters 6 and 7 of this title, providing for mediation, conciliation, and arbitration, and all Acts and parts of Acts in conflict with the provisions of this chapter are repealed, except that the members, secretary, officers, employees, and agents of the Railroad Labor Board, in office on May 20, 1926, shall receive their salaries for a period of 30 days from such date, in the same manner as though this chapter had not been passed.

# SUBCHAPTER II.     CARRIERS BY AIR

## § 201     (§ 181). Application of Subchapter I to Carriers by Air

All of the provisions of subchapter I of this chapter except section 153 of this title are extended to and shall cover every common carrier by air engaged in interstate or foreign commerce, and every carrier by air transporting mail for or under contract with the United States Government, and every air pilot or other person who performs any work as an employee or subordinate official of such carrier or carriers, subject to its or their continuing authority to supervise and direct the manner of rendition of his service.

## § 202   (§ 182). Duties, Penalties, Benefits, and Privileges of Subchapter I Applicable

The duties, requirements, penalties, benefits, and privileges prescribed and established by the provisions of subchapter I of this chapter except section 153 of this title shall apply to said carriers by air and their employees in the same manner and to the same extent as though such carriers and their employees were specifically included within the definition of "carrier" and "employee", respectively, in section 151 of this title.

## § 203   (§ 183). Disputes Within Jurisdiction of Mediation Board

The parties or either party to a dispute between an employee or a group of employees and a carrier or carriers by air may invoke the services of the National Mediation Board and the jurisdiction of said Mediation Board is extended to any of the following cases:

(a) A dispute concerning changes in rates of pay, rules, or working conditions not adjusted by the parties in conference.

(b) Any other dispute not referable to an adjustment board, as hereinafter provided, and not adjusted in conference between the parties, or where conferences are refused.

The National Mediation Board may proffer its services in case any labor emergency is found by it to exist at any time.

The services of the Mediation Board may be invoked in a case under this subchapter in the same manner and to the same extent as are the disputes covered by section 155 of this title.

## § 204   (§ 184). System, Group, or Regional Boards of Adjustment

The disputes between an employee or group of employees and a carrier or carriers by air growing out of grievances, or out of the interpretation or application of agreements concerning rates of pay, rules, or working conditions, including cases pending and unadjusted on April 10, 1936 before the National Labor Relations Board, shall be handled in the usual manner up to and including the chief operating officer of the carrier designated to handle such disputes; but, failing to reach an adjustment in this manner, the disputes may be referred by petition of the parties or by either party to an appropriate adjustment board, as hereinafter provided, with a full statement of the facts and supporting data bearing upon the disputes.

It shall be the duty of every carrier and of its employees, acting through their representatives, selected in accordance with the provisions of this subchapter, to establish a board of adjustment of jurisdiction not exceeding the jurisdiction which may be lawfully exercised by system, group, or regional boards of adjustment, under the authority of section 153 of this title.

Such boards of adjustment may be established by agreement between employees and carriers either on any individual carrier, or system, or group of carriers by air and any class or classes of its or their employees; or pending the establishment of a permanent National Board of Adjustment as hereinafter provided. Nothing in this chapter shall prevent said carriers by air, or any class or classes of their employees, both acting through their representatives selected in accordance with provisions of this subchapter, from mutually agreeing to the establishment of a National Board of Adjustment of temporary duration and of similarly limited jurisdiction.

## § 205    (§ 185). National Air Transport Adjustment Board

When, in the judgment of the National Mediation Board, it shall be necessary to have a permanent national board of adjustment in order to provide for the prompt and orderly settlement of disputes between said carriers by air, or any of them, and its or their employees, growing out of grievances or out of the interpretation or application of agreements between said carriers by air or any of them, and any class or classes of its or their employees, covering rates of pay, rules, or working conditions, the National Mediation Board is empowered and directed, by its order duly made, published, and served, to direct the said carriers by air and such labor organizations of their employees, national in scope, as have been or may be recognized in accordance with the provisions of this chapter, to select and designate four representatives who shall constitute a board which shall be known as the "National Air Transport Adjustment Board." Two members of said National Air Transport Adjustment Board shall be selected by said carriers by air and two members by the said labor organizations of the employees, within thirty days after the date of the order of the National Mediation Board, in the manner and by the procedure prescribed by section 153 of this title for the selection and designation of members of the National Railroad Adjustment Board. The National Air Transport Adjustment Board shall meet within forty days after the date of the order of the National Mediation Board directing the selection and designation of its members and shall organize and adopt rules for conducting its proceedings, in the manner prescribed in section 153 of this title. Vacancies in membership or office shall be filled, members shall be appointed in case of failure of the carriers or of labor organizations of the employees to select and designate representatives, members of the National Air Transport Adjustment Board shall be compensated, hearings shall be held, findings and awards made, stated, served, and enforced, and the number and compensation of any necessary assistants shall be determined and the compensation of such employees shall be paid, all in the same manner and to the same extent as provided with reference to the National Railroad Adjustment Board by section 153 of this title. The powers and duties prescribed and established by the provisions of section 153 of this title with reference to the National Railroad Adjustment Board and the several divisions thereof are conferred upon and shall be exercised and performed in like manner and to the same extent by the said National Air Transport Adjustment Board, not exceeding, however, the jurisdiction conferred upon said National Air Transport Adjustment Board by the provisions of this subchapter. From and after the organization of the National Air Transport Adjustment Board, if any system, group, or regional board of adjustment established by any carrier or carriers by air and any class or classes of its or their employees is not satisfactory to either party thereto, the said party, upon ninety days' notice to the other party, may elect to come under the jurisdiction of the National Air Transport Adjustment Board.

## § 207 (§ 187).   Separability

If any provision of this subchapter or application thereof to any person or circumstance is held invalid, the remainder of such sections and the application of such provision to other persons or circumstances shall not be affected thereby.

## § 208 (§ 188).   Authorization of Appropriations

There is authorized to be appropriated such sums as may be necessary for expenditure by the Mediation Board in carrying out the provisions of this chapter.

# NORRIS-LAGUARDIA ACT

■ ■ ■

47 Stat. 70 (1932), 29 U.S.C. §§ 101 et seq. (1976).

## § 1 (§ 101). Issuance of Restraining Orders and Injunctions; Limitation; Public Policy

No court of the United States, as herein defined, shall have jurisdiction to issue any restraining order or temporary or permanent injunction in a case involving or growing out of a labor dispute, except in a strict conformity with the provisions of this chapter; nor shall any such restraining order or temporary or permanent injunction be issued contrary to the public policy declared in this chapter.

## § 2 (§ 102). Public Policy in Labor Matters Declared

In the interpretation of this chapter and in determining the jurisdiction and authority of the courts of the United States, as such jurisdiction and authority are defined and limited in this chapter, the public policy of the United States is hereby declared as follows:

Whereas under prevailing economic conditions, developed with the aid of governmental authority for owners of property to organize in the corporate and other forms of ownership association, the individual unorganized worker is commonly helpless to exercise actual liberty of contract and to protect his freedom of labor, and thereby to obtain acceptable terms and conditions of employment, wherefore, though he should be free to decline to associate with his fellows, it is necessary that he have full freedom of association, self-organization, and designation of representatives of his own choosing, to negotiate the terms and conditions of his employment, and that he shall be free from the interference, restraint, or coercion of employers of labor, or their agents, in the designation of such representatives or in self-organization or in other concerted activities for the purpose of collective bargaining or other mutual aid or protection; therefore, the following definitions of, and limitations upon, the jurisdiction and authority of the courts of the United States are hereby enacted.

## § 3 (§ 103). Nonenforceability of Undertakings in Conflict With Public Policy; "Yellow Dog" Contracts

Any undertaking or promise, such as is described in this section, or any other undertaking or promise in conflict with the public policy declared in section 102 [§ 2] of this title, is declared to be contrary to the public policy of the United States, shall not be enforceable in any court of the United States and shall not afford any basis for the granting of legal or equitable relief by any such court, including specifically the following:

Every undertaking or promise hereafter made, whether written or oral, express or implied, constituting or contained in any contract or agreement of hiring or employment between any individual, firm, company, association, or corporation, and any employee or prospective employee of the same whereby

(a) Either party to such contract or agreement undertakes or promises not to join, become, or remain a member of any labor organization or of any employer organization; or

(b) Either party to such contract or agreement undertakes or promises that he will withdraw from an employment relation in the event that he joins, becomes, or remains a member of any labor organization or of any employer organization.

## § 4 (§ 104). Enumeration of Specific Acts Not Subject to Restraining Orders or Injunctions

No court of the United States shall have jurisdiction to issue any restraining order or temporary or permanent injunction in any case involving or growing out of any labor dispute to prohibit any person or persons participating or interested in such dispute (as these terms are herein defined) from doing, whether singly or in concert, any of the following acts:

(a) Ceasing or refusing to perform any work or to remain in any relation of employment;

(b) Becoming or remaining a member of any labor organization or of any employer organization, regardless of any such undertaking or promise as is described in Section 103 [Sec. 3] of this title;

(c) Paying or giving to, or withholding from, any person participating or interested in such labor dispute, any strike or unemployment benefits or insurance, or other moneys or things of value;

(d) By all lawful means aiding any person participating or interested in any labor dispute who is being proceeded against in, or is prosecuting, any action or suit in any court of the United States or of any State;

(e) Giving publicity to the existence of, or the facts involved in, any labor dispute, whether by advertising, speaking, patrolling, or by any other method not involving fraud or violence;

(f) Assembling peaceably to act or to organize to act in promotion of their interests in a labor dispute;

(g) Advising or notifying any person of an intention to do any of the Acts heretofore specified;

(h) Agreeing with other persons to do or not to do any of the acts heretofore specified; and

(i) Advising, urging, or otherwise causing or inducing without fraud or violence the acts heretofore specified, regardless of any such undertaking or promise as is described in section 103 [Sec. 3] of this title.

## § 5 (§ 105). Doing in Concert as Specific Acts as Constituting Unlawful Combination or Conspiracy Subjecting Person to Injunctive Remedies

No court of the United States shall have jurisdiction to issue a restraining order or temporary or permanent injunction upon the ground that any of the persons participating or interested in a labor dispute constitute or are engaged in an unlawful combination or conspiracy because of the doing in concert of the acts enumerated in section 104 [Sec. 4] of this title.

## § 6 (§ 106). Responsibility of Officers and Members of Associations or Their Organizations for Unlawful Acts of Individual Officers, Members, or Agents

No officer or member of any association or organization, and no association or organization participating or interested in a labor dispute, shall be held responsible or liable in any court of the United States for the unlawful acts of individual officers, members, or agents, except upon clear proof of actual participation in, or actual authorization of, such acts, or of ratification of such acts after actual knowledge thereof.

## § 7 (§ 107). Issuance of Injunctions in Labor Disputes; Hearing; Findings of Court; Notice to Affected Persons; Temporary Restraining Order; Undertakings

No court of the United States shall have jurisdiction to issue a temporary or permanent injunction in any case involving or growing out of a labor dispute, as defined in this chapter, except after hearing the testimony of witnesses in open court (with opportunity for cross-examination) in support of the allegations of a complaint made under oath, and testimony in opposition thereto, if offered, and except after findings of fact by the court, to the effect—

(a) That unlawful acts have been threatened and will be committed unless restrained or have been committed and will be continued unless restrained, but no injunction or temporary restraining order shall be issued on account of any threat or unlawful act excepting against the person or persons, association, or organization making the threat or committing the unlawful act or actually authorizing or ratifying the same after actual knowledge thereof;

(b) That substantial and irreparable injury to complainant's property will follow;

(c) That as to each item of relief granted greater injury will be inflicted upon complainant by the denial of relief than will be inflicted upon defendants by the granting of relief;

(d) That complainant has no adequate remedy at law; and

(e) That the public officers charged with the duty to protect complainant's property are unable or unwilling to furnish adequate protection.

Such hearing shall be held after due and personal notice thereof has been given, in such manner as the court shall direct, to all known persons against whom relief is sought, and also to the chief of those public officials of the county and city within which the unlawful acts have been threatened or committed charged with the duty to protect complainant's property: Provided, however, That if a complainant shall also allege that, unless a temporary restraining order shall be issued without notice, a substantial and irreparable injury to complainant's property will be unavoidable, such a temporary restraining order may be issued upon testimony under oath, sufficient, if sustained, to justify the court in issuing a temporary injunction upon a hearing after notice. Such a temporary restraining order shall be effective for no longer than five days and shall become void at the expiration of said five days. No temporary restraining order or temporary injunction shall be issued except on condition that complainant shall first file an undertaking with adequate security in an amount to be fixed by the court sufficient to recompense those enjoined for any loss, expense, or damage caused by the improvident or erroneous issuance of such order or injunction, including all reasonable costs (together with a reasonable attorney's fee) and expense of defense against the order or against the granting of any injunctive relief sought in the same proceeding and subsequently denied by the court.

The undertaking herein mentioned shall be understood to signify an agreement entered into by the complainant and the surety upon which a decree may be rendered in the same suit or proceeding against said complainant and surety, upon a hearing to assess damages of which hearing complainant and surety shall have reasonable notice, the said complainant and surety submitting themselves to the jurisdiction of the court for that purpose. But nothing in this section shall deprive any party having a claim or cause of action under or upon such undertaking from electing to pursue his ordinary remedy by suit at law or in equity.

## § 8 (§ 108). Noncompliance With Obligations Involved in Labor Disputes or Failure to Settle by Negotiation or Arbitration as Preventing Injunctive Relief

No restraining order or injunctive relief shall be granted to any complainant who has failed to comply with any obligation imposed by law which is involved in the labor dispute in question, or who has failed to make every reasonable effort to settle such dispute either by negotiation or with the aid of any available governmental machinery of mediation or voluntary arbitration.

## § 9 (§ 109). Granting of Restraining Order of Injunction as Dependent on Previous Findings of Fact; Limitations on Prohibitions Included in Restraining Orders and Injunctions

No restraining order or temporary or permanent injunction shall be granted in a case involving or growing out of a labor dispute, except on the basis of findings of fact made and filed by the court in the record of the case prior to the issuance of such restraining order or injunction; and every restraining order or injunction granted in a case involving or growing out of a labor dispute shall include only a prohibition of such specific act or acts as may be expressly complained of in the bill of complaint or petition filed in such case and as shall be expressly included in said findings of fact made and filed by the court as provided in this chapter.

## § 10 (§ 110). Review by Court of Appeals or Issuance of Denial of Temporary Injunctions; Record

Whenever any court of the United States shall issue or deny any temporary injunction in a case involving or growing out of a labor dispute, the court shall, upon the request of any party to the proceedings and on his filing the usual bond for costs, forthwith certify as in ordinary cases the record of the case to the court of appeals for its review. Upon the filing of such record in the court of appeals, the appeal shall be heard and the temporary injunctive order affirmed, modified, or set aside expeditiously.

## §§ 11 and 12 (§§ 111 and 112). Repealed June 25, 1948

## § 13 (§ 113). Definitions of Terms and Words Used in Act

When used in this Act, and for the purposes of this Act—

(a) A case shall be held to involve or to grow out of a labor dispute when the case involves persons who are engaged in the same industry, trade, craft, or occupation; or have direct or indirect interests therein; or who are employees of the same employer; or who are members of the same or an affiliated organization of employers or employees; whether such dispute is (1) between one or more employers or associations of employers and one or more employees or associations of employees; (2) between one or more employers or associations of employers and one or more employers or associations of employers; or (3) between one or more employees or associations of employees and one or more employees or associations of employees; or when the case involves any conflicting or competing interests in a "labor dispute" as defined in this section of "persons participating or interested" therein as defined in this section.

(b) A person or association shall be held to be a person participating or interested in a labor dispute if relief is sought against him or it, and if he or it is engaged in the same industry, trade, craft, or occupation in which such dispute occurs, or has a direct or indirect interest therein, or is a member, officer, or agent of any association composed in whole or in part of employers or employees engaged in such industry, trade, craft, or occupation.

(c) The term "labor dispute" includes any controversy concerning terms or conditions of employment, or concerning the association or representation of persons in negotiating, fixing, maintaining, changing, or seeking to arrange terms or conditions of employment, regardless of whether or not the disputants stand in the proximate relation of employer and employee.

(d) The term "court of the United States" means any court of the United States whose jurisdiction has been or may be conferred or defined or limited by Act of Congress, including the courts of the District of Columbia.

## § 14 (§ 114).    Separability of Provisions

If any provision of this chapter or the application thereof to any person or circumstance is held unconstitutional or otherwise invalid, the remaining provisions of the Act and the application of such provisions to other persons or circumstances shall not be affected thereby.

## § 15 (§ 115).    Repeal of Conflicting Laws

All Acts and parts of Acts in conflict with the provisions of this chapter are repealed.

# NATIONAL LABOR RELATIONS ACT*

■ ■ ■

49 Stat. 499 (1935) *as amended* 61 Stat. 136 (1947); 65 Stat. 601
(1951); 72 Stat. 945(1958); 73 Stat. 541 (1959); 88 Stat. 395
(1974); 92 Stat. 2678 (1978); 94 Stat. 347(1980); 94 Stat. 3452
(1980); 29 U.S.C. §§ 151–69.

## § 1 (§ 151). Findings and Policies

The denial by **some** employers of the right of employees to organize
and the refusal by **some** employers to accept the procedure of collective
bargaining lead to strikes and other forms of industrial strife or unrest,
which have the intent or the necessary effect of burdening or obstructing
commerce by (a) impairing the efficiency, safety, or operation of the
instrumentalities of commerce; (b) occurring in the current of commerce;
(c) materially affecting, restraining, or controlling the flow of raw
materials or manufactured or processed goods from or into the channels
of commerce, or the prices of such materials or goods in commerce; or (d)
causing diminution of employment and wages in such volume as
substantially to impair or disrupt the market for goods flowing from or
into the channels of commerce.

The inequality of bargaining power between employees who do not
possess full freedom of association or actual liberty of contract, and
employers who are organized in the corporate or other forms of ownership
association substantially burdens and affects the flow of commerce, and
tends to aggravate recurrent business depressions, by depressing wage
rates and the purchasing power of wage earners in industry and by
preventing the stabilization of competitive wage rates and working
conditions within and between industries.

Experience has proved that protection by law of the right of employees to
organize and bargain collectively safeguards commerce from injury,
impairment, or interruption, and promotes the flow of commerce by
removing certain recognized sources of industrial strife and unrest, by
encouraging practices fundamental to the friendly adjustment of
industrial disputes arising out of differences as to wages, hours, or other
working conditions, and by restoring equality of bargaining power
between employers and employees.

---

\* The provisions of the 1935 National Labor Relations Act (Wagner Act) are in roman type;
provisions added by the Labor Management Relations Act (1947) [Taft-Hartley amendments] are
in bold face; provisions added by the Labor-Management Reporting and Disclosure Act (1959)
[Landrum Griffin] are in italics; provisions added by Pub. L. No. 93–360 (enacted July 26, 1974)
are in bold-face italics. Material deleted by any of those statutes is enclosed by brackets.

**Experience has further demonstrated that certain practices by some labor organizations, their officers, and members have the intent or the necessary effect of burdening or obstructing commerce by preventing the free flow of goods in such commerce through strikes and other forms of industrial unrest or through concerted activities which impair the interest of the public in the free flow of such commerce. The elimination of such practices is a necessary condition to the assurance of the rights herein guaranteed.**

It is hereby declared to be the policy of the United States to eliminate the causes of certain substantial obstructions to the free flow of commerce and to mitigate and eliminate these obstructions when they have occurred by encouraging the practice and procedure of collective bargaining and by protecting the exercise by workers of full freedom of association, self organization, and designation of representatives of their own choosing, for the purpose of negotiating the terms and conditions of their employment or other mutual aid or protection.

## § 2  (§ 152). Definitions

When used in this Act—

(1) The term "person" includes one or more individuals, labor organizations, partnerships, associations, corporations, legal representatives, trustees, trustees in bankruptcy, or receivers.*

(2) The term "employer" includes any person acting [in the interest] **as an agent** of an employer, directly or indirectly, but shall not include the United States **or any wholly owned Government corporation, or any Federal Reserve Bank**, or any State or political subdivision thereof, **[or any corporation or association operating a hospital, if no part of the net earnings inures to the benefit of any private shareholder or individual,]** or any person subject to the Railway Labor Act, as amended from time to time, or any labor organization (other than when acting as an employer), or anyone acting in the capacity of officer or agent of such labor organization.

(3) The term "employee" shall include any employee, and shall not be limited to the employees of a particular employer, unless the Act explicitly states otherwise, and shall include any individual whose work has ceased as a consequence of, or in connection with, any current labor dispute or because of any unfair labor practice, and who has not obtained any other regular and substantially equivalent employment, but shall not include any individual employed as an

---

* Section 2(1) was amended by Pub. L. No. 95–598, effective October 1, 1979, to add the words "cases under Title II of the United States Code" and to delete the material enclosed in brackets.

agricultural laborer, or in the domestic service of any family or person at his home, or any individual employed by his parent or spouse, **or any individual having the status of an independent contractor, or any individual employed as a supervisor, or any individual employed by an employer subject to the Railway Labor Act, as amended from time to time, or by any other person who is not an employer as herein defined.**

(4) The term "representatives" includes any individual or labor organization.

(5) The term "labor organization" means any organization of any kind, or any agency or employee representation committee or plan, in which employees participate and which exists for the purpose, in whole or in part, of dealing with employers concerning grievances, labor disputes, wages, rates of pay, hours of employment, or conditions of work.

(6) The term "commerce" means trade, traffic commerce, transportation, or communication among the several States, or between the District of Columbia or any Territory of the United States and any State or other Territory, or between any foreign country and any State, Territory, or the District of Columbia, or within the District of Columbia or any Territory, or between points in the same State but through any other State or any Territory or the District of Columbia or any foreign country.

(7) The term "affecting commerce" means in commerce, or burdening or obstructing commerce or the free flow of commerce, or having led or tending to lead to a labor dispute burdening or obstructing commerce or the free flow of commerce.

(8) The term "unfair labor practice" means any unfair labor practice listed in section 8 [29 U.S.C. 158].

(9) The term "labor dispute" includes any controversy concerning terms, tenure or conditions of employment, or concerning the association or representation of persons in negotiating, fixing, maintaining, changing, or seeking to arrange terms or conditions of employment, regardless of whether the disputants stand in the proximate relation of employer and employee.

(10) The term "National Labor Relations Board" means the National Labor Relations Board provided for in section 3 of this Act.

**(11) The term "supervisor" means any individual having authority, in the interest of the employer, to hire, transfer, suspend, lay off, recall, promote, discharge, assign, reward, or discipline other employees, or responsibly to direct them, or to adjust their grievances, or effectively to recommend such action, if in connection with the foregoing the exercise of**

such authority is not of a merely routine or clerical nature, but requires the use of independent judgment.

(12) The term "professional employee" means—

(a) any employee engaged in work (i) predominantly intellectual and varied in character as opposed to routine mental, manual, mechanical, or physical work; (ii) involving the consistent exercise of discretion and judgment in its performance; (iii) of such a character that the output produced or the result accomplished cannot be standardized in relation to a given period of time; (iv) requiring knowledge of an advanced type in a field of science or learning customarily acquired by a prolonged course of specialized intellectual instruction and study in an institution of higher learning or a hospital, as distinguished from a general academic education or from an apprenticeship or from training in the performance of routine mental, manual, or physical processes; or

(b) any employee, who (i) has completed the courses of specialized intellectual instruction and study described in clause (iv) of paragraph (a), and (ii) is performing related work under the supervision of a professional person to qualify himself to become a professional employee as defined in paragraph (a).

(13) In determining whether any person is acting as an "agent" of another person so as to make such other person responsible for his acts, the question of whether the specific acts performed were actually authorized or subsequently ratified shall not be controlling.

*(14) The term "health care institution" shall include any hospital, convalescent hospital, health maintenance organization, health clinic, nursing home, extended care facility, or other institution devoted to the care of sick, infirm, or aged person.*

## § 3 (§ 153). The National Labor Relations Board

(a) The National Labor Relations Board (hereinafter called the "Board") created by this Act prior to its amendment by the Labor Management Relations Act, 1947, is hereby continued as an agency of the United States, except that the Board shall consist of five instead of three members, appointed by the President by and with the advice and consent of the Senate. Of the two additional members so provided for, one shall be appointed for a term of five years and the other for a term of two years. Their successors, and the successors of the other members, shall be appointed for terms of five years each, excepting that any individual chosen to fill a vacancy shall be appointed only for the unexpired term of the member whom he shall succeed. The President shall designate one member to serve as Chairman of the Board. Any member of the Board may be removed by the President, upon notice and hearing, for neglect of duty or malfeasance in office, but for no other cause.

**(b)** The Board is authorized to delegate to any group of three or more members any or all of the powers which it may itself exercise. *The Board is also authorized to delegate to its regional directors its powers under section 9 to determine the unit appropriate for the purpose of collective bargaining, to investigate and provide for hearings, and determine whether a question of representation exists, and to direct an election or take a secret ballot under subsection (c) or (e) of section 9 and certify the results thereof, except that upon the filing of a request therefor with the Board by any interested person, the Board may review any action of a regional director delegated to him under this paragraph, but such a review shall not, unless specifically ordered by the Board, operate as a stay of any action taken by the regional director.* A vacancy in the Board shall not impair the right of the remaining members to exercise all of the powers of the Board, and three members of the Board shall, at all times, constitute a quorum of the Board, except that two members shall constitute a quorum of any group designated pursuant to the first sentence thereof. The Board shall have an official seal which shall be judicially noticed.

**(c)** The Board shall at the close of each fiscal year make a report in writing to Congress and to the President (stating in detail the cases it has heard, the decisions it has rendered,) [the names, salaries, and duties of all employees and officers in the employ or under the supervision of the Board,]* (and an account of all moneys it has disbursed).**

**(d)** There shall be a General Counsel of the Board who shall be appointed by the President, by and with the advice and consent of the Senate, for a term of four years. The General Counsel of the Board shall exercise general supervision over all attorneys employed by the Board (other than administrative law judges and legal assistants to Board members) and over the officers and employees in the regional offices. He shall have final authority, on behalf of the Board, in respect of the investigation of charges

---

* Section 3(c) was amended by Pub. L. No. 93–608, approved January 2, 1975, to delete the material enclosed by brackets.

** Section 3 (c) was further amended by Pub. L. No. 97–375, enacted on December 21, 1982, to delete the material in parentheses and add "summarizing significant case activities and operations for the fiscal year."

and issuance of complaints under section 10, and in respect of the prosecution of such complaints before the Board, and shall have such other duties as the Board may prescribe or as may be provided by law. *In case of a vacancy in the office of the General Counsel the President is authorized to designate the officer or employee who shall act as General Counsel during such vacancy, but no person or persons so designated shall so act (1) for more than forty days when the Congress is in session unless a nomination to fill such vacancy shall have been submitted to the Senate, or (2) after the adjournment sine die of the session of the Senate in which such nomination was submitted.*

## § 4 (§ 154). The National Labor Relations Board; Eligibility for Reappointment; Officers and Employees; Payment of Expenses

(a) Each member of the Board and the General Counsel of the Board [shall receive a salary of $12,000* a year, shall be eligible for reappointment,]** and shall not engage in any other business, vocation, or employment. The Board shall appoint an executive secretary, and such attorneys, examiners, and regional directors, and such other employees as it may from time to time find necessary for the proper performance of its duties. The Board may not employ any attorneys for the purpose of reviewing transcripts of hearings or preparing drafts of opinions except that any attorney employed for assignment as a legal assistant to any Board member may for such Board member review such transcripts and prepare such drafts. No administrative law judge's report shall be reviewed, either before or after its publication, by any person other than a member of the Board or his legal assistant, and no administrative law judge shall advise or consult with the Board with respect to exceptions taken to his findings, rulings, or recommendations. The Board may establish or utilize such regional, local, or other agencies, and utilize such voluntary and uncompensated services, as may from time to time be needed. Attorneys appointed under this section may, at the direction of the Board, appear for and represent the Board in any case in court. Nothing in this Act shall be construed to authorize the Board to appoint individuals for the purpose of conciliation or mediation, or for economic analysis.

(b) All the expenses of the Board, including all necessary traveling and subsistence expenses outside the District of Columbia incurred by the members or employees of the Board under its orders, shall be allowed and paid on the presentation of

---

\*   See 5 U.S.C. §§ 5314 and 5315.

\*\*  Pursuant to the Federal Salary Schedule, member compensation was omitted.

itemized vouchers therefor approved by the Board or by any individual it designates for that purpose.

## § 5 (§ 155). National Labor Relations Board; Principal Office; Conducting Inquiries Throughout Country; Participation in Decisions or Inquiries Conducted by Member

The principal office of the Board shall be in the District of Columbia, but it may meet and exercise any or all of its powers at any other place. The Board may, by one or more of its members or by such agents or agencies as it may designate, prosecute any inquiry necessary to its functions in any part of the United States. A member who participates in such an inquiry shall not be disqualified from subsequently participating in a decision of the Board in the same case.

## § 6 (§ 156). Rules and Regulations

The Board shall have authority from time to time to make, amend, and rescind, **in the manner prescribed by subchapter II of chapter 5 of title 5**\*, such rules and regulations as may be necessary to carry out the provisions of this Act.

## § 7 (§ 157). Rights of Employees

Employees shall have the right to self organization, to form, join, or assist labor organizations, to bargain collectively through representatives of their own choosing, and to engage in **other** concerted activities for the purpose of collective bargaining or other mutual aid or protection, **and shall also have the right to refrain from any or all of such activities except to the extent that such right may be affected by an agreement requiring membership in a labor organization as a condition of employment as authorized in section 8(a)(3).**

## § 8 (§ 158). Unfair Labor Practices

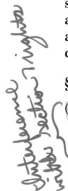

(a) It shall be an unfair labor practice for an employer—

(1) to interfere with, restrain, or coerce employees in the exercise of the rights guaranteed in section 7;

(2) to dominate or interfere with the formation or administration of any labor organization or contribute financial or other support to it: *Provided*, That subject to rules and regulations made and published by the Board pursuant to section 6, an employer shall not be prohibited from permitting employees to confer with him during working hours without loss of time or pay;

---

\* Pub. L. No. 89–554_7(b), enacted September 6, 1966 replaced "the Administrative Procedures Act" with "Subchapter II of chapter 5 of title 5."

*discriminatory intent*

(3) by discrimination in regard to hire or tenure of employment or any term or condition of employment to encourage or discourage membership in any labor organization: *Provided*, [ ] That nothing in this Act, or in any other statute of the United States, shall preclude an employer from making an agreement with a labor organization (not established, maintained, or assisted by any action defined in **section 8(a)** of this Act as an unfair labor practice) to require as a condition of employment membership therein **on or after the thirtieth day following the beginning of such employment or the effective date of such agreement, whichever is the later,** (i) if such labor organization is the representative of the employees as provided in section 9(a), in the appropriate collective bargaining unit covered by such agreement when made **[and has at the time the agreement was made or within the preceding twelve months received from the Board a notice of compliance with section 9(f), (g), (h)], and (ii) unless following an election held as provided in section 9(e) within one year preceding the effective date of such agreement, the Board shall have certified that at least a majority of the employees eligible to vote in such election have voted to rescind the authority of such labor organization to make such an agreement:** *Provided further*, **That no employer shall justify any discrimination against an employee for nonmembership in a labor organization (A) if he has reasonable grounds for believing that such membership was not available to the employee on the same terms and conditions generally applicable to other members, or (B) if he has reasonable grounds for believing that membership was denied or terminated for reasons other than the failure of the employee to tender the periodic dues and the initiation fees uniformly required as a condition of acquiring or retaining membership;**

(4) to discharge or otherwise discriminate against an employee because he has filed charges or given testimony under this Act;

(5) to refuse to bargain collectively with the representatives of his employees, subject to the provisions of section 9(a).

**(b) It shall be an unfair labor practice for a labor organization or its agents—**

*applies to union*

**(1) to restrain or coerce (A) employees in the exercise of the rights guaranteed in section 7:** *Provided*, **That this paragraph shall not impair the right of a labor organization to prescribe its own rules with respect to the acquisition or retention of membership therein; or (B) an employer in the selection of his representatives for the purposes of collective bargaining or the adjustment of grievances;**

(2) to cause or attempt to cause an employer to discriminate against an employee in violation of subsection (a)(3) or to discriminate against an employee with respect to whom membership in such organization has been denied or terminated on some ground other than his failure to tender the periodic dues and the initiation fees uniformly required as a condition of acquiring or retaining membership;

(3) to refuse to bargain collectively with an employer, provided it is the representative of his employees subject to the provisions of section 9(a);

(4)(i) to engage in, or to induce or encourage [the employees of any employer] *any individual employed by any person engaged in commerce or in an industry affecting commerce* to engage in, a strike or a [concerted] refusal in the course of [their] *his* employment to use, manufacture, process, transport, or otherwise handle or work on any goods, articles, materials, or commodities or to perform any services[,]; *or (ii) to threaten, coerce, or restrain any person engaged in commerce or in an industry affecting commerce,* where *in either case* an object thereof is:

(A) forcing or requiring any employer or self-employed person to join any labor or employer organization or [any employer or other person to cease using, selling, handling, transporting, or otherwise dealing in the products of any other producer, processor, or manufacturer, or to cease doing business with any other person] *to enter into any agreement which is prohibited by section 8(e);*

(B) *forcing or requiring any person to cease using, selling, handling, transporting, or otherwise dealing in the products of any other producer, processor, or manufacturer, or to cease doing business with any other person,* or forcing or requiring any other employer to recognize or bargain with a labor organization as the representative of his employees unless such labor organization has been certified as the representative of such employees under the provisions of section 9[;]: *Provided, That nothing contained in this clause (B) shall be construed to make unlawful, where not otherwise unlawful, any primary strike or primary picketing;*

(C) forcing or requiring any employer to recognize or bargain with a particular labor organization as the representative of his employees if another labor organization has been certified as the representative of such employees under the provisions of section 9;

**(D)** forcing or requiring any employer to assign particular work to employees in a particular labor organization or in a particular trade, craft, or class rather than to employees in another labor organization or in another trade, craft, or class, unless such employer is failing to conform to an order or certification of the Board determining the bargaining representative for employees performing such work;

*Provided*, That nothing contained in this subsection (b) shall be construed to make unlawful a refusal by any person to enter upon the premises of any employer (other than his own employer), if the employees of such employer are engaged in a strike ratified or approved by a representative of such employees whom such employer is required to recognize under this Act[;]: *Provided further, That for the purposes of this paragraph (4) only, nothing contained in such paragraph shall be construed to prohibit publicity, other than picketing, for the purpose of truthfully advising the public, including consumers and members of a labor organization, that a product or products are produced by an employer with whom the labor organization has a primary dispute and are distributed by another employer, as long as such publicity does not have an effect of inducing any individual employed by any person other than the primary employer in the course of his employment to refuse to pick up, deliver, or transport any goods, or not to perform any services, at the establishment of the employer engaged in such distribution;*

**(5)** to require of employees covered by an agreement authorized under subsection (a)(3) the payment, as a condition precedent to becoming a member of such organization, of a fee in an amount which the Board finds excessive or discriminatory under all the circumstances. In making such a finding, the Board shall consider, among other relevant factors, the practices and customs of labor organizations in the particular industry, and the wages currently paid to the employees affected; [and]

**(6)** to cause or attempt to cause an employer to pay or deliver or agree to pay or deliver any money or other thing of value, in the nature of an exaction, for services which are not performed or not to be performed[.]; *and*

*(7) to picket or cause to be picketed, or threaten to picket or cause to be picketed, any employer where an object thereof is forcing or requiring an employer to recognize or bargain with a labor organization as the representative of his employees, or forcing or requiring the employees of an employer to accept or select such labor organization as their*

*collective bargaining representative, unless such labor organization is currently certified as the representative of such employees:*

> (A) *where the employer has lawfully recognized in accordance with this Act any other labor organization and a question concerning representation may not appropriately be raised under section 9(c) of this Act,*
>
> (B) *where within the preceding twelve months a valid election under section 9(c) of this Act has been conducted, or*
>
> (C) *where such picketing has been conducted without a petition under section 9(c) being filed within a reasonable period of time not to exceed thirty days from the commencement of such picketing: Provided, That when such a petition has been filed the Board shall forthwith, without regard to the provisions of section 9(c)(1) or the absence of a showing of a substantial interest on the part of the labor organization, direct an election in such unit as the Board finds to be appropriate and shall certify the results thereof: Provided further, That nothing in this subparagraph (C) shall be construed to prohibit any picketing or other publicity for the purpose of truthfully advising the public (including consumers) that an employer does not employ members of, or have a contract with, a labor organization, unless an effect of such picketing is to induce any individual employed by any other person in the course of his employment, not to pick up, deliver or transport any goods or not to perform any services.*

*Nothing in this paragraph (7) shall be construed to permit any act which would otherwise be an unfair labor practice under this section 8(b).*

**(c)** The expressing of any views, argument, or opinion, or the dissemination thereof, whether in written, printed, graphic, or visual form, shall not constitute or be evidence of an unfair labor practice under any of the provisions of this Act, if such expression contains no threat of reprisal or force or promise of benefit.

**(d)** For the purposes of this section, to bargain collectively is the performance of the mutual obligation of the employer and the representative of the employees to meet at reasonable times, and confer in good faith with respect to wages, hours, and other terms and conditions of employment, or the negotiation of an agreement, or any question arising thereunder, and the execution of a written contract incorporating any agreement reached if requested by either party, but such obligation does not compel either party to agree to a proposal or require the making of a concession: *Provided,* That where there is in effect a collective

*applies to employer*

bargaining contract covering employees in an industry affecting commerce, the duty to bargain collectively shall also mean that no party to such contract shall terminate or modify such contract, unless the party desiring such termination or modification—

(1) serves a written notice upon the other party to the contract of the proposed termination or modification sixty days prior to the expiration date thereof, or in the event such contract contains no expiration date, sixty days prior to the time it is proposed to make such termination or modification;

(2) offers to meet and confer with the other party for the purpose of negotiating a new contract or a contract containing the proposed modifications;

(3) notifies the Federal Mediation and Conciliation Service within thirty days after such notice of the existence of a dispute, and simultaneously therewith notifies any State or Territorial agency established to mediate and conciliate disputes within the State or Territory where the dispute occurred, provided no agreement has been reached by that time; and

(4) continues in full force and effect, without resorting to strike or lockout, all the terms and conditions of the existing contract for a period of sixty days after such notice is given or until the expiration date of such contract, whichever occurs later:

The duties imposed upon employers, employees, and labor organizations by paragraphs (2), (3), and (4) shall become inapplicable upon an intervening certification of the Board, under which the labor organization or individual, which is a party to the contract, has been superseded as or ceased to be the representative of the employees subject to the provisions of section 9(a), and the duties so imposed shall not be construed as requiring either party to discuss or agree to any modification of the terms and conditions contained in a contract for a fixed period, if such modification is to become effective before such terms and conditions can be reopened under the provisions of the contract. Any employee who engages in a strike within [the sixty day] *any notice* period specified in this subsection, *or who engages in any strike within the appropriate period specified in subsection (g) of this section* shall lose his status as an employee of the employer engaged in the particular labor dispute, for the purposes of sections 8, 9, and 10 of this Act, as amended, but such loss of status for such employee shall terminate if and when he is reemployed by such employer. *Whenever the collective bargaining involves employees of a health care institution, the provisions of this section 8(d) shall be modified as follows:*

> *(A) The notice of section 8(d)(1) shall be ninety days; the notice of section 8(d)(3) shall be sixty days; and the contract period of section 8(d)(4) shall be ninety days.*
>
> *(B) Where the bargaining is for an initial agreement following certification or recognition, at least thirty days' notice of the existence of a dispute shall be given by the labor organization to the agencies set forth in section 8(d)(3).*
>
> *(C) After notice is given to the Federal Mediation and Conciliation Service under either clause (A) or (B) of this sentence, the Service shall promptly communicate with the parties and use its best efforts, by mediation and conciliation, to bring them to agreement. The parties shall participate fully and promptly in such meetings as may be undertaken by the Service for the purpose of aiding in a settlement of the dispute.*

(e) *It shall be an unfair labor practice for any labor organization and any employer to enter into any contract or agreement, express or implied, whereby such employer ceases or refrains or agrees to cease or refrain from handling, using, selling, transporting or otherwise dealing in any of the products of any other employer, or to cease doing business with any other person, and any contract or agreement entered into heretofore or hereafter containing such an agreement shall be to such extent unenforceable and void:* Provided, *That nothing in this subsection (e) shall apply to an agreement between a labor organization and an employer in the construction industry relating to the contracting or subcontracting of work to be done at the site of the construction, alteration, painting, or repair of a building, structure, or other work:* Provided further, *That for the purposes of this subsection (e) and section 8(b)(4)(B) the terms "any employer" "any person engaged in commerce or in industry affecting commerce", and "any person" when used in relation to the terms "any other producer, processor, or manufacturer", "any other employer", or "any other person" shall not include persons in the relation of a jobber, manufacturer, contractor, or subcontractor working on the goods or premises of the jobber or manufacturer or performing parts of an integrated process of production in the apparel and clothing industry:* Provided further, *That nothing in this Act shall prohibit the enforcement of any agreement which is within the foregoing exception.*

(f) *It shall not be an unfair labor practice under subsections (a) and (b) of this section for an employer engaged primarily in the building and construction industry to make an agreement covering employees engaged (or who, upon their employment, will be engaged) in the building and* *construction industry with a labor organization of which building and construction employees are members (not established, maintained, or assisted by any action defined in section 8(a) of this Act as an unfair labor practice) because (1) the majority status of such labor organization has not been established under the provisions of section 9 of this Act prior to the making of such agreement, or (2) such agreement requires as a condition of employment, membership in such labor organization after the seventh day following the beginning of such employment or the effective date of the agreement, whichever is later, or (3) such agreement requires the employer to notify such labor organization of opportunities for employment with such employer, or gives such labor organization an opportunity to refer qualified applicants for such employment, or (4) such agreement specifies minimum training or experience qualifications for employment or provides for priority in opportunities for employment based upon length of service with such employer, in the industry or in the particular geographical area: Provided, That nothing in this subsection shall set aside the final proviso to section 8(a)(3) of this Act: Provided further, That any agreement which would be invalid, but for clause (1) of this subsection, shall not be a bar to a petition filed pursuant to section 9(c) or 9(e).\**

**(g) A labor organization before engaging in any strike, picketing, or other concerted refusal to work at any health care institution shall, not less than ten days prior to such action, notify the institution in writing and the Federal Mediation and Conciliation Service of that intention, except that in the case of bargaining for an initial agreement following certification or recognition the notice required by this subsection shall not be given until the expiration of the period specified in clause (B) of the last sentence of section 8(d) of this Act. The notice shall state the date and time that such action will commence. The notice, once given, may be extended by the written agreement of both parties.**

## § 9 (§ 159). Representatives and Elections

(a) Representatives designated or selected for the purposes of collective bargaining by the majority of the employees in a unit appropriate for such purposes, shall be the exclusive representatives of all the employees in such unit for the purposes of collective bargaining in respect to rates of pay, wages, hours of employment, or other conditions of employment: *Provided,* That any individual employee or a group of employees shall have the right at any time to present grievances to their employer **and to**

---

\*    Section 8(f) was inserted in the Act by subsection (a) of Pub. L. No. 86–257 § 705, effective November 14, 1959. Section 705(b) provides "Nothing contained in the amendment made by subsection (a) shall be construed as authorizing the execution or application of agreements requiring membership in a labor organization as a condition of employment in any State or Territory in which such execution or application is prohibited by State or Territorial law."

have such grievances adjusted, without the intervention of the bargaining representative, as long as the adjustment is not inconsistent with the terms of a collective bargaining contract or agreement then in effect: *Provided further,* That the bargaining representative has been given opportunity to be present at such adjustment.

(b) The Board shall decide in each case whether, in order to assure to employees the fullest freedom in exercising the rights guaranteed by this Act, the unit appropriate for the purposes of collective bargaining shall be the employer unit, craft unit, plant unit, or subdivision thereof: *Provided,* **That the Board shall not (1) decide that any unit is appropriate for such purposes if such unit includes both professional employees and employees who are not professional employees unless a majority of such professional employees vote for inclusion in such unit; or (2) decide that any craft unit is inappropriate for such purposes on the ground that a different unit has been established by a prior Board determination, unless a majority of the employees in the proposed craft unit vote against separate representation or (3) decide that any unit is appropriate for such purposes if it includes, together with other employees, any individual employed as a guard to enforce against employees and other persons rules to protect property of the employer or to protect the safety of persons on the employer's premises; but no labor organization shall be certified as the representative of employees in a bargaining unit of guards if such organization admits to membership, or is affiliated directly or indirectly with an organization which admits to membership, employees other than guards.**

[(c) Whenever a question affecting commerce arises concerning the representation of employees, the Board may investigate such controversy and certify to the parties, in writing, the name or names of the representatives that have been designated or selected. In any such investigation, the Board shall provide for an appropriate hearing upon due notice, either in conjunction with a proceeding under section 10 or otherwise, and may take a secret ballot of employees, or utilize any other suitable method to ascertain such representatives.]

**(c)(1) Wherever a petition shall have been filed, in accordance with such regulations as may be prescribed by the Board—**

> **(A) by an employee or group of employees or any individual or labor organization acting in their behalf alleging that a substantial number of employees (i) wish to be represented for collective bargaining and that their employer declines to recognize their representative as the representative defined in section 9(a), or (ii) assert**

that the individual or labor organization, which has been certified or is being currently recognized by their employer as the bargaining representative, is no longer a representative as defined in section 9(a); or

(B) by an employer, alleging that one or more individuals or labor organizations have presented to him a claim to be recognized as the representative defined in section 9(a);

the Board shall investigate such petition and if it has reasonable cause to believe that a question of representation affecting commerce exists shall provide for an appropriate hearing upon due notice. Such hearing may be conducted by an officer or employee of the regional office, who shall not make any recommendations with respect thereto. If the Board finds upon the record of such hearing that such a question of representation exists, it shall direct an election by secret ballot and shall certify the results thereof.

(2) In determining whether or not a question of representation affecting commerce exists, the same regulations and rules of decision shall apply irrespective of the identity of the persons filing the petition or the kind of relief sought and in no case shall the Board deny a labor organization a place on the ballot by reason of an order with respect to such labor organization or its predecessor not issued in conformity with section 10(c).

(3) No election shall be directed in any bargaining unit or any subdivision within which, in the preceding twelve month period, a valid election shall have been held. Employees [on strike] *engaged in an economic strike* who are not entitled to reinstatement shall [not] be eligible to vote[.] *under such regulations as the Board shall find are consistent with the purposes and provisions of this Act in any election conducted within twelve months after the commencement of the strike.* In any election where none of the choices on the ballot receives a majority, a runoff shall be conducted, the ballot providing for a selection between the two choices receiving the largest and second largest number of valid votes cast in the election.

(4) Nothing in this section shall be construed to prohibit the waiving of hearings by stipulation for the purpose of a consent election in conformity with regulations and rules of decision of the Board.

(5) In determining whether a unit is appropriate for the purposes specified in subsection (b) the extent to which the employees have organized shall not be controlling.

(d) Whenever an order of the Board made pursuant to section 10(c) is based in whole or in part upon facts certified following an investigation pursuant to subsection (c) of this section and there is a petition for the enforcement or review of such order, such certification and the record of such investigation shall be included in the transcript of the entire record required to be filed under section 10(e) or 10(f), and thereupon the decree of the court enforcing, modifying, or setting aside in whole or in part the order of the Board shall be made and entered upon the pleadings, testimony, and proceedings set forth in such transcript.

**(e)(1) Upon the filing with the Board, by 30 per centum or more of the employees in a bargaining unit covered by an agreement between their employer and a labor organization made pursuant to section 8(a)(3), of a petition alleging they desire that such authority be rescinded, the Board shall take a secret ballot of the employees in such unit and certify the results thereof to such labor organization and to the employer.**

> **(2) No election shall be conducted pursuant to this subsection in any bargaining unit or any subdivision within which, in the preceding twelve month period, a valid election shall have been held.**

## § 10 (§ 160).   Prevention of Unfair Labor Practices

(a) The Board is empowered, as hereinafter provided, to prevent any person from engaging in any unfair labor practice (listed in section 8) affecting commerce. This power shall not be affected by any other means of adjustment or prevention that has been or may be established by agreement, law, or otherwise: *Provided,* **That the Board is empowered by agreement with any agency of any State or Territory to cede to such agency jurisdiction over any cases in any industry (other than mining, manufacturing, communications, and transportation except where predominantly local in character) even though such cases may involve labor disputes affecting commerce, unless the provision of the State or Territorial statute applicable to the determination of such cases by such agency is inconsistent with the corresponding provision of this Act or has received a construction inconsistent therewith.**

(b) Whenever it is charged that any person has engaged in or is engaging in any such unfair labor practice, the Board, or any agent or agency designated by the Board for such purposes, shall have power to issue and cause to be served upon such person a complaint stating the charges in that respect, and containing a notice of hearing before the Board or a member thereof, or before a designated agent or agency, at a place therein fixed, not less than five days after the serving of said complaint:

*Provided,* **That no complaint shall issue based upon any unfair labor practice occurring more than six months prior to the filing of the charge with the Board and the service of a copy thereof upon the person against whom such charge is made, unless the person aggrieved thereby was prevented from filing such charge by reason of service in the armed forces, in which event the six-month period shall be computed from the day of his discharge.** Any such complaint may be amended by the member, agent, or agency conducting the hearing or the Board in its discretion at any time prior to the issuance of an order based thereon. The person so complained of shall have the right to file an answer to the original or amended complaint and to appear in person or otherwise and give testimony at the place and time fixed in the complaint. In the discretion of the member, agent, or agency conducting the hearing or the Board, any other person may be allowed to intervene in the said proceeding and to present testimony. [In any such proceeding the rules of evidence prevailing in courts of law or equity shall not be controlling.] **Any such proceeding shall, so far as practicable, be conducted in accordance with the rules of evidence applicable in the district courts of the United States under the rules of civil procedure for the district courts of the United States, adopted by the Supreme Court of the United States pursuant to [the Act of June 19, 1934 (28 U.S.C. §§ 723BB, 723BC)].**\*

(c) The testimony taken by such member, agent, or agency or the Board shall be reduced to writing and filed with the Board. Thereafter, in its discretion, the Board upon notice may take further testimony or hear argument. If upon [all] **the preponderance of** the testimony taken the Board shall be of the opinion that any person named in the complaint has engaged in or is engaging in any such unfair labor practice, then the Board shall state its findings of fact and shall issue and cause to be served on such person an order requiring such person to cease and desist from such unfair labor practice, and to take such affirmative action including reinstatement of employees with or without back pay, as will effectuate the policies of this Act: *Provided,* **That where an order directs reinstatement of an employee, back pay may be required of the employer or labor organization, as the case may be, responsible for the discrimination suffered by him:** *And provided further,* **That in determining whether a complaint shall issue alleging a violation of section 8(a)(1) or section 8(a)(2), and in deciding such cases, the same regulations and rules of decision shall apply irrespective of whether or not the labor organization affected is affiliated with a labor organization national or international in scope. Such order may further require such**

---

\*     Section 10(c) was amended to replace the material in brackets with "Section 2072 of Title 28."

**person to make reports from time to time showing the extent to which it has complied with the order.** If upon [all] **the preponderance of** the testimony taken the Board shall not be of the opinion that the person named in the complaint has engaged in or is engaging in any such unfair labor practice, then the Board shall state its findings of fact and shall issue an order dismissing the said complaint. **No order of the Board shall require the reinstatement of any individual as an employee who has been suspended or discharged, or the payment to him of any back pay, if such individual was suspended or discharged for cause. In case the evidence is presented before a member of the Board, or before an administrative law judge or judges thereof, such member, or such judge or judges, as the case may be, shall issue and cause to be served on the parties to the proceeding a proposed report, together with a recommended order, which shall be filed with the Board, and if no exceptions are filed within twenty days after service thereof upon such parties, or within such further period as the Board may authorize, such recommended order shall become the order of the Board and become effective as therein prescribed.**

(d) Until **[a transcript of]** the record in a case shall have been filed in a court, as hereinafter provided, the Board may at any time, upon reasonable notice and in such manner as it shall deem proper, modify or set aside, in whole or in part, any finding or order made or issued by it.

(e) The Board shall have power to petition any court of appeals of the United States, or if all the courts of appeals to which application may be made are in vacation, any district court of the United States, within any circuit or district, respectively, wherein the unfair labor practice in question occurred or wherein such person resides or transacts business, for the enforcement of such order and for appropriate temporary relief or restraining order, and shall file in the court the record in the proceedings, as provided in section 2112 of title 28, United States Code. Upon the filing of such petition, the court shall cause notice thereof to be served upon such person, and thereupon shall have jurisdiction of the proceeding and of the question determined therein, and shall have power to grant such temporary relief or restraining order as it deems just and proper, and to make and enter a decree enforcing, modifying, and enforcing as so modified, or setting aside in whole or in part the order of the Board. No objection that has not been urged before the Board, its member, agent, or agency, shall be considered by the court, unless the failure or neglect to urge such objection shall be excused because of extraordinary circumstances. The findings of the Board with respect to questions of fact if supported by **substantial** evidence **on the record considered as a whole** shall be conclusive. If either party shall apply to the court for leave to adduce additional evidence and shall show to the satisfaction of the court that such additional evidence is material and that there were reasonable grounds for the failure to adduce such evidence in the hearing before the Board, its member, agent, or agency, the court may order such additional evidence to be taken before the Board, its member, agent, or agency, and to be made a part of the record. The Board may modify its findings as to the facts, or make new findings, by reason of additional evidence so taken and filed, and it shall file such modified or new findings, which findings with respect to questions of fact if supported by **substantial** evidence **on the record considered as a whole** shall be conclusive, and shall file its recommendations, if any, for the modification or setting aside of its original order. Upon the filing of the record with it the jurisdiction of the court shall be exclusive and its judgment and decree shall be final, except that the same shall be subject to review by the appropriate United States court of appeals if application was made to the district court as hereinabove provided, and by the Supreme Court of the United States upon writ of certiorari or certification as provided in section 1254 of title 28.

(f) Any person aggrieved by a final order of the Board granting or denying in whole or in part the relief sought may obtain a review of such order in any circuit court of appeals of the United States in the circuit wherein the unfair labor practice in question was alleged to have been engaged in or wherein such person resides or transacts business, or in the United States Court of Appeals for the District of Columbia, by filing in such court a written petition praying that the order of the Board be modified or set aside. A copy of such petition shall be forthwith transmitted by the clerk of the court to the Board, and thereupon the aggrieved party shall file in the court the record in the proceeding, certified by the Board, as provided in section 2112 of title 28, United States Code. Upon the filing of such petition, the court shall proceed in the same manner as in the case of an application by the Board under subsection (e) of this section, and shall have the same jurisdiction to grant to the Board such temporary relief or restraining order as it deems just and proper, and in like manner to make and enter a decree enforcing, modifying, and enforcing as so modified, or setting aside in whole or in part the order of the Board; the findings of the Board with respect to questions of fact if supported by **substantial** evidence **on the record considered as a whole** shall in like manner be conclusive.

(g) The commencement of proceedings under subsection (e) or (f) of this section shall not, unless specifically ordered by the court, operate as a stay of the Board's order.

(h) When granting appropriate temporary relief or a restraining order, or making and entering a decree enforcing, modifying, and enforcing as so modified, or setting aside in whole or in part an order of the Board, as provided in this section, the jurisdiction of courts sitting in equity shall not be limited by the Act entitled "An Act to amend the Judicial Code and to define and limit the jurisdiction of courts sitting in equity, and for other purposes," approved March 23, 1932 (29 U.S.C. §§ 101–115 (Supp. VII)).

(i) Petitions filed under this Act shall be heard expeditiously, and if possible within ten days after they have been docketed.*

**(j) The Board shall have power, upon issuance of a complaint as provided in subsection (b) charging that any person has engaged in or is engaging in an unfair labor practice, to petition any United Stated district court, within any district wherein the unfair labor practice in question is alleged to have occurred or wherein such person resides or transacts business, for appropriate temporary relief or restraining order. Upon the filing of any such petition the court shall cause notice thereof to be served upon such person, and thereupon shall have jurisdiction to grant to the Board such temporary relief or restraining order as it deems just and proper.**

**(k) Whenever it is charged that any person has engaged in an unfair labor practice within the meaning of paragraph (4)(D) of section 8(b), the Board is empowered and directed to hear and determine the dispute out of which such unfair labor practice shall have arisen, unless, within ten days after notice that such charge has been filed, the parties to such dispute submit to the Board satisfactory evidence that they have adjusted, or agreed upon methods for the voluntary adjustment of, the dispute. Upon compliance by the parties to the dispute with the decision of the Board or upon such voluntary adjustment of the dispute, such charge shall be dismissed.**

**(*l*) Whenever it is charged that any person has engaged in an unfair labor practice within the meaning of paragraphs (4)(A), (B), or (C) of section 8(b),** *or section 8(e) or section 8(b)(7),* **the preliminary investigation of such charge shall be made forthwith and given priority over all other cases except cases of like character in the office where it is filed or to which it is referred. If, after such investigation, the officer or regional attorney to whom the matter may be referred has reasonable cause to believe such charge is true and that a complaint should issue, he shall, on behalf of the Board, petition any United States district court within any district where the unfair labor practice in question has occurred, is alleged to have occurred, or wherein such person resides or transacts business, for appropriate injunctive relief**

---

\*   Repealed by Pub. L. No. 98–620 on November 8, 1984.

pending the final adjudication of the Board with respect to such matter. Upon the filing of any such petition the district court shall have jurisdiction to grant such injunctive relief or temporary restraining order as it deems just and proper, notwithstanding any other provision of law: *Provided further*, That no temporary restraining order shall be issued without notice unless a petition alleges that substantial and irreparable injury to the charging party will be unavoidable and such temporary restraining order shall be effective for no longer than five days and will become void at the expiration of such period [.]: *Provided further, That such officer or regional attorney shall not apply for any restraining order under section 8(b)(7) if a charge against the employer under section 8(a)(2) has been filed and after the preliminary investigation, he has reasonable cause to believe that such charge is true and that a complaint should issue.* Upon filing of any such petition the courts shall cause notice thereof to be served upon any person involved in the charge and such person, including the charging party, shall be given an opportunity to appear by counsel and present any relevant testimony: *Provided further*, That for the purposes of this subsection district courts shall be deemed to have jurisdiction of a labor organization (1) in the district in which such organization maintains its principal office, or (2) in any district in which its duly authorized officers or agents are engaged in promoting or protecting the interests of employee members. The service of legal process upon such officer or agent shall constitute service upon the labor organization and make such organization a party to the suit. In situations where such relief is appropriate the procedure specified herein shall apply to charges with respect to section 8(b)(4)(D).

*(m) Whenever it is charged that any person has engaged in an unfair labor practice within the meaning of subsection (a)(3) or (b)(2) of section 8, such charge shall be given priority over all other cases except cases of like character in the office where it is filed or to which it is referred and cases given priority under subsection (l).*

## § 11 (§ 161).    Investigatory Powers

For the purpose of all hearings and investigations, which, in the opinion of the Board, are necessary and proper for the exercise of the powers vested in it by section 9 and section 10—

(1) The Board, or its duly authorized agents or agencies, shall at all reasonable times have access to, for the purpose of examination, and the right to copy any evidence of any person being investigated or proceeded against that relates to any matter under investigation or in question. [Any member of the Board shall have power to issue

subpoenas requiring the attendance and testimony of witnesses and the production of any evidence that relates to any matter under investigation or in question, before the Board, its member, agent or agency conducting the hearing or investigation.] **The Board, or any member thereof, shall upon application of any party to such proceedings, forthwith issue to such party subpoenas requiring the attendance and testimony of witnesses or the production of any evidence in such proceeding or investigation requested in such application. Within five days after the service of a subpoena on any person requiring the production of any evidence in his possession or under his control, such person may petition the Board to revoke, and the Board shall revoke, such subpoena if in its opinion the evidence whose production is required does not relate to any matter under investigation, or any matter in question in such proceedings, or if in its opinion such subpoena does not describe with sufficient particularity the evidence whose production is required**. Any member of the Board, or any agent or agency designated by the Board for such purposes, may administer oaths and affirmations, examine witnesses, and receive evidence. Such attendance of witnesses and the production of such evidence may be required from any place in the United States or any Territory or possession thereof, at any designated place of hearing.

(2) In case of contumacy or refusal to obey a subpoena issued to any person, any district court of the United States or the United States courts of any Territory or possession, within the jurisdiction of which the inquiry is carried on or within the jurisdiction of which said person guilty of contumacy or refusal to obey is found or resides or transacts business, upon application by the Board shall have jurisdiction to issue to such person an order requiring such person to appeal before the Board, its member, agent, or agency, there to produce evidence if so ordered, or there to give testimony touching the matter under investigation or in question; and any failure to obey such order of the court may be punished by said court as a contempt thereof.

[(3) No person shall be excused from attending and testifying or from producing books, records, correspondence, documents, or other evidence in obedience to the subpoena of the Board, on the ground that the testimony or evidence required of him may tend to incriminate him or subject him to a penalty or forfeiture; but no individual shall be prosecuted or subjected to any penalty or forfeiture for or on account of any transaction, matter, or thing concerning which he is compelled, after having claimed his privilege against self-incrimination, to testify or produce evidence, except that such individual so testifying shall not be exempt from prosecution and punishment for perjury committed in so testifying.]*

(4) Complaints, orders and other process and papers of the Board, its member, agent, or agency, may be served either personally or by registered or certified mail or by telegraph or by leaving a copy thereof at the principal office or place of business of the person required to be served. The verified return by the individual so serving the same setting forth the manner of such service shall be proof of the same, and the return post office receipt or telegraph receipt thereof when registered or certified and mailed or when telegraphed as aforesaid shall be proof of service of the same. Witnesses summoned before the Board, its member, agent, or agency, shall be paid the same fees and mileage that are paid witnesses in the courts of the United States, and witnesses whose depositions are taken and the persons taking the same shall severally be entitled to the same fees as are paid for like services in the courts of the United States.**

(5) All process of any court to which application may be made under this Act may be served in the judicial district wherein the defendant or other person required to be served resides or may be found.

(6) The several departments and agencies of the Government, when directed by the President, shall furnish the Board, upon its request, all records, papers, and information in their possession relating to any matter before the Board.

## § 12 (§ 162).    Offenses and Penalties

Any person who shall willfully resist, prevent, impede, or interfere with any member of the Board or any of its agents or agencies in the performance of duties pursuant to this Act shall be punished by a fine of not more than $5,000 or by imprisonment for not more than one year, or both.

## § 13 (§ 163).    Limitations

Nothing in this Act, **except as specifically provided for herein,** shall be construed so as either to interfere with or impede or diminish in any way the right to strike, **or to affect the limitations or qualifications on that right.**

## § 14 (§ 164).    Construction of Provisions

**(a) Nothing herein shall prohibit any individual employed as a supervisor from becoming or remaining a member of a labor**

---

\*    Repealed by § 259 of the Organized Crime Control Act of 1970, 18 U.S.C. § 6001 et seq. See 18 U.S.C. §§ 6003–04.

\*\*    Section 11(4) was amended by Pub. L. No. 96–245, effective May 21, 1980.

organization, but no employer subject to this Act shall be compelled to deem individuals defined herein as supervisors as employees for the purpose of any law, either national or local, relating to collective bargaining.

**(b)** Nothing in this Act shall be construed as authorizing the execution or application of agreements requiring membership in a labor organization as a condition of employment in any State or Territory in which such execution or application is prohibited by State or Territorial law.

(c)(1) *The Board, in its discretion, may, by rule of decision or by published rules adopted pursuant to the Administrative Procedure Act, decline to assert jurisdiction over any labor dispute involving any class or category of employers, where, in the opinion of the Board, the effect of such labor dispute on commerce is not sufficiently substantial to warrant the exercise of its jurisdiction:* Provided, *That the Board shall not decline to assert jurisdiction over any labor dispute over which it would assert jurisdiction under the standards prevailing upon August 1, 1959.*

(2) *Nothing in this Act shall be deemed to prevent or bar any agency or the courts of any State or Territory (including the Commonwealth of Puerto Rico, Guam, and the Virgin Islands), from assuming and asserting jurisdiction over labor disputes over which the Board declines, pursuant to paragraph (1) of this subsection, to assert jurisdiction.*

## § 15 (§ 165).    Conflict of Laws

Wherever the application of the provisions of section 272 of chapter 10 of the Act entitled "An Act to establish a uniform system of bankruptcy throughout the United States," approved July 1, 1898, and Acts amendatory thereof and supplementary thereto (11 U.S.C. § 672), conflicts with the application of the provisions of this Act, this Act shall prevail: *Provided*, That in any situation where the provisions of this Act cannot be validly enforced, the provisions of such other Acts shall remain in full force and effect.

## § 16 (§ 166).    Separability

If any provision of this Act, or the application of such provision to any person or circumstances, shall be held invalid, the remainder of this Act, or the application of such provision to persons or circumstances other than those as to which it is held invalid, shall not be affected thereby.

## § 17 (§ 167).    Short Title

This Act may be cited as the "National Labor Relations Act."

## § 18 (§ 168).   Validation of Certificates and Other Board Actions

No petition entertained, no investigation made, no election held, and no certification issued by the National Labor Relations Board, under any of the provisions of section 9 of the National Labor Relations Act, as amended, shall be invalid by reason of the failure of the Congress of Industrial Organizations to have complied with the requirements of section 9(f), (g), or (h) of the aforesaid Act prior to December 22, 1949, or by reason of the failure of the American Federation of Labor to have complied with the provisions of section 9(f), (g), or (h) of the aforesaid Act prior to November 7, 1947: *Provided,* That no liability shall be imposed under any provision of this Act upon any person for failure to honor any election or certificate referred to above, prior to the effective date of this amendment: *Provided, however,* That this proviso shall not have the effect of setting aside or in any way affecting judgments or decrees heretofore entered under section 10(e) or (f) and which have become final.*

## § 19 (§ 169).   Employees with Religious Convictions

*Any employee [of a health care institution] who is a member of and adheres to established and traditional tenets or teachings of a bona fide religion, body, or sect which has historically held conscientious objections to joining or financially supporting labor organizations shall not be required to join or financially support any labor organization as a condition of employment; except that such employee may be required* in a contract between such employees' employer and a labor organization *in lieu of periodic dues and initiation fees, to pay sums equal to such dues and initiation fees to a nonreligious* nonlabor organization *charitable fund exempt from taxation under section 501(c)(3) of title 26 of the Internal Revenue Code, chosen by such employee from a list of at least three such funds, designated in such [a] contract [between such institution and a labor organization,] or if the contract fails to designate such funds, then to any such fund chosen by the employee.* If such employee who holds conscientious objections pursuant to this section requests the labor organization to use the grievance-arbitration procedure on the employee's behalf, the labor organization is authorized to charge the employee for the reasonable cost of using such procedure.**

---

\*   Section 18 was added by Pub. L. No. 82–189, enacted October 22, 1951.

\*\*   Section 19 was amended by Pub. L. No. 96–593, approved December 24, 1980, to add the material in roman type and to delete the material enclosed in brackets.

# LABOR MANAGEMENT RELATIONS ACT

■ ■ ■

Act of June 23, 1947, 61 Stat. 136,
*as amended,* 29 U.S.C. §§ 141 et seq.

## § 1 (§ 141). Short Title; Congressional Declaration of Purpose and Policy

(a) This chapter may be cited as the "Labor Management Relations Act, 1947."

(b) Industrial strife which interferes with the normal flow of commerce and with the full production of articles and commodities for commerce, can be avoided or substantially minimized if employers, employees, and labor organizations each recognize under law one another's legitimate rights in their relations with each other, and above all recognize under law that neither party has any right in its relations with any other to engage in acts or practices which jeopardize the public health, safety, or interest.

It is the purpose and policy of this chapter, in order to promote the full flow of commerce, to prescribe the legitimate rights of both employees and employers in their relations affecting commerce, to provide orderly and peaceful procedures for preventing the interference by either with the legitimate rights of the other, to protect the rights of individual employees in their relations with labor organizations whose activities affect commerce, to define and proscribe practices on the part of labor and management which affect commerce and are inimical to the general welfare, and to protect the rights of the public in connection with labor disputes affecting commerce.

## § 2 (§ 142). Definitions

When used in this chapter—

> (1) The term "industry affecting commerce" means any industry or activity in commerce or in which a labor dispute would burden or obstruct commerce or tend to burden or obstruct commerce or the free flow of commerce.

> (2) The term "strike" includes any strike or other concerted stoppage of work by employees (including a stoppage by reason of the expiration of a collective-bargaining agreement) and any concerted slowdown or other concerted interruption of operations by employees.

(3) The terms "commerce", "labor disputes", "employer", "employee", "labor organization", "representative", "person", and "supervisor" shall have the same meaning as when used in subchapter II of this chapter.

## § 3  (§ 143). Saving Provisions

Nothing in this chapter shall be construed to require an individual employee to render labor or service without his consent, nor shall anything in this chapter be construed to make the quitting of his labor by an individual employee an illegal act; nor shall any court issue any process to compel the performance by an individual employee of such labor or service, without his consent; nor shall the quitting of labor by an employee or employees in good faith because of abnormally dangerous conditions for work at the place of employment of such employee or employees be deemed a strike under this chapter.

## § 4  (§ 144). Separability

If any provision of this chapter, or the application of such provision to any person or circumstance, shall be held invalid, the remainder of this chapter, or the application of such provision to persons or circumstances other than those as to which it is held invalid, shall not be affected thereby.

## TITLE I—NATIONAL LABOR RELATIONS ACT
## (49 STAT. 449 (1935))

### 29 U.S.C. §§ 151–169

**§ 101**    The National Labor Relations Act is hereby amended to read as follows:

(The National Labor Relations Act with these and later amendments is set out separately)

## TITLE II—CONCILIATION OF LABOR DISPUTES IN INDUSTRIES AFFECTING COMMERCE; NATIONAL EMERGENCIES

### 29 U.S.C. §§ 171–183

## § 201    (§ 171). Declaration of Purpose and Policy

It is the policy of the United States that—

(a) sound and stable industrial peace and the advancement of the general welfare, health, and safety of the Nation and of the best interests of employers and employees can most satisfactorily be secured by the settlement of issues between employers and employees through the processes of conference and collective bargaining between employers and the representatives of their employees;

(b) the settlement of issues between employers and employees through collective bargaining may be advanced by making available full and adequate governmental facilities for conciliation, mediation, and voluntary arbitration to aid and encourage employers and the representatives of their employees to reach and maintain agreements concerning rates of pay, hours, and working conditions, and to make all reasonable efforts to settle their differences by mutual agreement reached through conferences and collective bargaining or by such methods as may be provided for in any applicable agreement for the settlement of disputes; and

(c) certain controversies which arise between parties to collective-bargaining agreements may be avoided or minimized by making available full and adequate governmental facilities for furnishing assistance to employers and the representatives of their employees in formulating for inclusion within such agreements provision for adequate notice of any proposed changes in the terms of such agreements, for the final adjustment of grievances or questions regarding the application or interpretation of such agreements, and other provisions designed to prevent the subsequent arising of such controversies.

## § 202    (§ 172). Federal Mediation and Conciliation Services

(a) There is created an independent agency to be known as the Federal Mediation and Conciliation Service (herein referred to as the "Service", except that for sixty days after June 23, 1947, such term shall refer to the Conciliation Service of the Department of Labor). The Service shall be under the direction of a Federal Mediation and Conciliation Director (hereinafter referred to as the "Director"), who shall be appointed by the President by and with the advice and consent of the Senate. The Director shall not engage in any other business, vocation, or employment.

(b) The Director is authorized, subject to the civil service laws, to appoint such clerical and other personnel as may be necessary for the execution of the functions of the Service, and shall fix their compensation in accordance with chapter 51 and subchapter III of chapter 53 of title 5 [the Classification Act of 1949], and may, without regard to the provisions of the civil service laws, appoint such conciliators and mediators as may be necessary to carry out the functions of the Service. The Director is authorized to make such expenditures for supplies, facilities, and services as he deems necessary. Such expenditures shall be allowed and paid upon presentation of itemized vouchers therefor approved by the Director or by any employee designated by him for that purpose.

(c) The principal office of the Service shall be in the District of Columbia, but the Director may establish regional offices convenient to localities in which labor controversies are likely to arise. The Director may by order, subject to revocation at any time, delegate any authority and discretion conferred upon him by this chapter to any regional director, or other officer or employee of the Service. The Director may establish suitable procedures for cooperation with State and local mediation agencies. The Director shall make an annual report in writing to Congress at the end of the fiscal year.

(d) All mediation and conciliation functions of the Secretary of Labor or the United States Conciliation Service under section 51 of this title ["An Act to create a Department of Labor"], and all functions of the United States Conciliation Service under any other law are transferred to the Federal Mediation and Conciliation Service, together with the personnel and records of the United States Conciliation Service. Such transfer shall take effect upon the sixtieth day after June 23, 1947. Such transfer shall not affect any proceedings pending before the United States Conciliation Service or any certification, order, rule, or regulation theretofore made by it or by the Secretary of Labor. The Director and the Service shall not be subject in any way to the jurisdiction or authority of the Secretary of Labor or any official or division of the Department of Labor.

## § 203    (§ 173). Functions of the Service

(a) It shall be the duty of the Service, in order to prevent or minimize interruptions of the free flow of commerce growing out of labor disputes, to assist parties to labor disputes in industries affecting commerce to settle such disputes through conciliation and mediation.

(b) The Service may proffer its services in any labor dispute in any industry affecting commerce, either upon its own motion or upon the request of one or more of the parties to the dispute, whenever in its judgment such dispute threatens to cause a substantial interruption of commerce. The Director and the Service are directed to avoid attempting to mediate disputes which would have only a minor effect on interstate commerce if State or other conciliation services are available to the parties. Whenever the Service does proffer its services in any dispute, it shall be the duty of the Service promptly to put itself in communication with the parties and to use its best efforts, by mediation and conciliation, to bring them to agreement.

(c) If the Director is not able to bring the parties to agreement by conciliation within a reasonable time, he shall seek to induce the parties voluntarily to seek other means of settling the dispute without resort to strike, lock-out, or other coercion, including submission to the employees in the bargaining unit of the employer's last offer of settlement for approval or rejection in a secret ballot. The failure or refusal of either party to agree to any procedure suggested by the Director shall not be deemed a violation of any duty or obligation imposed by this chapter.

(d) Final adjustment by a method agreed upon by the parties is declared to be the desirable method for settlement of grievance disputes arising over the application or interpretation of an existing collective-bargaining agreement. The Service is directed to make its conciliation and mediation services available in the settlement of such grievance disputes only as a last resort and in exceptional cases.

(e) The Service is authorized and directed to encourage and support the establishment and operation of joint labor management activities conducted by plant, area, and industry-wide committees designed to improve labor management relationships, job security and organizational effectiveness, in accordance with the provisions of section 175a of this title.

(f) The Service may make its services available to Federal agencies to aid in the resolution of disputes under the provision of subchapter IV of chapter 5 of Title 5. Functions performed by the Service may include assisting parties to disputes related to administrative programs, training persons in skills and procedures employed in alternative means of dispute resolution, and furnishing officers and employees of the Service to act as neutrals. Only officers and employees who are qualified in accordance with section 573 of Title 5 may be assigned to act as neutrals. The Service shall consult with the agency designated by, or the interagency committee designated or established by, the President under section 573 of Title 5 in maintaining rosters of neutrals and arbitrators, and to adopt such procedures and rules as are necessary to carry out the services authorized in this subsection.

## § 204   (§ 174). Co-Equal Obligations of Employees, Their Representatives, and Management to Minimize Labor Disputes

(a) In order to prevent or minimize interruptions of the free flow of commerce growing out of labor disputes, employers and employees and their representatives, in any industry affecting commerce, shall—

(1) exert every reasonable effort to make and maintain agreements concerning rates of pay, hours, and working conditions, including provision for adequate notice of any proposed change in the terms of such agreements;

(2) whenever a dispute arises over the terms or application of a collective-bargaining agreement and a conference is requested by a party or prospective party thereto, arrange promptly for such a conference to be held and endeavor in such conference to settle such dispute expeditiously; and

(3) in case such dispute is not settled by conference, participate fully and promptly in such meetings as may be undertaken by the Service under this Act for the purpose of aiding in a settlement of the dispute.

## § 205  (§ 175). National Labor-Management Panel; Creation and Composition; Appointment, Tenure, and Compensation; Duties

(a) There is created a National Labor-Management Panel which shall be composed of twelve members appointed by the President, six of whom shall be selected from among persons outstanding in the field of management and six of whom shall be selected from among persons outstanding in the field of labor. Each member shall hold office for a term of three years, except that any member appointed to fill a vacancy occurring prior to the expiration of the term for which his predecessor was appointed shall be appointed for the remainder of such term, and the terms of office of the members first taking office shall expire, as designated by the President at the time of appointment, four at the end of the first year, four at the end of the second year, and four at the end of the third year after the date of appointment. Members of the panel, when serving on business of the panel, shall be paid compensation at the rate of $25 per day, and shall also be entitled to receive an allowance for actual and necessary travel and subsistence expenses while so serving away from their places of residence.

(b) It shall be the duty of the panel, at the request of the Director, to advise in the avoidance of industrial controversies and the manner in which mediation and voluntary adjustment shall be administered, particularly with reference to controversies affecting the general welfare of the country.

## § 205A (§ 175a).   Assistance to Plant, Area, and Industrywide Labor Management Committees

(a)(1) The Service is authorized and directed to provide assistance in the establishment and operation of plant, area and industry-wide labor management committees which—

> (A) have been organized jointly by employers and labor organizations representing employees in that plant, area, or industry; and
>
> (B) are established for the purpose of improving labor management relationships, job security, organizational effectiveness, enhancing economic development or involving workers in decisions affecting their jobs including improving

communication with respect to subjects of mutual interest and concern.

(2) The Service is authorized and directed to enter into contracts and to make grants, where necessary or appropriate, to fulfill its responsibilities under this section.

(b)(1) No grant may be made, no contract may be entered into and no other assistance may be provided under the provisions of this section to a plant labor management committee unless the employees in that plant are represented by a labor organization and there is in effect at that plant a collective bargaining agreement.

(2) No grant may be made, no contract may be entered into and no other assistance may be provided under the provisions of this section to an area or industrywide labor management committee unless its participants include any labor organizations certified or recognized as the representative of the employees of an employer participating in such committee. Nothing in this clause shall prohibit participation in an area or industrywide committee by an employer whose employees are not represented by a labor organization.

(3) No grant may be made under the provisions of this section to any labor management committee which the Service finds to have as one of its purposes the discouragement of the exercise of rights contained in section 157 of this title [section 7 the National Labor Relations Act (29 U.S.C. 157)], or the interference with collective bargaining in any plant, or industry.

(c) The Service shall carry out the provisions of this section through an office established for that purpose.

(d) There are authorized to be appropriated to carry out the provisions of this section $10,000,000 for the fiscal year 1979, and such sums as may be necessary thereafter.

## § 206   (§ 176). National Emergencies; Appointment of Board of Inquiry by President; Report; Contents; Filing With Service

Whenever in the opinion of the President of the United States, a threatened or actual strike or lock-out affecting an entire industry or a substantial part thereof engaged in trade, commerce, transportation, transmission, or communication among the several States or with foreign nations, or engaged in the production of goods for commerce, will, if permitted to occur or to continue, imperil the national health or safety, he may appoint a board of inquiry to inquire into the issues involved in the dispute and to make a written report to him within such time as he shall prescribe. Such report shall include a statement of the facts with respect to the dispute, including each party's statement of its position but shall not contain any recommendations. The President shall file a copy of such report with the Service and shall make its contents available to the public.

## § 207     (§ 177). Board of Inquiry

(a) A board of inquiry shall be composed of a chairman and such other members as the President shall determine, and shall have power to sit and act in any place within the United States and to conduct such hearings either in public or in private, as it may deem necessary or proper, to ascertain the facts with respect to the causes and circumstances of the dispute.

(b) Members of a board of inquiry shall receive compensation at the rate of $50 for each day actually spent by them in the work of the board, together with necessary travel and subsistence expenses.

(c) For the purpose of any hearing or inquiry conducted by any board appointed under this title, the provisions of sections 49 and 50 of title 15 (relating to the attendance of witnesses and the production of books, papers, and documents), are hereby made applicable to the powers and duties of such board.

## § 208     (§ 178). Injunctions During National Emergency

(a) Upon receiving a report from a board of inquiry the President may direct the Attorney General to petition any district court of the United States having jurisdiction of the parties to enjoin such strike or lock-out or the continuing thereof, and if the court finds that such threatened or actual strike or lock-out—

> (i) affects an entire industry or a substantial part thereof engaged in trade, commerce, transportation, transmission, or communication among the several States or with foreign nations, or engaged in the production of goods for commerce; and
>
> (ii) if permitted to occur or to continue, will imperil the national health or safety, it shall have jurisdiction to enjoin any such strike or lock-out, or the continuing thereof, and to make such other orders as may be appropriate.

(b) In any case, the provisions of chapter 6 of this title [An Act entitled "An Act to amend the Judicial Code and to define and limit the jurisdiction of courts sitting in equity, and for other purposes"] shall not be applicable.

(c) The order or orders of the court shall be subject to review by the appropriate United States court of appeals and by the Supreme Court upon writ of certiorari or certification as provided in section 1254 of Title 28.

## § 209 (§ 179). Injunctions During National Emergency; Adjustment Efforts by Parties During Injunction Period

(a) Whenever a district court has issued an order under section 178 of this title enjoining acts or practices which imperil or threaten to imperil the national health or safety, it shall be the duty of the parties to the labor dispute giving rise to such order to make every effort to adjust and settle their differences, with the assistance of the Service created by this chapter. Neither party shall be under any duty to accept, in whole or in part, any proposal of settlement made by the Service.

(b) Upon the issuance of such order, the President shall reconvene the board of inquiry which has previously reported with respect to the dispute. At the end of a sixty-day period (unless the dispute has been settled by that time), the board of inquiry shall report to the President the current position of the parties and the efforts which have been made for settlement, and shall include a statement by each party of its position and a statement of the employer's last offer of settlement. The President shall make such report available to the public. The National Labor Relations Board, within the succeeding fifteen days, shall take a secret ballot of the employees of each employer involved in the dispute on the question of whether they wish to accept the final offer of settlement made by their employer as stated by him and shall certify the results thereof to the Attorney General within five days thereafter.

## § 210 (§ 180). Discharge of Injunction Upon Certification of Results of Election; Report to Congress

Upon the certification of the results of such ballot or upon a settlement being reached, whichever happens sooner, the Attorney General shall move the court to discharge the injunction, which motion shall then be granted and the injunction discharged. When such motion is granted, the President shall submit to the Congress a full and comprehensive report of the proceedings, including the findings of the board of inquiry and the ballot taken by the National Labor Relations Board, together with such recommendations as he may see fit to make for consideration and appropriate action.

## § 211 (§ 181). Compilation of Collective-Bargaining Agreements, etc.; Use of Data

(a) For the guidance and information of interested representatives of employers, employees, and the general public, the Bureau of Labor Statistics of the Department of Labor shall maintain a file of copies of all available collective bargaining agreements and other available agreements and actions thereunder settling or adjusting labor disputes. Such file shall be open to inspection under appropriate conditions prescribed by the Secretary of Labor, except that no specific information submitted in confidence shall be disclosed.

(b) The Bureau of Labor Statistics in the Department of Labor is authorized to furnish upon request of the Service, or employers, employees, or their representatives, all available data and factual information which may aid in the settlement of any labor dispute, except that no specific information submitted in confidence shall be disclosed.

## § 212     (§ 182). Exemption of Railway Labor Act From Title

The provisions of this title shall not be applicable with respect to any matter which is subject to the provisions of the Railway Labor Act [45 U.S.C. §§ 151 et seq.], as amended from time to time.

## § 213     (§ 183). Conciliation of Labor Disputes in the Health Care Industry

(a) If, in the opinion of the Director of the Federal Mediation and Conciliation Service a threatened or actual strike or lockout affecting a health care institution will, if permitted to occur or to continue, substantially interrupt the delivery of health care in the locality concerned, the Director may further assist in the resolution of the impasse by establishing within 30 days after the notice to the Federal Mediation and Conciliation Service under clause (A) of the last sentence of section 158(d) of this title (which is required by clause (3) of such section 158(d) of this title), or within 10 days after the notice under clause (B), an impartial Board of Inquiry to investigate the issues involved in the dispute and to make a written report thereon to the parties within fifteen (15) days after the establishment of such a Board. The written report shall contain the findings of fact together with the Board's recommendations for settling the dispute, with the objective of achieving a prompt, peaceful and just settlement of the dispute. Each such Board shall be composed of such number of individuals as the Director may deem desirable. No member appointed under this section shall have any interest or involvement in the health care institutions or the employee organizations involved in the dispute.

(b)(1) Members of any board established under this section who are otherwise employed by the Federal Government shall serve without compensation but shall be reimbursed for travel, subsistence, and other necessary expenses incurred by them in carrying out its duties under this section.

(2) Members of any board established under this section who are not subject to paragraph (1) shall receive compensation at a rate prescribed by the Director but not to exceed the daily rate prescribed for GSB18 of the General Schedule under section 5332 of title 5,

including travel for each day they are engaged in the performance of their duties under this section and shall be entitled to reimbursement for travel, subsistence, and other necessary expenses incurred by them in carrying out their duties under this section.

(c) After the establishment of a board under subsection (a) of this section and for 15 days after any such board has issued its report, no change in the status quo in effect prior to the expiration of the contract in the case of negotiations for a contract renewal, or in effect prior to the time of the impasse in the case of an initial bargaining negotiation, except by agreement, shall be made by the parties to the controversy.

(d) There are authorized to be appropriated such sums as may be necessary to carry out the provisions of this section.

# TITLE III—LIABILITIES OF AND RESTRICTIONS ON LABOR AND MANAGEMENT

29 U.S.C. §§ 185–187
2 U.S.C. § 441b

## § 301 (§ 185). Suits by and Against Labor Organizations

(a) Suits for violation of contracts between an employer and a labor organization representing employees in an industry affecting commerce as defined in this chapter, or between any such labor organizations, may be brought in any district court of the United States having jurisdiction of the parties, without respect to the amount in controversy or without regard to the citizenship of the parties.

(b) Any labor organization which represents employees in an industry affecting commerce as defined in this Act and any employer whose activities affect commerce as defined in this chapter shall be bound by the acts of its agents. Any such labor organization may sue or be sued as an entity and in behalf of the employees whom it represents in the courts of the United States. Any money judgment against a labor organization in a district court of the United States shall be enforceable only against the organization as an entity and against its assets, and shall not be enforceable against any individual member or his assets.

(c) For the purposes of actions and proceedings by or against labor organizations in the district courts of the United States, district courts shall be deemed to have jurisdiction of a labor organization (1) in the district in which such organization maintains its principal office, or (2) in any district in which its duly authorized officers or agents are engaged in representing or acting for employee members.

(d) The service of summons, subpoena, or other legal process of any court of the United States upon an officer or agent of a labor organization, in his capacity as such, shall constitute service upon the labor organization.

(e) For the purposes of this section, in determining whether any person is acting as an "agent" of another person so as to make such other person responsible for his acts, the question of whether the specific acts performed were actually authorized or subsequently ratified shall not be controlling.

## § 302    (§ 186). Restrictions on Financial Transactions

(a) Payment or lending, etc., of money by employer or agent to employees, representatives, or labor organizations

It shall be unlawful for any employer or association of employers or any person who acts as a labor relations expert, adviser, or consultant to an employer or who acts in the interest of an employer to pay, lend, or deliver, or agree to pay, lend, or deliver, any money or other thing of value—

> (1) to any representative of any of his employees who are employed in an industry affecting commerce; or

> (2) to any labor organization, or any officer or employee thereof, which represents, seeks to represent, or would admit to membership, any of the employees of such employer who are employed in an industry affecting commerce; or

> (3) to any employee or group or committee of employees of such employer employed in an industry affecting commerce in excess of their normal compensation for the purpose of causing such employee or group or committee directly or indirectly to influence any other employees in the exercise of the right to organize and bargain collectively through representatives of their own choosing; or

> (4) to any officer or employee of a labor organization engaged in an industry affecting commerce with intent to influence him in respect to any of his actions, decisions, or duties as a representative of employees or as such officer or employee of such labor organization,

(b)(1) It shall be unlawful for any person to request, demand, receive or accept, or agree to receive or accept any payment, loan, or delivery of any money or other thing of value prohibited by subsection (a) of this section.

> (2) It shall be unlawful for any labor organization, or for any person acting as an officer, agent, representative, or employee of such labor organization, to demand or accept from the operator of any motor vehicle (as defined in section 13102 of Title 49) employed in the transportation of property in commerce, or the employer of any such operator, any money or other thing of value payable to such organization or to an officer, agent, representative or employee

thereof as a fee or charge for the unloading, or in connection with the unloading, of the cargo of such vehicle: Provided, That nothing in this paragraph shall be construed to make unlawful any payment by an employer to any of his employees as compensation for their services as employees.

(c) The provisions of this section shall not be applicable

(1) in respect to any money or other thing of value payable by an employer to any of his employees whose established duties include acting openly for such employer in matters of labor relations or personnel administration or to any representative of his employees, or to any officer or employee of a labor organization, who is also an employee or former employee of such employer, as compensation for, or by reason of, his service as an employee of such employer;

(2) with respect to the payment or delivery of any money or other thing of value in satisfaction of a judgment of any court or a decision or award of an arbitrator or impartial chairman or in compromise, adjustment, settlement, or release of any claim, complaint, grievance, or dispute in the absence of fraud or duress;

(3) with respect to the sale or purchase of an article or commodity at the prevailing market price in the regular course of business;

(4) with respect to money deducted from the wages of employees in payment of membership dues in a labor organization: Provided, That the employer has received from each employee, on whose account such deductions are made, a written assignment which shall not be irrevocable for a period of more than one year, or beyond the termination date of the applicable collective agreement, whichever occurs sooner;

(5) with respect to money or other thing of value paid to a trust fund established by such representative, for the sole and exclusive benefit of the employees of such employer, and their families and dependents (or of such employees, families, and dependents jointly with the employees of other employers making similar payments, and their families and dependents): Provided, That

(A) such payments are held in trust for the purpose of paying, either from principal or income or both, for the benefit of employees, their families and dependents, for medical or hospital care, pensions or retirement or death of employees, compensation for injuries or illness resulting from occupational activity or insurance to provide any of the foregoing, or unemployment benefits or life insurance, disability and sickness insurance, or accident insurance;

(B) the detailed basis on which such payments are to be made is specified in a written agreement with the employer, and employees and employers are equally represented in the administration of such fund, together with such neutral persons as the representatives of the employers and the representatives of employees may agree upon and in the event the employer and employee groups deadlock on the administration of such fund and there are no neutral persons empowered to break such deadlock, such agreement provides that the two groups shall agree on an impartial umpire to decide such dispute, or in the event of their failure to agree within a reasonable length of time, an impartial umpire to decide such dispute shall, on petition of either group, be appointed by the district court of the United States for the district where the trust fund has its principal office, and shall also contain provisions for an annual audit of the trust fund, a statement of the results of which shall be available for inspection by interested persons at the principal office of the trust fund and at such other places as may be designated in such written agreement; and

(C) such payments as are intended to be used for the purpose of providing pensions or annuities for employees are made to a separate trust which provides that the funds held therein cannot be used for any purpose other than paying such pensions or annuities;

(6) with respect to money or other thing of value paid by any employer to a trust fund established by such representative for the purpose of pooled vacation, holiday, severance or similar benefits, or defraying costs of apprenticeship or other training programs: Provided, That the requirements of clause (B) of the proviso to clause (5) of this subsection shall apply to such trust funds;

(7) with respect to money or other thing of value paid by any employer to a pooled or individual trust fund established by such representative for the purpose of

(A) scholarships for the benefit of employees, their families, and dependents for study at educational institutions, or

(B) child care centers for preschool and school age dependents of employees, or

(C) financial assistance for employee housing. Provided, that no labor organization or employer shall be required to bargain on the establishment of any such trust fund, and refusal to do so shall not constitute an unfair labor practice: Provided further, That the requirements of clause (B) of the proviso to clause (5) of this subsection shall apply to such trust funds;

(8) with respect to money or any other thing of value paid by any employer to a trust fund established by such representative for the purpose of defraying the costs of legal services for employees, their

families, and dependents for counsel or plan of their choice: Provided, that the requirements of clause (B) of the proviso to clause (5) of this subsection shall apply to such trust funds: Provided further, that no such legal services shall be furnished:

    (A) to initiate any proceeding directed (i) against any such employer or its officers or agents except in workman's compensation cases, or (ii) against such labor organization, or its parent or subordinate bodies, or their officers or agents, or (iii) against any other employer or labor organization, or their officers or agents, in any matter arising under subchapter II of this chapter [the National Labor Relations Act],, or this chapter; and

    (B) in any proceeding where a labor organization would be prohibited from defraying the costs of legal services by the provisions of the Labor-Management Reporting and Disclosure Act of 1959 [29 U.S.C. § 401 et seq.]; or

(9) with respect to money or other things of value paid by an employer to a plant, area or industrywide labor management committee established for one or more of the purposes set forth in section 5(b) of the Labor Management Cooperation Act of 1978.

(d)(1) Any person who participates in a transaction involving a payment, loan, or delivery of money or other thing of value to a labor organization in payment of membership dues or to a joint labor-management trust fund as defined in clause (B) of the proviso to clause (5) of subsection (c) of this section or to a plant, area, or industry-wide labor-management committee that is received and used by such labor organization, trust fund, or committee, which transaction does not satisfy all the applicable requirements of subsections (c)(4) through (c)(9) of this section, and willfully and with intent to benefit himself or to benefit other persons he knows are not permitted to receive a payment, loan, money, or other thing of value under subsections (c)(4) through (c)(9) violates this subsection, shall, upon conviction thereof, be guilty of a felony and be subject to a fine of not more than $15,000, or imprisoned for not more than five years, or both; but if the value of the amount of money or thing of value involved in any violation of the provisions of this section does not exceed $1,000, such person shall be guilty of a misdemeanor and be subject to a fine of not more than $10,000, or imprisoned for not more than one year, or both.

(2) Except for violations involving transactions covered by subsection (d)(1) of this section, any person who willfully violates this section shall, upon conviction thereof, be guilty of a felony and be subject of a fine of not more than $15,000, or imprisoned for not more than five years, or both; but if the value of the amount of money or thing of value involved in any violation of the provisions of this section does

not exceed $1,000, such person shall be guilty of a misdemeanor and be subject to a fine of not more than $10,000, or imprisoned for not more than one year or both.

(e) The district courts of the United States and the United States courts of the Territories and possessions shall have jurisdiction, for cause shown, and subject to the provisions of section 381 of title 28 (relating to notice to opposite party) to restrain violations of this section, without regard to the provisions of sections 17 of title 15 and section 52 of this title, and the provisions of chapter 6 of this title [29 U.S.C. §§ 101–115].

(f) This section shall not apply to any contract in force on June 23, 1947, until the expiration of such contract, or until July 1, 1948, whichever first occurs.

(g) Compliance with the restrictions contained in subsection (c)(5)(B) of this section upon contributions to trust funds, otherwise lawful, shall not be applicable to contributions to such trust funds established by collective agreement prior to January 1, 1946, nor shall subsection (c)(5)(A) of this section be construed as prohibiting contributions to such trust funds if prior to January 1, 1947, such funds contained provisions for pooled vacation benefits.

## § 303 (§ 187). Unlawful Activities or Conduct; Right to Sue; Jurisdiction; Limitations; Damages

(a) It shall be unlawful, for the purpose of this section only, in an industry or activity affecting commerce, for any labor organization to engage in any activity or conduct defined as an unfair labor practice in section 158(b)(4) of this title [Section 8(b)(4) of the National Labor Relations Act].

(b) Whoever shall be injured in his business or property by reason of any violation of subsection (a) of this section may sue therefor in any district court of the United States subject to the limitations and provisions of section 185 of this title without respect to the amount in controversy, or in any other court having jurisdiction of the parties, and shall recover the damages by him sustained and the cost of the suit.

## § 304 (2 U.S.C. § 441b). Contributions or Expenditures by National Banks, Corporations, or Labor Organizations

(a) It is unlawful for any national bank, or any corporation organized by authority of any law of Congress, to make a contribution or expenditure in connection with any election to any political office, or in connection with any primary election or political convention or caucus held to select candidates for any political office, or for any corporation whatever, or any labor organization, to make a contribution or expenditure in connection with any election at which presidential and vice presidential electors or a Senator or Representative in, or a Delegate or Resident Commissioner to,

Congress are to be voted for, or in connection with any primary election or political convention or caucus held to select candidates for any of the foregoing offices, or for any candidate, political committee, or other person knowingly to accept or receive any contribution prohibited by this section, or any officer or any director of any corporation or any national bank or any officer of any labor organization to consent to any contribution or expenditure by the corporation, national bank, or labor organization, as the case may be, prohibited by this section.

(b)(1) For the purposes of this section the term "labor organization" means any organization of any kind, or any agency or employee representation committee or plan, in which employees participate and which exists for the purpose, in whole or in part, of dealing with employers concerning grievances, labor disputes, wages, rates of pay, hours of employment, or conditions of work.

(2) For purposes of this section and section, * * * the term "contribution or expenditure" includes a contribution or expenditures, as those terms are defined in section 431 of this title, and also includes any direct or indirect payment, distribution, loan, advance, deposit, or gift of money, or any services, or anything of value (except a loan of money by a national or State bank made in accordance with the applicable banking laws and regulations and in the ordinary course of business) to any candidate, campaign committee, or political party or organization, in connection with any election to any of the offices referred to in this section or for any applicable electioneering communication, but shall not include

(A) communications by a corporation to its stockholders and executive or administrative personnel and their families or by a labor organization to its members and their families on any subject;

(B) nonpartisan registration and get-out-the-vote campaigns by a corporation aimed at its stockholders and executive or administrative personnel and their families, or by a labor organization aimed at its members and their families; and

(C) the establishment, administration, and solicitation of contributions to a separate segregated fund to be utilized for political purposes by a corporation, labor organization, membership organization, cooperative, or corporation without capital stock.

(3) It shall be unlawful—

(A) for such a fund to make a contribution or expenditure by utilizing money or anything of value secured by physical force, job discrimination, financial reprisals, or the threat of force, job discrimination, or financial reprisal; or by dues, fees, or other moneys required as a condition of membership in a labor organization or as a condition of employment, or by moneys obtained in any commercial transaction;

(B) for any person soliciting an employee for a contribution to such a fund to fail to inform such employee of the political purposes of such fund at the time of such solicitation; and

(C) for any person soliciting an employee for a contribution to such a fund to fail to inform such employee, at the time of such solicitation, of his right to refuse to so contribute without any reprisal.

(4)(A) Except as provided in subparagraphs (B), (C), and (D), it shall be unlawful—

(i) for a corporation, or a separate segregated fund established by a corporation, to solicit contributions to such a fund from any person other than its stockholders and their families and its executive or administrative personnel and their families, and

(ii) for a labor organization, or a separate segregated fund established by a labor organization, to solicit contributions to such a fund from any person other than its members and their families.

(B) It shall not be unlawful under this section for a corporation, a labor organization, or a separate segregated fund established by such corporation or such labor organization, to make 2 written solicitations for contributions during the calendar year from any stockholder, executive or administrative personnel, or employee of a corporation or the families of such persons. A solicitation under this subparagraph may be made only by mail addressed to stockholders, executive or administrative personnel, or employees at their residence and shall be so designed that the corporation, labor organization, or separate segregated fund conducting such solicitation cannot determine who makes a contribution of $50 or less as a result of such solicitation and who does not make such a contribution.

(C) This paragraph shall not prevent a membership organization, cooperative, or corporation without capital stock, or a separate segregated fund established by a membership organization, cooperative, or corporation without capital stock, from soliciting contributions to such a fund from members of such organization, cooperative, or corporation without capital stock.

(D) This paragraph shall not prevent a trade association or a separate segregated fund established by a trade association from soliciting contributions from the stockholders and executive or administrative personnel of the member corporations of such trade association and the families of such stockholders or personnel to the extent that such solicitation of such stockholders and personnel, and their families, has been separately and specifically approved by the member corporation involved, and such member corporation does not approve any such solicitation by more than one such trade association in any calendar year.

(5) Notwithstanding any other law, any method of soliciting voluntary contributions or of facilitating the making of voluntary contributions to a separate segregated fund established by a corporation, permitted by law to corporations with regard to stockholders and executive or administrative personnel, shall also be permitted to labor organizations with regard to their members.

(6) Any corporation, including its subsidiaries, branches, divisions, and affiliates, that utilizes a method of soliciting voluntary contributions or facilitating the making of voluntary contributions, shall make available such method, on written request and at a cost sufficient only to reimburse the corporation for the expenses incurred thereby, to a labor organization representing any members working for such corporation, its subsidiaries, branches, divisions, and affiliates.

(7) For purposes of this section, the term "executive or administrative personnel" means individuals employed by a corporation who are paid on a salary, rather than hourly, basis and who have policymaking, managerial, professional, or supervisory responsibilities.

* * *

## TITLE IV—CREATION OF JOINT COMMITTEE TO STUDY AND REPORT ON BASIC PROBLEMS AFFECTING FRIENDLY LABOR RELATIONS AND PRODUCTIVITY

[Omitted]

* * *

## TITLE V

29 U.S.C. §§ 142–44

### § 501   (§ 142). Definitions

When used in this Act—

(1) The term "industry affecting commerce" means any industry or activity in commerce or in which a labor dispute would burden or

obstruct commerce or tend to burden or obstruct commerce or the free flow of commerce.

(2) The term "strike" includes any strike or other concerted stoppage of work by employees (including a stoppage by reason of the expiration of a collective-bargaining agreement) and any concerted slow-down or other concerted interruption of operations by employees.

(3) The terms "commerce," "labor disputes," "employer," "employee," "labor organization," "representative," "person," and "supervisor" shall have the same meaning as when used in subchapter II of this chapter [the National Labor Relations Act, as amended].

## § 502    (§ 143). Saving Provision

Nothing in this chapter shall be construed to require an individual employee to render labor or service without his consent, nor shall anything in this chapter be construed to make the quitting of his labor by an individual employee an illegal act; nor shall any court issue any process to compel the performance by an individual employee of such labor or service, without his consent; nor shall the quitting of labor by an employee or employees in good faith because of abnormally dangerous conditions for work at the place of employment of such employee or employees be deemed a strike under this chapter.

## § 503    (§ 144). Separability

If any provision of this chapter, or the application of such provision to any person or circumstance, shall be held invalid, the remainder of this chapter, or the application of such provision to persons or circumstances other than those as to which it is held invalid, shall not be affected thereby.

# WORKPLACE FAIRNESS ACT

■ ■ ■

(Striker Replacement Bill)

103rd CONGRESS

1st Session

S. 55

1993

## SUMMARY OF THE ACT

The Workplace Fairness Act or Striker Replacement Bill was introduced in the House by William Clay (D–Mo), and in the Senate by Howard Metzenbaum (D–Oh) in 1992 and again in 1993. The House approved the bill but the Senate failed to achieve cloture despite a last minute amendment by Senators Packwood and Metzenbaum that conditioned the ban on permanent replacements on the striking union agreeing to accept binding arbitration. Although President Bush had indicated he would veto the bill, in 1993 President Clinton indicated he would have signed the bill if the Senate had ended the filibuster.

The Act was intended to amend the National Labor Relations Act to make it an unfair labor practice for an employer to promise, threaten, or take other action to hire a permanent replacement for an employee who: (1) at the beginning of a labor dispute was in a bargaining unit in which a labor organization either was the certified or recognized exclusive representative or was seeking to be so certified or recognized, on the basis of written authorizations by a majority of unit employees; and (2) in connection with that dispute has engaged in concerted activities for collective bargaining or other mutual aid and protection through that labor organization. The Act would have also made it an unfair labor practice for an employer to withhold or deny any other employment right or privilege to such an employee who is working for or has unconditionally offered to return to work for the employer, out of preference for any other individual based on that individual's performing, having performed, or having indicated a willingness to perform bargaining unit work for the employer during the dispute. The Act would have also amended the Railway Labor Act to prohibit any carrier or its officer or agent from discriminating against an employee in a craft or class in any of the above ways prohibited to employers under the National Labor Relations Act.

The following presents the provisions of the Workplace Fairness Act by incorporating its provisions into the existing language of the National

Labor Relations Act and the Railway Labor Act. The additional language of the Workplace Fairness Act is shown in bold face italics, while the existing statutory language that would have been deleted by the act is shown struck.

## AMENDMENTS TO THE NATIONAL LABOR RELATIONS ACT

### § 8 (§ 158). Unfair Labor Practices

(a) It shall be an unfair labor practice for an employer—

\* \* \*

(5) to refuse to bargain collectively with the representatives of his employees, subject to the provisions of section 9(a).; *or*

*(6) to promise, to threaten, or take other action—*

*(i) to hire a permanent replacement for an employee who—*

*(A) at the commencement of a labor dispute was an employee of the employer in a bargaining unit in which a labor organization was the certified or recognized exclusive representative or, on the basis of written authorizations by a majority of the unit employees, was seeking to be so certified or recognized; and*

*(B) in connection with that dispute has engaged in concerted activities for the purpose of collective bargaining or other mutual aid or protection through that labor organization; or*

*(ii) to withhold or deny any other employment right or privilege to an employee, who meets the criteria of subparagraph (A) and (B) of clause (i) and who is working for or has unconditionally offered to return to work for the employer, out of a preference for any other individual that is based on the fact that the individual is performing, has performed or has indicated a willingness to perform bargaining unit work for the employer during the labor dispute.*

## AMENDMENTS TO THE RAILWAY LABOR ACT

### Sec. 2 General duties

### Fourth. Organization and collective bargaining; freedom from interference by carrier; assistance in organizing or maintaining organization by carrier forbidden; deduction of dues from wages forbidden

*(a)* Employees shall have the right to organize and bargain collectively through representatives of their own choosing. The majority of any craft or class of employees shall have the right to determine who shall be the representative of the craft or class for the purposes of this chapter. No carrier, its officers, or agents shall deny or in any way question the right of its employees to join, organize, or assist in organizing the labor organization of their choice, and it shall be unlawful for any carrier to interfere in any way with the organization of its employees, or to use the funds of the carrier in maintaining or assisting or contributing to any labor organization, labor representative, or other agency of collective bargaining, or in performing any work therefor, or to influence or coerce employees in an effort to induce them to join or remain or not to join or remain members of any labor organization, or to deduct from the wages of employees any dues, fees, assessments, or other contributions payable to labor organizations, or to collect or to assist in the collection of any such dues, fees, assessments, or other contributions: *Provided*, That nothing in this chapter shall be construed to prohibit a carrier from permitting an employee, individually, or local representatives of employees from conferring with management during working hours without loss of time, or to prohibit a carrier from furnishing free transportation to its employees while engaged in the business of a labor organization.

*(b) No carrier, or officer or agent of the carrier, shall promise, threaten or take other action—*

> *(1) to hire a permanent replacement for an employee who—*
>
>> *(A) at the commencement of a dispute was an employee of the carrier in a craft or class in which a labor organization was the designated or authorized representative or, on the basis of written authorizations by a majority of the craft or class, was seeking to be so designated or authorized; and*
>>
>> *(B) in connection with that dispute has exercised the right to join, to organize, to assist in organizing, or to bargain collectively through that labor organization; or*
>
> *(2) to withhold or deny any other employment right or privilege to an employee, who meets the criteria of subparagraphs (A) and (B) of paragraph (1) and who is working for or has unconditionally offered to return to work*

*for the carrier, out of a preference for any other individual that is based on the fact that the individual is employed, was employed, or indicated a willingness to be employed during the dispute.*

# TEAMWORK FOR EMPLOYEES AND MANAGERS ACT

■ ■ ■

104th CONGRESS
1st Session
H. R. 743
1995

## SUMMARY OF THE ACT

The Teamwork for Employees and Managers Act (TEAM Act) was introduced by Representative Steve Gunderson (R–Wi) on January 30, 1995. It passed the U.S. House of Representatives 221–202 on September 27, 1995 and passed the Senate 53–46 on July 10, 1996, but was vetoed by President Clinton. No attempt was made to over-ride the veto.

The Act was intended to amend the National Labor Relations Act to allow employers to establish, assist, maintain, or participate in an organization or entity in which employees participate, to at least the same extent practicable as do representatives of management, to address matters of mutual interest (including, but not limited to, issues of quality, productivity, efficiency, and safety and health), if such organizations or entities do not have, claim, or seek authority to: (1) be the exclusive bargaining representative of the employees; or (2) negotiate, enter into, or amend collective bargaining agreements. The Act also made these amendments inapplicable in any case in which a labor organization is the representative of such employees (any unionized workplace).

The following presents the provisions of the TEAM Act by incorporating its provisions into the existing language of the National Labor Relations Act. The additional language of the TEAM Act is shown in bold face italics, while the existing statutory language that would have been deleted by the act is shown struck.

## AMENDMENTS TO THE NATIONAL LABOR RELATIONS ACT

### § 8 (§ 158). Unfair Labor Practices

(a) It shall be an unfair labor practice for an employer—

(1) to interfere with, restrain, or coerce employees in the exercise of the rights guaranteed in section 7;

(2) to dominate or interfere with the formation or administration of any labor organization or contribute financial or other support to it: *Provided,* That subject to rules and regulations made and

95

published by the Board pursuant to section 6, an employer shall not be prohibited from permitting employees to confer with him during working hours without loss of time or pay: *Provided further, That it shall not constitute or be evidence of an unfair labor practice under this paragraph for an employer to establish, assist, maintain, or participate in any organization or entity of any kind, in which employees participate, to at least the same extent practicable as representatives of management participate to address matters of mutual interest, including, but not limited to, issues of quality, productivity, efficiency, and safety and health, and which does not have, claim, or seek authority to be the exclusive bargaining representative of the employees or to negotiate or enter into collective bargaining agreements with the employer or to amend existing collective bargaining agreements between the employer and any labor organization, except that in a case in which a labor organization is the representative of such employees as provided in section 9(a), this proviso shall not apply;*

# EMPLOYEE FREE CHOICE ACT

■ ■ ■

110th CONGRESS
1st Session
H. R. 800
2007

## SUMMARY OF THE ACT

The Employee Free Choice Act was introduced by Senator Edward Kennedy (D–Mass) and Representatives George Miller (D–Calif) and Peter King (R–NY) in the first session of the 110th Congress, 2007. It passed the U.S. House of Representatives 241–185 on March 1, 2007 and gained majority support in the Senate, but could not overcome a Republican led filibuster.

The Act seeks to amend the National Labor Relations Act to achieve three major objectives: to allow employees to choose and an exclusive bargaining representative by signing authorization cards without going through a formal election; to provide for mediation and arbitration of first contract disputes; and to establish stronger penalties for unfair labor practices including up to $20,000 in civil penalties per offense, triple backpay awards and the greater use of injunctive relief.

The following presents the provisions of the Employee Free Choice Act by incorporating its provisions into the existing language of the National Labor Relations Act. The additional language of the Employee Free Choice Act is shown in bold face italics, while the existing statutory language that would be deleted by the act is shown struck.

## AMENDMENTS TO THE NATIONAL LABOR RELATIONS ACT

### § 3 (§ 153). The National Labor Relations Board

(a) * * *

(b) The Board is authorized to delegate to any group of three or more members any or all of the powers which it may itself exercise. The Board is also authorized to delegate to its regional directors its powers under section 9 to determine the unit appropriate for the purpose of collective bargaining, to investigate and provide for hearings, and determine whether a question of representation exists, and to direct an election or take a secret ballot under subsection (c) or (e) of section 9 and certify the results thereof, *and to issue certifications as provided for in that section,* except that upon the filing of a request therefor with the Board by any interested person, the Board may review any action of a regional director delegated to him under this paragraph, but such a review shall not, unless specifically ordered by the Board, operate as a stay of any action taken by the regional director. A vacancy in the Board shall not impair the right of the remaining members to exercise all of the powers of the Board, and three members of the Board shall, at all times, constitute a quorum of the Board, except that two members shall constitute a quorum of any group designated pursuant to the first sentence hereof. The Board shall have an official seal which shall be judicially noticed.

\* \* \*

## § 8  (§ 158). Unfair Labor Practices

(a) \* \* \*

(b) It shall be an unfair labor practice for a labor organization or its agents—

(1) \* \* \*

\* \* \*

(7) to picket or cause to be picketed, or threaten to picket or cause to be picketed, any employer where an object thereof is forcing or requiring an employer to recognize or bargain with a labor organization as the representative of his employees, or forcing or requiring the employees of an employer to accept or select such labor organization as their collective bargaining representative, unless such labor organization is currently certified as the representative of such employees:

(A) \* \* \*

(B) where within the preceding twelve months a valid election under section 9(c) of this Act has been conducted *or a petition has been filed under section 9(c)(6)*, or

(C) where such picketing has been conducted without a petition under section 9(c) being filed within a reasonable period of time not to exceed thirty days from the commencement of such picketing: *Provided,* That ~~when such a petition has been filed~~*when such a petition other than a petition under section 9(c)(6) has been filed* the Board shall forthwith, without regard to the provisions of section 9(c)(1) or the absence of a showing of a substantial interest on the part of the labor organization, direct an election in such unit as the Board finds to be appropriate and shall certify the results thereof: *Provided further,* That nothing in this subparagraph (C) shall be construed to prohibit any picketing or other publicity for the purpose of truthfully advising the public (including consumers) that an employer does not employ members of, or have a contract with, a labor organization, unless an effect of such picketing is to induce any individual employed by any other person in the course of his employment, not to pick up, deliver or transport any goods or not to perform any services.

\* \* \*

*(h) Whenever collective bargaining is for the purpose of establishing an initial agreement following certification or recognition, the provisions of subsection (d) shall be modified as follows:*

*(1) Not later than 10 days after receiving a written request for collective bargaining from an individual or labor organization that has been newly organized or certified as a representative as defined in section 9(a), or within such further period as the parties agree upon, the parties shall meet and commence to bargain collectively and shall make every reasonable effort to conclude and sign a collective bargaining agreement.*

*(2) If after the expiration of the 90-day period beginning on the date on which bargaining is commenced, or such additional period as the parties may agree upon, the parties have failed to reach an agreement, either party may notify the Federal Mediation and Conciliation Service of the existence of a dispute and request mediation. Whenever such a request is received, it shall be the duty of the Service promptly to put itself in communication with the parties and to use its best efforts, by mediation and conciliation, to bring them to agreement.*

*(3) If after the expiration of the 30-day period beginning on the date on which the request for mediation is made under paragraph (2), or such additional period as the parties may agree upon, the Service is not able to bring the parties to agreement by conciliation, the Service shall refer the dispute to an arbitration board established in accordance with such regulations as may be prescribed by the Service. The arbitration panel shall render a decision settling the dispute and such decision shall be binding upon the parties for a period of 2 years, unless amended during such period by written consent of the parties.*

## § 9  (§ 159). Representatives and Elections

(a) * * *

* * *

(c)(1) * * *

* * *

*(6) Notwithstanding any other provision of this section, whenever a petition shall have been filed by an employee or group of employees or any individual or labor organization acting in their behalf alleging that a majority of employees in a unit appropriate for the purposes of collective bargaining wish to be represented by an individual or labor organization for such purposes, the Board shall investigate the petition. If the Board finds that a majority of the employees in a unit appropriate for bargaining has signed valid authorizations designating the individual or labor organization specified in the petition as their bargaining representative and that no other individual or labor organization is currently certified or recognized as the exclusive representative of any of the employees in the unit, the Board shall not direct an election but shall certify the individual or labor organization as the representative described in subsection (a).*

*(7) The Board shall develop guidelines and procedures for the designation by employees of a bargaining representative in the manner described in paragraph (6). Such guidelines and procedures shall include—*

*(A) model collective bargaining authorization language that may be used for purposes of making the designations described in paragraph (6); and*

*(B) procedures to be used by the Board to establish the validity of signed authorizations designating bargaining representatives.*

* * *

## § 10  (§ 160).    Prevention of Unfair Labor Practices

(a) * * *

* * *

(c) The testimony taken by such member, agent, or agency or the Board shall be reduced to writing and filed with the Board. Thereafter, in its discretion, the Board upon notice may take further testimony or hear argument. If upon the preponderance of the testimony taken the Board shall be of the opinion that any person named in the complaint has engaged in or is engaging in any such unfair labor practice, then the Board shall state its findings of fact and shall issue and cause to be served on such person an order requiring such person to cease and desist from such unfair labor practice, and to take such affirmative action including reinstatement of employees with or without back pay, as will effectuate the policies of this Act: *Provided,* That where an order directs reinstatement of an employee, back pay may be required of the employer or labor organization, as the case may be, responsible for the discrimination suffered by him: ~~And provided further,~~*Provided further, That if the Board finds that an employer has discriminated against an employee in violation of subsection (a)(3) of section 8 while employees of the employer were seeking representation by a labor organization, or during the period after a labor organization was recognized as a representative defined in subsection (a) of section 9 until the first collective bargaining contract was entered into between the employer and the representative, the Board in such order shall award the employee back pay and, in addition, 2 times that amount as liquidated damages: Provided further,* That in determining whether a complaint shall issue alleging a violation of section 8(a)(1) or section 8(a)(2), and in deciding such cases, the same regulations and rules of decisions shall apply irrespective of whether or not the labor organization affected is affiliated with a labor organization national or international in scope. Such order may further require such person to make reports from time to time showing the extent to which it has complied with the order. If upon the preponderance of the testimony taken the Board shall not be of the opinion that the person named in the complaint has engaged in or is engaging in any such unfair labor practice, then the Board shall state its findings of fact and shall issue an order dismissing the said complaint. No order of the Board shall require the reinstatement of any individual as an employee who has been suspended or discharged, or the payment to him of any back pay, if such individual was suspended or discharged for cause. In case the evidence is presented before a member of the Board, or before an examiner or examiners thereof, such member, or such examiner or examiners, as the case may be, shall issue and cause to be served on the parties to the proceeding a proposed report, together with a recommended order, which shall be filed with the Board, and if no exceptions are filed within twenty days after service thereof upon such parties, or within such further period as the Board may authorize, such recommended order shall become the order of the Board and become effective as therein prescribed.

\* \* \*

(l) ~~Whenever it is charged that any person has engaged in an unfair labor practice within the meaning of paragraph (4)(A), (B), or (C) of section 8(b), or section 8(e) or section 8(b)(7), the preliminary investigation of such charge shall be made forthwith and given priority over all other cases except cases of like character in the office where it is filed or to which it is referred.~~*Whenever it is charged—*

*(A) that any employer—*

*(i) discharged or otherwise discriminated against an employee in violation of subsection (a)(3) of section 8;*

*(ii) threatened to discharge or to otherwise discriminate against an employee in violation of subsection (a)(1) of section 8; or*

*(iii) engaged in any other unfair labor practice within the meaning of subsection (a)(1) that significantly interferes with, restrains, or coerces employees in the exercise of the rights guaranteed in section 7;*

*while employees of that employer were seeking representation by a labor organization or during the period after a labor organization was recognized as a representative defined in section 9(a) until the first collective bargaining contract is entered into between the employer and the representative; or*

*(B) that any person has engaged in an unfair labor practice within the meaning of subparagraph (A), (B) or (C) of section 8(b)(4), section 8(e), or section 8(b)(7);*

*the preliminary investigation of such charge shall be made forthwith and given priority over all other cases except cases of like character in the office where it is filed or to which it is referred.*

*(2)* If, after such investigation, the officer or regional attorney to whom the matter may be referred has reasonable cause to believe such charge is true and that a complaint should issue, he shall, on behalf of the Board, petition any district court of the United States (including the United States District Court for the District of Columbia) within any district where the unfair labor practice in question has occurred, is alleged to have occurred, or wherein such person resides or transacts business, for appropriate injunctive relief pending the final adjudication of the Board with respect to such matter. Upon the filing of any such

petition the district court shall have jurisdiction to grant such injunctive relief or temporary restraining order as it deems just and proper, notwithstanding any other provision of law: *Provided further,* That no temporary restraining order shall be issued without notice unless a petition alleges that substantial and irreparable injury to the charging party will be unavoidable and such temporary restraining order shall be effective for no longer than five days and will become void at the expiration of such period: *Provided further,* That such officer or regional attorney shall not apply for any restraining order under section 8(b)(7) if a charge against the employer under section 8(a)(2) has been filed and after the preliminary investigation, he has reasonable cause to believe that such charge is true and that a complaint should issue. Upon filing of any such petition other courts shall cause notice thereof to be served upon any person involved in the charge and such person, including the charging party, shall be given an opportunity to appear by counsel and present any relevant testimony: *Provided further,* That for the purposes of this subsection district courts shall be deemed to have jurisdiction of a labor organization (1) in the district in which such organization maintains its principal office, or (2) in any district in which its duly authorized officers or agents are engaged in promoting or protecting the interests of employee members. The service of legal process upon such officer or agent shall constitute service upon the labor organization and make such organization a party to the suit. In situations where such relief is appropriate the procedure specified herein shall apply to charges with respect to section 8(b)(4)(D).

(m) Whenever it is charged that any person has engaged in an unfair labor practice within the meaning of subsection (a)(3) or (b)(2) of section 8 **under circumstances not subject to section 10(l)**, such charge shall be given priority over all other cases except cases of like character in the office where it is filed or to which it is referred and cases given priority under subsection (i).

* * *

## § 12 (§ 162). Offenses and Penalties

~~Any~~*(a) Any* **person** who shall willfully resist, prevent, impede, or interfere with any member of the Board or any of its agents or agencies in the performance of duties pursuant to this Act shall be punished by a fine of not more than $5,000 or by imprisonment for not more than one year, or both.

*(b) Any employer who willfully or repeatedly commits any unfair labor practice within the meaning of subsections (a)(1)*

*or (a)(3) of section 8 while employees of the employer are seeking representation by a labor organization or during the period after a labor organization has been recognized as a representative defined in subsection (a) of section 9 until the first collective bargaining contract is entered into between the employer and the representative shall, in addition to any make-whole remedy ordered, be subject to a civil penalty of not to exceed $20,000 for each violation. In determining the amount of any penalty under this section, the Board shall consider the gravity of the unfair labor practice and the impact of the unfair labor practice on the charging party, on other persons seeking to exercise rights guaranteed by this Act, or on the public interest.*

\* \* \*

# FORMS AND DOCUMENTS

■ ■ ■

## THE NLRB AND YOU

http://www.nlrb.gov/

http://www.ppgbuffalo.org/wp-content/uploads/2010/06/NLRB-Unfair-Labor-Practices.pdf

# The National Labor Relations Board and YOU

Representation Cases

This pamphlet contains a general explanation of what the National Labor Relations Board (NLRB) is and what it does concerning the processing of representation petitions. For future information, contact the nearest NLRB office and ask to speak with the Information Officer.

### What is the National Labor Relations Board?

We are an independent Federal agency established to enforce the National Labor Relations Act (NLRA). As an independent agency, we are not part of any other government agency—such as the Department of Labor.

Congress has empowered the NLRB to conduct secret-ballot elections so employees may exercise a free choice whether a union should represent them for bargaining purposes. A secret-ballot election will be conducted only when a petition requesting an election is filed. Such a petition should be filed with the Regional Office in the area where the unit of employees is located. All Regional Offices have petition forms that are available on request and without cost.

### Types of Petitions

1) *Certification of Representative (RC)*

This petition, which is normally filed by a union, seeks an election to determine whether employees wish to be represented by a union. It must be supported by the signatures of 30 percent or more of the employees in the bargaining unit being sought. These signatures may be on paper. Generally, this designation or "showing of interest" contains a statement that the employees want to be represented for collective-bargaining purposes by a specific labor organization. The showing of interest must be signed by each employee and each employee's signature must be dated.

2) *Decertification (RD)*

This petition, which can be filed by an individual, seeks an election to determine whether the authority of a union to act as a bargaining representative of employees should continue. It must be supported by the signatures of 30 percent or more of the employees in the bargaining unit represented by the union. These signatures may be on separate cards or on a single piece of paper. Generally, this showing of interest contains a statement that the employees do not wish to be represented for collective-bargaining purposes by the existing labor organization. The showing of interest must be signed by each employee and each employee's signature must be dated.

3) *Withdrawal of Union-Security Authority (UD)*

This petition, which can also be filed by an individual, seeks an election to determine whether to continue the union's contractual authority to require that employees make certain lawful payments to the union in order to retain their jobs. It must be supported by the signatures of 30 percent or more of the employees in the bargaining unit covered by the union security agreement. These signatures may be on separate cards or on a single piece of paper. Generally, this showing of interest states that the employees no longer want their collective-bargaining agreement to contain a union-security provision. The showing of interest must be signed by each employee and each employee's signature must be dated.

4) *Employer Petition (RM)*

This petition is filed by an employer for an election when one or more unions claim to represent the employer's employees or when the employer has reasonable grounds for believing that the union, which is the current collective bargaining representative,

no longer represents a majority of employees. In the latter case, the petition must be supported by the evidence or "objective considerations" relied on by the employer for believing that the union no longer represents a majority of its employees.

5) *Unit Clarification (UC)*

This petition seeks to clarify the scope of an existing bargaining unit by, for example, determining whether a new classification is properly a part of that unit. The petition may be filed by either the employer or the union.

6) *Amendment of Certification (AC)*

This petition seeks the amendment of an outstanding certification of a union to reflect changed circumstances, such aschanges in the name or affiliation of the union. This petition may be filed by a union or an employer.

## What is a Bargaining Unit?

A bargaining unit is a group of two or more employees who share a "community of interest" and may reasonably be grouped together for collective-bargaining purposes. The NLRB is responsible for ensuring that any election in a representation case is conducted in an appropriate unit. A unit is usually described by the type of work done or job classification of employees-for example, production and maintenance employees or truckdrivers. In some cases, the number of facilities to be included in a bargaining unit is at issue, and a unit may be described by the number of locations to be involved. For example, in the retail industry, the NLRB may need to determine whether employees at a single or whether a bargaining unit consisting of several stores is appropriate. Generally, the appropriateness of a bargaining unit is determined on the basis of the community of interest of the employees involved. The NLRB may also consider factors such as any history of collective bargaining and the desires of the affected employees.

## What Can You Expect, If You File a Petition?

The Information Officer in the NLRB Regional Office nearest you can answer your questions regarding representation petitions and can assist you in completing the petition forms.

If you file a petition, you should be prepared to tell us the name and address of the employer and any labor organization(s) involved. In addition, you must describe the bargaining unit that is the subject of the petition, and the approximate number of employees in the unit. You also will need to tell us whether there is a labor organization that represents you, any other interested labor organization, or any collective-bargaining agreements in effect. If available, you should provide a copy of any current contract between the employer and the union.

You will need to state your current address on the petition form as well as sign it. A copy of the petition will be served on all parties involved.

The showing of interest in support of an RC, RD, or UD petition or the objective considerations in support of an RM petition (whichever is applicable) must be filed with the petition, or within 48 hours after its filing and, when RC and RD petitions are involved, no later than the last day on which the petition might timely be filed. If such proof is not timely submitted, or if the NLRB considers the showing of interest or objective considerations to be insufficient, the petition is subject to dismissal.

After the petition is filed, the case will be assigned to an NLRB agent for processing. If the Region determines that the petition should be processed further, the agent will attempt to secure agreement of the parties regarding the appropriate unit and the eligibility of voters as well as the date, time, and place of the election.

If all parties reach an agreement that is approved by a Regional Director, an election will be conducted. If agreement cannot be reached, a representation hearing will be conducted before an NLRB Hearing Officer. All parties will have the opportunity to appear and present evidence about the issues in dispute. After the hearing closes, a Regional Director's or Board decision will issue in which an election will be ordered or the petition will be dismissed. Exceptions to a Regional Director's decision can be filed by any party with the NLRB in Washington, D.C.

## NLRB Offices

Our office addresses are located in the telephone directory under the United States Government-National Labor Relations Board.

The address and phone number of the office closest to you is:

# NLRB CHARGE AGAINST EMPLOYER
# (NLRB FORM 501)

https://www.nlrb.gov/sites/default/files/attachments/basic-page/node-3040/nlrbform501.pdf

FORM EXEMPT UNDER 44 U.S.C 3512

FORM NLRB-501
(8-87)

UNITED STATES OF AMERICA
NATIONAL LABOR RELATIONS BOARD
**CHARGE AGAINST EMPLOYER**

| DO NOT WRITE IN THIS SPACE | |
|---|---|
| Case | Date Filed |
| | / / |

**INSTRUCTIONS:**
File an original together with four copies and a copy for each additional charged party named in item 1 with NLRB Regional Director for the region in which the alleged unfair labor practice occurred or is occurring.

### 1. EMPLOYER AGAINST WHOM CHARGE IS BROUGHT

| a. Name of Employer | | b. Number of workers employed |
|---|---|---|
| c. Address (Street, city, state, and ZIP code) | d. Employer Representative | e. Telephone No. ( ) - <br> Fax No. ( ) - |
| f. Type of Establishment (factory, mine, wholesaler, etc.) | g. Identify principal product or service | |

h. The above-named employer has engaged in and is engaging in unfair labor practices within the meaning of section 8(a), subsections (1) and (list subsections) _____ of the National Labor Relations Act, and these unfair labor practices are practices affecting commerce within the meaning of the Act, or these unfair labor practices are unfair practices affecting commerce within the meaning of the Act and the Postal Reorganization Act.

2. Basis of the Charge (set forth a clear and concise statement of the facts constituting the alleged unfair labor practices)

3. Full name of party filing charge (if labor organization, give full name, including local name and number)

| 4a. Address (Street and number, city, state, and ZIP code) | 4b. Telephone No. ( ) - <br> Fax No. ( ) - |
|---|---|

5. Full name of national or international labor organization of which it is an affiliate or constituent unit (to be filled in when charge is filed by a labor organization)

### 6. DECLARATION
I declare that I have read the above charge and that the statements are true to the best of my knowledge and belief.

By _____
(signature of representative or person making charge)       (Print/type name and title or office, if any)

     (fax) ( ) - _____

Address _____ ( ) - _____    / /
                                    (Telephone No.)          (date)

**WILLFUL FALSE STATEMENTS ON THIS CHARGE CAN BE PUNISHED BY FINE AND IMPRISONMENT (U.S. CODE, TITLE 18, SECTION 1001)**

**PRIVACY ACT STATEMENT**

Solicitation of the information on this form is authorized by the National Labor Relations Act (NLRA), 29 U.S.C. § 151 et seq. The principal use of the information is to assist the National Labor Relations Board (NLRB) in processing unfair labor practice and related proceedings or litigation. The routine uses for the information are fully set forth in the Federal Register, 71 Fed. Reg. 74942-43 (Dec. 13, 2006). The NLRB will further explain these uses upon request. Disclosure of this information to the NLRB is voluntary; however, failure to supply the information will cause the NLRB to decline to invoke its processes.

# NLRB CHARGE AGAINST UNION (NLRB FORM 508)

https://www.nlrb.gov/sites/default/files/attachments/basic-page/node-3040/nlrbform508.pdf

FORM NLRB-508
(8-87)

UNITED STATES OF AMERICA
NATIONAL LABOR RELATIONS BOARD
**CHARGE AGAINST LABOR ORGANIZATIONS
OR ITS AGENTS**

FORM EXEMPT UNDER 44 U.S.C 3512

**DO NOT WRITE IN THIS SPACE**

| Case | Date Filed |
|------|------------|
|      | / /        |

**INSTRUCTIONS:** File an original together with four copies and a copy for each additional charged party named in item 1 with NLRB Regional Director for the region in which the alleged unfair labor practice occurred or is occurring.

**1. LABOR ORGANIZATION OR ITS AGENTS AGAINST WHICH CHARGE IS BROUGHT**

a. Name

b. Union Representative to contact

c. Telephone No.
( ) -
Fax No.
( ) -

d. Address (Street, city, state, and ZIP code)

e. The above-named organization(s) or its agents has (have) engaged in and is (are) engaging in unfair labor practices within the meaning of section 8(b), subsection(s) (list subsections) _____ of the National Labor Relations Act, and these unfair labor practices are unfair practices affecting commerce within the meaning of the Act, or these unfair labor practices are unfair practices affecting commerce within the meaning of the Act and the Postal Reorganization Act.

2. Basis of the Charge (set forth a clear and concise statement of the facts constituting the alleged unfair labor practices)

| 3. Name of Employer | 4. Telephone No.<br>( ) -<br>Fax No.<br>( ) - |
|---|---|
| 5. Location of plant involved (street, city, state and ZIP code) | 6. Employer representative to contact |

| 7. Type of establishment (factory, mine, wholesaler, etc.) | 8. Identify principal product or service | 9. Number of workers employed |
|---|---|---|

10. Full name of party filing charge

| 11. Address of party filing charge (street, city, state and ZIP code.) | 12. Telephone No.<br>( )<br>Fax No.<br>( ) - |
|---|---|

**13. DECLARATION**

I declare that I have read the above charge and that the statements therein are true to the best of my knowledge and belief.

By _____
(signature of representative or person making charge)

(Print/type name and title or office, if any)

(Fax) ( ) -

Address _____

( ) -
(Telephone No.)

/ /
(date)

**WILLFUL FALSE STATEMENTS ON THIS CHARGE CAN BE PUNISHED BY FINE AND IMPRISONMENT (U.S. CODE, TITLE 18, SECTION 1001)**

**PRIVACY ACT STATEMENT**

Solicitation of the information on this form is authorized by the National Labor Relations Act (NLRA), 29 U.S.C. § 151 et seq. The principal use of the information is to assist the National Labor Relations Board (NLRB) in processing unfair labor practice and related proceedings or litigation. The routine uses for the information are fully set forth in the Federal Register, 71 Fed. Reg. 74942-43 (Dec. 13, 2006). The NLRB will further explain these uses upon request. Disclosure of this information to the NLRB is voluntary; however, failure to supply the information will cause the NLRB to decline to invoke its processes.

## ANATOMY OF AN **NLRB** CASE

Dennis O. Lynch, Deferral, Waiver, and Arbitration Under the NLRA: From Status to
Contract and Back Again, 44 U. Miami L. Rev. 237, 247–255 (1989).

In enacting the NLRA, Congress chose to create an administrative board staffed by labor relations experts who were to be appointed by the president and confirmed by Congress. The Board was charged with the responsibility of adjudicating unfair labor practice charges, with all final orders subject to judicial review by the United States Courts of Appeals before enforcement under a court's contempt power. Thus, the statutory structure contemplated the initial formulation of statutory policy by an administrative board responsive to changing political currents within the executive branch and Congress. At the same time, the federal courts were to provide an independent source of continuity in the development of labor policy through judicial review of final Board orders.

There are now two additional avenues by which the federal courts shape labor policies governing collective bargaining. First, under Section 301 of the LMRA, the courts have jurisdiction to enforce collective bargaining agreements through actions filed in the federal district courts. As a part of this power to enforce collective agreements, they also review arbitration awards as a precursor to deciding if an award should be enforced by a court order. Second, the federal courts share jurisdiction with the Board over claims by individual employees that their union has failed to represent them fairly either in bargaining or in the processing of grievances under a collective agreement.

In all three avenues of this involvement with the formulation of labor policy, the federal courts have been careful to project a contractarian image of labor policy. Court doctrine points to the role of both the Board and the courts as neutral adjudicators who encourage the parties to define workplace rights through collective bargaining and as avenues through which the parties enforce their bargain. Their actual decisions, however, establish initial statutory entitlements, fill in gaps in agreements, and balance bargaining power by regulating forms of concerted pressure. Thus, both the Board and the courts play prominent roles in the formulation of labor policy in ways that impact on the substantive terms of collective bargaining agreements.

Although theoretically neutral contract interpreters, private arbitrators also play a role in shaping and implementing statutory policy. The source of a labor arbitrator's jurisdiction over disputes is the parties' collective bargaining agreement. These agreements normally include an arbitration clause that defines the scope of the arbitrator's power to hear disputes arising under the agreement and that delineates the remedies that the arbitrator may include in an award. This consensual image of labor arbitration is, however, only a partial explanation for the expansive role of labor arbitration. To understand fully the role of labor arbitration, it is necessary to examine the doctrine shaping the interlocking relationship among the Board, the federal courts, and arbitrators.

Through their jurisdiction to enforce collective bargaining agreements, the federal courts have developed a substantial body of federal common law making labor arbitration the centerpiece of a democratic workplace in which workers and employers jointly agree on a set of rules governing the conduct of management representatives and employees. For example, if a union has waived its statutory right to strike during the term of an agreement, federal courts will presume that disputes arising under the agreement are subject to arbitration. Similarly, if a dispute is subject to arbitration, federal common law will imply a union obligation not to strike. Federal courts assume a coterminous relationship between the breadth of a grievance arbitration clause and a union's pledge not to strike. Finally, the autonomy of arbitrators in the interpretation of agreements is also protected by the limited nature of judicial review of arbitration awards. Consequently, federal courts ordinarily enforce arbitration awards as long as the arbitrator's opinion draws its essence from the agreement.

Implicit in this model of labor relations, with arbitration as the central means by which unions control employer discretion on a dispute-by-dispute basis, is the assumption that the union way waive employees' statutory rights. Section 7 of the NLRA guarantees to employees the right to engage in concerted activity for mutual aid and protection, which includes the right to strike. Although an individual employee may not contract with his employer to waive that employee's Section 7 right to engage in concerted activity, once employees have banded together into a union, their bargaining agent may waive this right in a collective bargaining agreement encompassing all the employees within the bargaining unit.

The "waiver" doctrine inevitably leads to shared jurisdiction between the Board and arbitrators in the adjudication of potential Section 7 violations. Consequently, the interpretation of the collective bargaining agreement becomes the central issue in determining both the extent of the protection provided by the agreement and whether the agreement waived the protection that the employees would otherwise enjoy under Section 7. Two similar cases, *NLRB v. City Disposal Systems*, 465 U.S. 822 (1984) and American Freight System v. NLRB, 722 F.2d 828 (D.C. Cir. 1983) provide useful examples of this overlap.

In each of these cases, an employee refused to drive a truck that he thought was unsafe and, as a result, was discharged by the employer for refusing to follow the order to drive. Illustration 1 sets forth the employee's options at this point: Most employees would immediately file a grievance claiming that the discharge was not for just cause, arguing that there was a contractual right to refuse to drive an unsafe truck [Box D]. Alternatively, or simultaneously, the employee might file an unfair labor practice charge with a regional office of the Board, alleging that he had been disciplined for engaging in protected concerted activity [Box B]. Should the employee attempt to go directly to court under Section 301 in order to enforce his claimed contractual right [Box E] to refuse to drive an unsafe truck, however, the court would dismiss the complaint and require the employee to first exhaust his remedies under the collective bargaining agreement. *Republic Steel Corp. v. Maddox*, 379 U.S. 650 (1965).

If the grievances is resolved in the employee's favor prior to arbitration and if the employee is content with the result, that would end the matter. If the grievance is arbitrated and the employee wins, the employer's only alternative is to seek to set aside the award in a court, but the court would normally treat the award as final and hence binding. *United Paperworkers Int'l Union v. Misco, Inc.*, 108 S.Ct. 364, 370–71 (1987); *United Steelworkers v. Enterprise Wheel & Car Corp.*, 363 U.S. 593,597 (1960). The situation becomes more complex, however, if the grievance is resolved against the employee.

Illustration 1

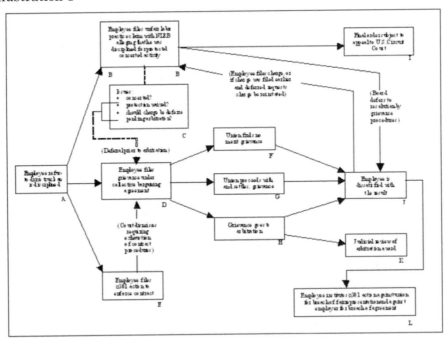

Illustration 1 depicts three different ways in which a decision adverse to the grievant may be made. First, the union could decide that the grievance lacks merit and thus decline to grieve; this was the case in *City*

*Disposal Systems*, 465 U.S. at 827 [Box F]. Second, the union might initiate grievance procedures and either settle the grievance because it decides that the employer was justified or because the grievance is not of sufficient merit to justify the expenditure of union resources to arbitrate. Alternatively, the union may agree to a compromise remedy, such as the employee's reinstatement without back pay [Box G]. If the union either settles the grievance or declines to grieve, the employee-if he is dissatisfied with the union's decision-may elect to pursue an alternative remedy by initiating a complaint in another forum [Boxes B and L]. Third, the grievance could go to arbitration and be denied by the arbitrator [Box H]. In *American Freight System*, for example, the grievance was denied after a hearing by a bipartite grievance committee which the court treated as equivalent to arbitration. *American Freight Sys. v. NLRB*, 722 F.2d 822, 832–33 (D.C. Cir. 1983). At this point, the employee in Illustration 1 must seek redress in a public forum to challenge the resolution of the dispute that occurred through private ordering [Boxes J–B, H–K, and J–L].

The employee has two options in public forums if the grievance ends short of arbitration, and an additional third option if it is denied by the arbitrator: (1) He can file an unfair labor practice charge if one is not already pending; [NLRA § 10(a), 29 U.S.C. § 160(a); Illustration 1, Boxes J–B] (2) he can file a Section 301 action alleging that the union breached its duty of fair representation [Boxes J–L] and that the employer breached the collective bargaining agreement; or (3) if the grievance has been denied by the arbitrator, he can additionally seek (through an action filed by the union) to have the award set aside by a federal district court. *United Steelworkers v. Enterprise Wheel & Car Corp.*, 363 U.S. 593 (1960). Thus, the nature of the cause of action is distinct in each forum, even though the action arises from the same underlying set of facts.

The discharged truck driver may also pursue the unfair labor practice charge before the Board either without first filing a grievance or after he has exhausted his available contract grievance procedures, as long as the six month statute of limitations for such charges has not run. The unfair labor practice charge poses three issues for the Board: (1) whether the driver was discharged for engaging in protected concerted activity; (2) whether the collective bargaining agreement waived the employee's statutory protection by establishing a contractual standard for the protection of employees who refuse to drive a truck that is less protective of bargaining unit employees than is Section 7 or whether the standard is equivalent to the statutory protection, *NLRB v. City Disposal Sys.*, 465 U.S. 822, 828, 835–37 (1984); and (3) whether the Board should defer the charge to arbitration. *American Freight Sys. v. NLRB*, 722 F.2d 828, 831 (D.C. Cir. 1983).

If the employee goes to the Board first or pursues a grievance and unfair labor practice charge simultaneously, either the General Counsel or the Board, if formal proceedings against the employer have reached the point of a hearing before an Administrative Law Judge (ALJ), will apply the standards for deferral prior to arbitration. Because the same underlying facts of the driver's discharge are the source of both the grievance and the unfair labor practice charge, the unfair labor practice proceedings will normally be stayed pending arbitration, as long as the employer is willing both to arbitrate and to be bound by the arbitral award.

If the employee is unhappy with the arbitrator's award and requests reinstatement of the unfair labor practice charge subsequent to the award, the issue posed will be the same as it would have been had the employee exhausted the contract grievance procedures before filing the charge. Under current Board standards, as long as the grievance proceeding are "fair and regular" and the arbitrator's award is not "palpably" inconsistent with the policies and purposes of the Act, the charge will be dismissed. *Olin Corp.,* 268 N.L.R.B. 573, 574 (1984).

Following the arbitrator's award in the case of the discharged driver, the employer can also make a narrower collateral estoppel argument for deferral based on the similarity of the issues posed in both forums. The employer will claim that the arbitrator's decision regarding the level of protection that the collective bargaining agreement provides the employee is essentially addressing the same issue that the Board would face in deciding whether the agreement waived the employee's statutory protection. Therefore, the employer will argue that the Board should respect the parties' agreement to have the arbitrator interpret the contract. *Darr v. NLRB,* 801 F.2d 1404, 1408 (D.C. Cir. 1986).

In response to either a broad deferral standard based on the same underlying facts or a more narrow collateral estoppel defense, the driver will argue that his access to the Board should not be waived on the basis of the overlap of his contract and statutory rights because the protection that Section 7 provides an employee who refuses to drive an unsafe truck reflects statutory policies that are independent of the collective bargaining agreement. The employee will claim that he is entitled to a de novo hearing on the facts and the law because the Board is charged with the responsibility to enforce statutory rights. In practice, the Board tends to favor the employer's position, but some federal courts have reversed the Board based on reasoning that is more sympathetic to the employee's argument.

When a grievance is decided short of arbitration, such as when the union decides either not to grieve or to settle the grievance, the Board's position on deferral is not as clear, but it appears to be moving toward treating a union settlement the same as an arbitration award. The fact pattern of *NLRB v. City Disposal Systems* posed the most difficult case for deferral to grievance proceedings because the union refused at the outset to grieve on the employee's behalf. *NLRB v. City Disposal Sys.*, 465 U.S. 822, 839–41 (1984). In *City Disposal Systems*, the charged party did not plead deferral as an affirmative defense; instead, the employer argued for dismissal based on the driver's failure to exhaust internal union procedures that permitted him to challenge the union's refusal to grieve. The ALJ dismissed the exhaustion argument with a reference to the statutory language that states that the Board's powers are not "affected by any other means of adjustment." Thus, the central issue of the case became whether the refusal to drive by a sole truck driver, without any aid or support by fellow employees, constituted protected concerted activity. Consequently, the Supreme Court majority opinion in City Disposal Systems focused only on the meaning of "concerted" under Section 7. The union's refusal to grieve is mentioned, but it played no apparent part in the majority's reasoning.

The dissent, in contrast, focused primarily on the need to contain this type of dispute within contract grievance procedures and suggested that the Board, even assuming that the refusal was protected, should have deferred to the union's initial decision to decline to grieve. *Id.* at 844 n.4. (O'Connor, J., dissenting).The general theory of collective bargaining is more consistent with the dissent in the sense that, under the theory, the Board should defer to a union's decision as long as no conflict between the union and the employee raises a question of whether the union's decision was made either in bad faith or arbitrarily. Thus, the dissent's approach implicitly suggests that fair representation protections should be incorporated into the deferral doctrine and that, if the union has not breached its duty by declining to grieve, the employee has no statutory right to a Board hearing.

This description of the relationships among the forums is primarily aimed at emphasizing the critical roles that waiver and deferral play in making arbitration the central forum for resolving claims involving both statutory and contract rights. The substance of the deferral and waiver doctrines and their implications for the protection and development of statutory rights are addressed in more detail in subsequent sections.

# SAMPLE AUTHORIZATION CARD

WORKERS LOCAL NO. 88
Authorization for Representation Form

Authorization for Representation
I, the undersigned employee of

COMPANY

ADDRESS _____

authorize Workers Local No.88 to represent me in negotiations for
better wages, hours, benefits and working conditions.

NAME _____

ADDRESS _____

CITY/STATE _____

HOME PHONE ( _____ ) _____

PRESENT WAGE RATE:_____

KIND OF WORK:

SHIFT:    day                    swing                    graveyard


SIGNATURE: _____

This information is strictly confidential
All information is kept confidential by the Workers Union and the
U.S. Government. All information shall be kept in absolute confidence
by the Union and the National Labor Relations Board.

THE FEDERAL LAW UPHOLDS YOUR RIGHT TO ORGANIZE
PLEASE SIGN NOW!

# NLRB PETITION FOR ELECTION (NLRB FORM 502)

https://www.nlrb.gov/sites/default/files/attachments/basic-page/node-3040/nlrbform502.pdf

# SAMPLE COLLECTIVE BARGAINING AGREEMENT

### Representative Sections

## PREAMBLE

This Agreement is entered into as of July 21 2008 by and between Enderby Industries, hereinafter referred to as the "Company", and Local 147 of the United Factory Workers of America (UFWA), hereinafter referred to as the "Union".

## ARTICLE I—RECOGNITION

The Company agrees to recognize the Union as the exclusive collective bargaining agent for those employees at the Esopus River Plant of Enderby Industries in River City, New York who are included in the bargaining unit as determined by the National Labor Relations Board in NLRB Case 2–R–3909, for the purpose of collective bargaining in respect to rates of pay, hours of work and other conditions of employment.

## ARTICLE II—UNION SECURITY

### Section 1. Union Shop

A.   Subject to applicable law, all employees who as of the date of this Agreement are members of the Union in good standing in accordance with the constitution and bylaws of the Union or who become members of the Union following the effective date of this Agreement, shall, as a condition of employment, remain members of the Union in good standing insofar as the payment of an amount equal to the periodic dues and initiation fees, uniformly required, is concerned.

B.   Subject to applicable law, all present employees who are not members of the Union and all individuals hired after the effective date of this agreement, shall, beginning on the thirtieth (30th) day following the effective date of this agreement or the thirtieth (30th) day following employment, whichever is later, as a condition of employment, either become and remain members of the Union in good standing insofar as the payment of an amount equal to the periodic dues and initiation fees, uniformly required, is concerned, or, in lieu of such Union membership, pay to the Union an equivalent service charge.

### Section 2. Union Dues Deduction or Service Charge Authorization.

A.   The Company, for each of its employees included within the bargaining unit recognized by the Company pursuant to Article I hereof, who individually, in writing, duly authorizes the Company Paymaster to do so, will deduct from the earnings payable to such employee the dues (including initiation fee, if any) for such employees' membership in the Local, or the equivalent service charge, and shall remit promptly to the Local all such deductions.

## ARTICLE III—WORKING CONDITIONS

Section 1. Safety and Health

The Company will continue to provide for the safety and health of its employees on its premises.

## ARTICLE IV—DISCRIMINATION AND COERCION

Section 1. There shall be no discrimination by supervisors or other agents of the Company against any employee because of the employee's membership in the Union or because the employee is acting as a representative of the Union.

Section 2. The Union agrees that neither its officers nor its members, nor persons employed directly or indirectly by the Union will intimidate or coerce any employee; nor solicit members or funds on Company premises during working hours.

Section 3. The Company shall not discriminate against any of the employees in the payment of wages, assignment of jobs, seniority, promotion, transfer, layoff, discipline, discharge or any other term or condition of employment because of race, creed, color, religion, marital status, sex, age, or national origin.

Section 4. The Union shall not discriminate against any employee on account of race, creed, color, religion, marital status, sex, age, national origin, or membership or nonmembership in the Union.

Section 5. The Company and the Union shall not discriminate against any employee because of physical or mental disability or because he or she is a disabled veteran or veteran of the Vietnam era in regard to any position for which the employee is qualified.

## ARTICLE V—HOURS OF WORK AND PREMIUM PAYMENTS

Section 1. Workweek—Workday

A. Workweek. The normal working week shall be forty (40) hours, five (5) days, eight (8) consecutive hours per day exclusive of the lunch period, Monday through Friday inclusive.

Section 2. Overtime Assignment and Equalization

A. In the interest of properly serving customers, the Union and the Company recognize the need for, and advantage to all concerned from, performance of assigned work outside of normal, schedules. The Company agrees to give notice of such assigned work to the extent reasonably practicable in the particular circumstances. Overtime shall be divided as equally as proficient operations permit among the qualified employees who are performing similar work in a work group. The supervisor will review, upon request, the record with his designated representative.

## ARTICLE VI—BULLETIN BOARDS

The Company agrees that the Union may post on Company bulletin boards factual and non-controversial material which a responsible representative of the Union wishes to post. If the Company contends that a posted notice is not within the spirit of this Article, the responsible Union representative, if available, will remove the notice. If the Union representative is not available, the Company reserves the right to remove such material.

## ARTICLE VII—PROBATIONARY PERIOD

New employees shall serve a probationary period of 60 working days, during which their performance shall be evaluated. An employee may be terminated or disciplined at the discretion of the company at any time during this probationary period, and during that period the provisions of Article VII, on discharge and discipline, shall not apply. Discipline, including discharge, of a probationary employee shall not be subject to binding arbitration.

## ARTICLE VIII—DISCIPLINE AND DISCHARGE

No employee who has completed the probationary period shall be suspended or discharged, or otherwise disciplined, except for just cause.

For the purposes of this provision, just cause for dismissal includes, but is not limited to, theft, fighting, use of banned substances, coming to work under the influence of alcohol, two unexcused absences and being late more than five times in one year.

## ARTICLE IX—RIGHT TO REPRESENTATIVE

At any meeting between a representative of the Company and an employee at which discipline (including warnings which are to be recorded in the personnel file, suspension, demotion or discharge) is to be considered or announced, a Union representative may be present if the employee so requests. The Company representative in charge of such meeting must advise the employee of this right.

## ARTICLE X—UNION REPRESENTATION

Section 1. Notification. The Union will give the Company written notice of the names of Representatives, Negotiating Committees and Officers of the Union, and will promptly advise the Company of any changes in such office or position. The Company will give the Union written notice of the supervisors designated to deal with the respective representatives of the Union, and will advise the Union, generally the Second Level Negotiating Committee Chairman, of changes in such designation in a timely manner.

Union Representatives shall be given permission to leave their work for Union business providing they make such request from their Supervisor, and the time so spent shall be properly accounted for.

Section 2. Layoff Deferment

(a) An employee who is an Official of the Union, and who has accumulated twelve (12) months or more of service shall credits, on written request of the Union be deferred from layoff (except temporary layoffs) from her or his job so long as work for which the employee is qualified is available and so long as the official's duties would permit such layoff deferment under applicable law.

ARTICLE XI—GRIEVANCE PROCEDURE

Section 1. Definition. A grievance is a claim involving the application or interpretation of any provision of the Agreement.

Section 2. Initiation of Grievances. Grievances may be filed by an employee or group of employees, a Representative or the Union. Grievances of a general nature filed by the Union may be initiated at the second step of the grievance procedure.

Section 3. Grievance Procedure.

Step 1. (a) Within two (2) weeks after the employee becomes aware or should become aware of the situation, condition, or action of management giving rise to a grievance, the employee affected thereby, or the employee's Representative, may present an oral or written grievance to the supervisor for settlement. The supervisor shall give an answer within two (2) working days. If on an oral grievance no oral agreement is reached, the grievance will be reduced to writing and presented to the supervisor within five working days.

(b) The written grievance will indicate the nature of the grievance, adjustment requested, and any other pertinent information. Each of the parties should retain a copy of the grievance.

(c) The supervisor will give to the Representative a written answer, within two (2) working days from the time the grievance is received. Additional time may be allowed by mutual agreement of the Representative and supervisor.

(d) If the grievance is not processed in writing to the second step of the grievance procedure within two (2) calendar weeks from receipt of the supervisor's written answer, the case shall be considered closed. Additional time may be allowed by mutual agreement.

(e) After a written grievance has been submitted, all negotiations and settlements with respect to this grievance shall be handled through the designated Union representative.

Step 2. [the subsequent steps, set out in great detail, are omitted]

ARTICLE XII—ARBITRATION

Section 1. Any grievance which remains unsettled after having been fully processed pursuant to the provisions Of Article XI, and which involves either,

    (a) the interpretation or application of a provision of this Agreement, or

    (b) a disciplinary penalty (including discharge) imposed on or after the effective date of this Agreement, which is alleged to have been imposed without just cause,

may be submitted to arbitration upon written request of either the Union or the Company, provided such request is made within 60 days after the final decision of the Company has been given to the Union pursuant to Article XI, Step 3. For the purpose of proceedings within the scope of (b) above, the standard to be applied by an arbitrator to cases involving disciplinary penalties (including discharge) is that such penalties shall be imposed only for just cause.

Section 2. A request for arbitration may be made by either the Company or the Union on any or all of the issues which it believes to be involved in a grievance specifically related to (a) or (b) above, and must state in reasonable detail the issue or issues sought to be arbitrated and the specific relief sought as to each such issue and must specifically state the contract provisions alleged to have been violated.

Section 3. (a) Within 10 days following a request for arbitration of a grievance, the Company or the Union may request the American Arbitration Association to submit a Panel of names from which an arbitrator may be chosen. In the selection of an arbitrator, the Voluntary Labor Arbitration Rules of the American Arbitration Association shall control.

Section 5. The award of an arbitrator so selected upon any grievance subject to arbitration as herein provided shall be final and binding upon all parties to this Agreement, provided that no arbitrator shall have any authority or jurisdiction to add to, detract from, or in any way alter the provisions of this Agreement.

[ECONOMIC PROVISIONS—This sample agreement does not list typical provisions for economic benefits, such as wages, health insurance, pensions (including contributions to 401K accounts), vacations, and holidays.]

ARTICLE XIII—ABSENCES

Section 1. Full time employees shall be entitled to the following absences with pay:

Personal Illness. Up to 15 working days per calendar year. Unused sick days may be accumulated and accrued into subsequent years.

Personal Business. Up to 3 working days.

Death of Immediate Relative. Up to 5 working days for any such death. Immediate Relatives are considered to include your wife or husband, children and grandchildren, parents, brothers, sisters, brothers-in-law, sisters-in-law and grandparents, plus the parents, brothers, sisters, brothers-in-law, sisters-in-law and grandparents of your spouse, foster child (if living in the employee's home), stepchildren, stepbrother, stepsister, son-in-law and daughter-in-law.

## ARTICLE XIV—STRIKES AND LOCKOUTS

Section 1. During the term of this Agreement, there shall be no strike, sitdown, slowdown, employee demonstration or any other organized or concerted interference with work of any kind, and no strike or interference with work shall be directly or indirectly authorized or sanctioned by the Union or any of its respective officers, officials, or Representatives.

Section 2. The Company will not lock out any employee or transfer any job under dispute from the local Plant or between Departments within the Plant while a disputed job is under discussion at any of the steps of the Grievance Procedure as set forth in Article XI, or if the matter is submitted to arbitration as provided in Article XII.

## ARTICLE XV—MANAGEMENT RESPONSIBILITY

The Company retains the exclusive right to manage its business, including (but not limited to) the right to determine the methods and means by which its operations are to be carried out, to direct the work force and determine its qualifications and to maintain safety, efficiency and order in its plants and operations.

## ARTICLE XVII—DECREASING FORCES

Section 1. When a lack of work condition arises, an effort will be made to reduce subcontracting and overtime before applying Section 3 of this Article.

(a) The Company will discuss with the Union the status of Apprentices before draftsmen having more than one year of seniority are laid off due to a reduction of forces.

(b) The Company will discuss with the Union any rotation schedule or reduced workweek below forty (40) hours after all employees in the Department with less than one (1) year of seniority have been given notice of layoff.

Section 2. When a reduction of forces is to be made:

(a) The Union will be given advance notice when a reduction of forces becomes necessary together with the reasons for such reduction.

(b) Each Representative in the affected groups shall be given duplicate lists which will show the length of seniority and classification of all the employees she or he represents.

(c) The employee to be laid off due to lack of work for an extended or indefinite period will be given at least two (2) week's notice. The employee will be advised personally of the reasons therefore and may, if she or he desires, have a Representative present at the time the reasons are given.

Section 3. The objective in cases of layoff or transfer due to lack of work is to avoid moving employees with the longest seniority from the department and to avoid reducing their pay while shorter service people remain in the department and suffer no pay reduction; similarly, the objective is to avoid laying off long service people while employees with less seniority remain employed in the Plant. At the same time it is the objective to recognize the need of the Company to have necessary work performed in a satisfactory manner.

## ARTICLE XVIII—INCREASING FORCES

When openings occur, first consideration will be given to employees with the longest seniority who are capable of performing the work in a satisfactory manner within a reasonable period of job familiarization from either those who are on recall or those who have been laid off due to lack of work and are currently working on lower classifications.

## ARTICLE XXIII—NOTIFICATION AND PUBLICITY

Section 1. The Company agrees to notify the Union of any matter affecting employees generally and concerning which the Union is the certified bargaining representative as soon as the supervisors are notified.

Section 2. On any matter which has been negotiated between the Company and the Union, the Company will notify the Union of its decision before it notifies the employees.

## ARTICLE XXIV—SUBCONTRACTING

The Company retains the right to subcontract work in accordance with sound business practice and without unduly affecting bargaining unit jobs.

## ARTICLE XXVI—NEUTRALITY

Section 1. Over the years, the Company and the Union have attempted to develop a constructive and harmonious relationship built on trust, integrity and mutual respect.

To underscore the Company's commitment in this matter, it agrees to adopt a position of neutrality in the event that the Union seeks to represent any non-represented employees of the Company.

Neutrality means that the Company shall neither help nor hinder the Union's conduct of an organizing campaign, nor shall it demean the Union as an organization or its representatives as individuals. Also, the Company shall not provide any support or assistance of any kind to any person or group opposed to Union organization.

Section 2. Consistent with the above, the Company reserves the right:

To challenge any issues relating to the scope and makeup of the unit sought by the Union through the Dispute Resolution procedure set forth below.

To communicate fairly and factually to employees in the unit sought concerning the terms and conditions of their employment with the Company and concerning legitimate issues in the campaign.

Section 3. For its part, the Union agrees that all facets of its organizing campaign will be conducted in a constructive and positive manner which does not misrepresent their employment and in a manner which neither demeans the Company as an organization nor its representatives as individuals.

The Company's commitment to remain neutral shall cease if the Union or its agents intentionally or repeatedly (after having the matter called to the Union's attention) misrepresent to the employees the facts and circumstances surrounding their employment or conduct a campaign which comments on the motives, integrity or character of the Company or its representatives.

Section 4. Upon written request, the Company shall grant access to its facilities to the Union for the purpose of distributing literature and meeting with unrepresented employees. Distribution of Union literature at entrances and exits of facilities shall not compromise safety or disrupt access or egress.

## ARTICLE XXVII—COMPLETE AGREEMENT

The parties acknowledge that during the negotiations that led to this Agreement, each had the unlimited right and opportunity to make demands and proposals with respect to any subject or matter not removed by law from the area of collective negotiations, and that the understandings and agreements arrived at by the parties after the exercise of such rights are fully set forth in this Agreement. No waiver or modification shall be effective unless signed by the parties hereto, and any such waiver shall be strictly limited to the situation presented therein.

## ARTICLE XXVIII—GOVERNMENT REQUIREMENTS

Nothing contained in this Agreement shall be deemed to impose upon either party the obligation to take any action, or refrain from taking any action, in violation of any existing or future law, or rule, regulation or directive issued by a government department or agency.

## ARTICLE XXIX—TERMINATION

This Agreement shall continue in full force and effect until July 20, 2004 and thereafter from year to year unless not more than ninety (90) days and not less than sixty (60) days prior to July 20, 2004 or prior to July 20 of any subsequent year, either party notifies the other in writing of its intention to terminate this Agreement, in which event the Agreement shall terminate on the July 20 following such notice.

Within thirty (30) days after such notice is given, collective bargaining negotiations shall commence for the purpose of considering the terms of a new Agreement.

S<small>IGNED:</small>

_____

F<small>OR THE</small> C<small>OMPANY</small>

_____

F<small>OR THE</small> U<small>NION</small>

# ILLINOIS PUBLIC LABOR RELATIONS ACT

■ ■ ■

5 Ill. Comp. Stat. 315/1–315/18
(selections)

## § 1 (5 ILCS 315/1).

This Act shall be known and may be cited as the "Illinois Public Labor Relations Act".

## § 2 (5 ILCS 315/2). Policy

It is the public policy of the State of Illinois to grant public employees full freedom of association, self-organization, and designation of representatives of their own choosing for the purpose of negotiating wages, hours and other conditions of employment or other mutual aid or protection.

It is the purpose of this Act to regulate labor relations between public employers and employees, including the designation of employee representatives, negotiation of wages, hours and other conditions of employment, and resolution of disputes arising under collective bargaining agreements.

It is the purpose of this Act to prescribe the legitimate rights of both public employees and public employers, to protect the public health and safety of the citizens of Illinois, and to provide peaceful and orderly procedures for protection of the rights of all. To prevent labor strife and to protect the public health and safety of the citizens of Illinois, all collective bargaining disputes involving persons designated by the Board as performing essential services and those persons defined herein as security employees shall be submitted to impartial arbitrators, who shall be authorized to issue awards in order to resolve such disputes. It is the public policy of the State of Illinois that where the right of employees to strike is prohibited by law, it is necessary to afford an alternate, expeditious, equitable and effective procedure for the resolution of labor disputes subject to approval procedures mandated by this Act. To that end, the provisions for such awards shall be liberally construed.

## § 2.5 (5 ILCS 315/2.5). Findings and Declarations; Court Reporters

The General Assembly finds and declares:

(1) It is the public policy of the State of Illinois and the intent of the General Assembly that State employees, including the Illinois official certified court reporters, are granted collective bargaining rights as provided in this Act.

(2) The Illinois Supreme Court in the case of *AOIC v. Teamsters 726* ruled that the Illinois Public Labor Relations Board could not assert jurisdiction over the Illinois official certified court reporters because the Supreme Court is their co-employer together with the Chief Judges of each judicial circuit.

(3) As a result of the Supreme Court's decision, the Illinois official certified court reporters have been denied the labor rights afforded all other State employees, including the rights to organize, to obtain recognition of their chosen collective bargaining representative, and to negotiate with respect to the wages, terms, and conditions of their employment.

(4) The General Assembly intends to create a statutory framework to allow Illinois official court reporters to enjoy the same collective bargaining and other labor rights granted to other public employees.

(5) Senate Resolution 431 and House Resolution 706, both of the 92nd General Assembly, were adopted, and in enacting this amendatory Act of the 94th General Assembly, the General Assembly is implementing the intent of those resolutions.

## § 3 (5 ILCS 315/3). Definitions

As used in this Act, unless the context otherwise requires:

(a) "Board" means the Illinois Labor Relations Board or, with respect to a matter over which the jurisdiction of the Board is assigned to the State Panel or the Local Panel under Section 5, the panel having jurisdiction over the matter.

(b) "Collective bargaining" means bargaining over terms and conditions of employment, including hours, wages, and other conditions of employment, as detailed in Section 7 and which are not excluded by Section 4.

(c) "Confidential employee" means an employee who, in the regular course of his or her duties, assists and acts in a confidential capacity to persons who formulate, determine, and effectuate management policies with regard to labor relations or who, in the regular course of his or her duties, has authorized access to information relating to the effectuation or review of the employer's collective bargaining policies.

(d) "Craft employees" means skilled journeymen, crafts persons, and their apprentices and helpers.

(e) "Essential services employees" means those public employees performing functions so essential that the interruption or termination of the function will constitute a clear and present danger to the health and safety of the persons in the affected community.

(f) "Exclusive representative", except with respect to non-State fire fighters and paramedics employed by fire departments and fire protection districts, non-State peace officers, and peace officers in the Department of State Police, means the labor organization that has been (i) designated by the Board as the representative of a majority of public employees in an appropriate bargaining unit in accordance with the procedures contained in this Act, (ii) historically recognized by the State of Illinois or any political subdivision of the State before July 1, 1984 (the effective date of this Act) as the exclusive representative of the employees in an appropriate bargaining unit, (iii) after July 1, 1984 (the effective date of this Act) recognized by an employer upon evidence, acceptable to the Board, that the labor organization has been designated as the exclusive representative by a majority of the employees in an appropriate bargaining unit; (iv) recognized as the exclusive representative of personal care attendants or personal assistants under Executive Order 2003–8 prior to the effective date of this amendatory Act of the 93rd General Assembly, and the organization shall be considered to be the exclusive representative of the personal care attendants or personal assistants as defined in this Section; or (v) recognized as the exclusive representative of child and day care home providers, including licensed and license exempt providers, pursuant to an election held under Executive Order 2005–1 prior to the effective date of this amendatory Act of the 94th General Assembly, and the organization shall be considered to be the exclusive representative of the child and day care home providers as defined in this Section.

With respect to non-State fire fighters and paramedics employed by fire departments and fire protection districts, non-State peace officers, and peace officers in the Department of State Police, "exclusive representative" means the labor organization that has been (i) designated by the Board as the representative of a majority of peace officers or fire fighters in an appropriate bargaining unit in accordance with the procedures contained in this Act, (ii) historically recognized by the State of Illinois or any political subdivision of the State before January 1, 1986 (the effective date of this amendatory Act of 1985) as the exclusive representative by a majority of the peace officers or fire fighters in an appropriate bargaining unit, or (iii) after January 1, 1986 (the effective date of this amendatory Act of 1985) recognized by an employer upon evidence, acceptable to the Board, that the labor organization has been designated as the exclusive representative by a majority of the peace officers or fire fighters in an appropriate bargaining unit.

Where a historical pattern of representation exists for the workers of a water system that was owned by a public utility, as defined in Section 3–105 of the Public Utilities Act, prior to becoming certified employees of a municipality or municipalities once the municipality or municipalities have acquired the water system as authorized in Section 11–124–5 of the Illinois Municipal Code, the Board shall find the labor organization that has historically represented the workers to be the exclusive representative under this Act, and shall find the unit represented by the exclusive representative to be the appropriate unit.

(g) "Fair share agreement" means an agreement between the employer and an employee organization under which all or any of the employees in a collective bargaining unit are required to pay their proportionate share of the costs of the collective bargaining process, contract administration, and pursuing matters affecting wages, hours, and other conditions of employment, but not to exceed the amount of dues uniformly required of members. The amount certified by the exclusive representative shall not include any fees for contributions related to the election or support of any candidate for political office. Nothing in this subsection (g) shall preclude an employee from making voluntary political contributions in conjunction with his or her fair share payment.

(i) "Labor organization" means any organization in which public employees participate and that exists for the purpose, in whole or in part, of dealing with a public employer concerning wages, hours, and other terms and conditions of employment, including the settlement of grievances.

(j) "Managerial employee" means an individual who is engaged predominantly in executive and management functions and is charged with the responsibility of directing the effectuation of management policies and practices. With respect only to State employees in positions under the jurisdiction of the Attorney General, Secretary of State, Comptroller, or Treasurer (i) that were certified in a bargaining unit on or after December 2, 2008, (ii) for which a petition is filed with the Illinois Public Labor Relations Board on or after April 5, 2013 (the effective date of Public Act 97–1172), or (iii) for which a petition is pending before the Illinois Public Labor Relations Board on that date, "managerial employee" means an individual who is engaged in executive and management functions or who is charged with the effectuation of management policies and practices or who represents management interests by taking or recommending discretionary actions that effectively control or implement policy. Nothing in this definition prohibits an individual from also meeting the definition of "supervisor" under subsection (r) of this Section.

(m) "Professional employee" means any employee engaged in work predominantly intellectual and varied in character rather than routine mental, manual, mechanical or physical work; involving the consistent exercise of discretion and adjustment in its performance; of such a character that the output produced or the result accomplished cannot be standardized in relation to a given period of time; and requiring advanced knowledge in a field of science or learning customarily acquired by a prolonged course of specialized intellectual instruction and study in an institution of higher learning or a hospital, as distinguished from a general academic education or from apprenticeship or from training in the performance of routine mental, manual, or physical processes; or any employee who has completed the courses of specialized intellectual instruction and study prescribed in this subsection (m) and is performing related work under the supervision of a professional person to qualify to become a professional employee as defined in this subsection (m).

(n) "Public employee" or "employee", for the purposes of this Act, means any individual employed by a public employer, including (i) interns and residents at public hospitals, (ii) as of the effective date of this amendatory Act of the 93rd General Assembly, but not before, personal care attendants and personal assistants working under the Home Services Program under Section 3 of the Disabled Persons Rehabilitation Act, subject to the limitations set forth in this Act and in the Disabled Persons Rehabilitation Act, (iii) as of the effective date of this amendatory Act of the 94th General Assembly, but not before, child and day care home providers participating in the child care assistance program under Section 9A-11 of the Illinois Public Aid Code, subject to the limitations set forth in this Act and in Section 9A-11 of the Illinois Public Aid Code, (iv) as of January 29, 2013 (the effective date of Public Act 97–1158), but not before except as otherwise provided in this subsection (n), home care and home health workers who function as personal care attendants, personal assistants, and individual maintenance home health workers and who also work under the Home Services Program under Section 3 of the Disabled Persons Rehabilitation Act, no matter whether the State provides those services through direct fee-for-service arrangements, with the assistance of a managed care organization or other intermediary, or otherwise, (v) beginning on the effective date of this amendatory Act of the 98th General Assembly and notwithstanding any other provision of this Act, any person employed by a public employer and who is classified as or who holds the employment title of Chief Stationary Engineer, Assistant Chief Stationary Engineer, Sewage Plant Operator, Water Plant Operator, Stationary Engineer, Plant Operating Engineer, and any other employee who holds the position of: Civil Engineer V, Civil Engineer VI, Civil Engineer VII, Technical Manager I, Technical Manager II, Technical Manager III, Technical Manager IV, Technical Manager V, Technical Manager VI, Realty Specialist III, Realty Specialist IV, Realty Specialist V, Technical Advisor I, Technical Advisor II, Technical Advisor III, Technical Advisor IV, or Technical Advisor V employed by the Department of Transportation who is in a position which is certified in a bargaining unit on or before the effective date of this amendatory Act of the 98th General Assembly, and (vi) beginning on the effective date of this amendatory Act of the 98th General Assembly and notwithstanding any other provision of this Act, any mental health administrator in the Department of Corrections who is classified as or who holds the position of Public Service Administrator (Option 8K), any employee of the Office of the Inspector General in the Department of Human Services who is classified as or who holds the position of Public Service Administrator (Option 7), any Deputy of Intelligence in the Department of Corrections who is classified as or who holds the position of Public Service Administrator (Option 7), and any employee of the Department of State Police who handles issues concerning the Illinois State Police Sex Offender Registry and who is classified as or holds the position of Public Service Administrator (Option 7), but excluding all of the following: employees of the General Assembly of the State of Illinois; elected officials; executive heads of a department; members of boards or commissions; the Executive Inspectors General; any special Executive Inspectors General; employees of each Office of an Executive Inspector General; commissioners and employees of the Executive Ethics Commission; the Auditor General's Inspector General; employees of the Office of the Auditor General's Inspector General; the Legislative Inspector General; any special Legislative Inspectors General; employees of the Office of the Legislative Inspector General; commissioners and employees of the Legislative Ethics Commission; employees of any agency, board or commission created by this Act; employees appointed to State positions of a temporary or emergency nature; all employees of school districts and higher education institutions except firefighters and peace officers employed by a state university and except peace officers employed by a school district in its own police department in existence on the effective date of this amendatory Act of the 96th General Assembly; managerial employees; short-term employees; legislative liaisons; a person who is a State employee under the jurisdiction of the Office of the Attorney General who is licensed to practice law or whose position authorizes, either directly or indirectly, meaningful input into government decision-making on issues where there is room for principled disagreement on goals or their implementation; a person who is a State employee under the jurisdiction of the Office of the Comptroller who holds the position of Public Service Administrator or whose position is otherwise exempt under the Comptroller Merit Employment Code; a person who is a State employee under the jurisdiction of the Secretary of State who holds the position classification of Executive I or higher, whose position authorizes, either directly or indirectly, meaningful input into government decision-making on issues where there is room for principled disagreement on goals or their implementation, or who is otherwise exempt under the Secretary of State Merit Employment Code; employees in the Office of the Secretary of State who are completely exempt from jurisdiction B of the Secretary of State Merit Employment Code and who are in Rutan-exempt positions on or after April 5, 2013 (the effective date of Public Act 97–1172); a person who is a State employee under the jurisdiction of the Treasurer who holds a position that is exempt from the State Treasurer Employment Code; any employee of a State agency who (i) holds the title or position of, or exercises substantially similar duties as a legislative liaison, Agency General Counsel, Agency Chief of Staff, Agency Executive Director, Agency Deputy Director, Agency Chief Fiscal Officer, Agency Human Resources Director, Public Information Officer, or Chief Information Officer and (ii) was neither included in a bargaining unit nor subject to an active petition for certification in a bargaining unit; any employee of a State agency who (i) is in a position that is Rutan-exempt, as designated by the employer, and completely exempt from jurisdiction B of the Personnel Code and (ii) was neither included in a bargaining unit nor subject to an active petition for certification in a bargaining unit; any term appointed employee of a State agency pursuant to Section 8b.18 or 8b.19 of the Personnel Code who was neither included in a bargaining unit nor subject to an active petition for certification in a bargaining unit; any employment position properly designated pursuant to Section 6.1 of this Act; confidential employees; independent contractors; and supervisors except as provided in this Act.

Home care and home health workers who function as personal care attendants, personal assistants, and individual maintenance home health workers and who also work under the Home Services Program under Section 3 of the Disabled Persons Rehabilitation Act shall not be considered public employees for any purposes not specifically provided for in Public Act 93–204 or Public Act 97–1158, including but not limited to, purposes of vicarious liability in tort and purposes of statutory retirement or health insurance benefits. Home care and home health workers who function as personal care attendants, personal assistants, and individual maintenance home health workers and who also work under the Home Services Program under Section 3 of the Disabled Persons Rehabilitation Act shall not be covered by the State Employees Group Insurance Act of 1971 (5 ILCS 375).

Child and day care home providers shall not be considered public employees for any purposes not specifically provided for in this amendatory Act of the 94th General Assembly, including but not limited to, purposes of vicarious liability in tort and purposes of statutory retirement or health insurance benefits. Child and day care home providers shall not be covered by the State Employees Group Insurance Act of 1971.

Notwithstanding Section 9, subsection (c), or any other provisions of this Act, all peace officers above the rank of captain in municipalities with more than 1,000,000 inhabitants shall be excluded from this Act.

(o) Except as otherwise in subsection (o-5), "public employer" or "employer" means the State of Illinois; any political subdivision of the State, unit of local government or school district; authorities including departments, divisions, bureaus, boards, commissions, or other agencies of the foregoing entities; and any person acting within the scope of his or her authority, express or implied, on behalf of those entities in dealing with its employees. As of the effective date of the amendatory Act of the 93rd General Assembly, but not before, the State of Illinois shall be considered the employer of the personal care attendants and personal assistants working under the Home Services Program under Section 3 of the Disabled Persons Rehabilitation Act, subject to the limitations set forth in this Act and in the Disabled Persons Rehabilitation Act. As of January 29, 2013 (the effective date of Public Act 97–1158), but not before except as otherwise provided in this subsection (o), the State shall be considered the employer of home care and home health workers who function as personal care attendants, personal assistants, and individual maintenance home health workers and who also work under the Home Services Program under Section 3 of the Disabled Persons Rehabilitation Act, no matter whether the State provides those services through direct fee-for-service arrangements, with the assistance of a managed care organization or other intermediary, or otherwise, but subject to the limitations set forth in this Act and the Disabled Persons Rehabilitation Act. The State shall not be considered to be the employer of home care and home health workers who function as personal care attendants, personal assistants, and individual maintenance home health workers and who also work under the Home Services Program under Section 3 of the Disabled Persons Rehabilitation Act, for any purposes not specifically provided for in Public Act 93–204 or Public Act 97–1158, including but not limited to, purposes of vicarious liability in tort and purposes of statutory retirement or health insurance benefits. Home care and home health workers who function as personal care attendants, personal assistants, and individual maintenance home health workers and who also work under the Home Services Program under Section 3 of the Disabled Persons Rehabilitation Act shall not be covered by the State Employees Group Insurance Act of 1971 (5 ILCS 375/). As of the effective date of this amendatory Act of the 94th General Assembly but not before, the State of Illinois shall be considered the employer of the day and child care home providers participating in the child care assistance program under Section 9A-11 of the Illinois Public Aid Code, subject to the limitations set forth in this Act and in Section 9A-11 of the Illinois Public Aid Code. The State shall not be considered to be the employer of child and day care home providers for any purposes not specifically provided for in this amendatory Act of the 94th General Assembly, including but not limited to, purposes of vicarious liability in tort and purposes of statutory retirement or health insurance benefits. Child and day care home providers shall not be covered by the State Employees Group Insurance Act of 1971.

"Public employer" or "employer" as used in this Act, however, does not mean and shall not include the General Assembly of the State of Illinois, the Executive Ethics Commission, the Offices of the Executive Inspectors General, the Legislative Ethics Commission, the Office of the Legislative Inspector General, the Office of the Auditor General's Inspector General, the Office of the Governor, the Governor's Office of Management and Budget, the Illinois Finance Authority, the Office of the Lieutenant Governor, the State Board of Elections, and educational employers or employers as defined in the Illinois Educational Labor Relations Act, except with respect to a state university in its employment of firefighters and peace officers and except with respect to a school district in the employment of peace officers in its own police department in existence on the effective date of this amendatory Act of the 96th General Assembly. County boards and county sheriffs shall be designated as joint or co-employers of county peace officers appointed under the authority of a county sheriff. Nothing in this subsection (o) shall be construed to prevent the State Panel or the Local Panel from determining that employers are joint or co-employers.

(o-5) With respect to wages, fringe benefits, hours, holidays, vacations, proficiency examinations, sick leave, and other conditions of employment, the public employer of public employees who are court reporters, as defined in the Court Reporters Act, shall be determined as follows:

(1) For court reporters employed by the Cook County Judicial Circuit, the chief judge of the Cook County Circuit Court is the public employer and employer representative.

(2) For court reporters employed by the 12th, 18th, 19th, and, on and after December 4, 2006, the 22nd judicial circuits, a group consisting of the chief judges of those circuits, acting jointly by majority vote, is the public employer and employer representative.

(3) For court reporters employed by all other judicial circuits, a group consisting of the chief judges of those circuits, acting jointly by majority vote, is the public employer and employer representative.

(p) "Security employee" means an employee who is responsible for the supervision and control of inmates at correctional facilities. The term also includes other non-security employees in bargaining units having the majority of employees being responsible for the supervision and control of inmates at correctional facilities.

(q) "Short-term employee" means an employee who is employed for less than 2 consecutive calendar quarters during a calendar year and who does not have a reasonable assurance that he or she will be rehired by the same employer for the same service in a subsequent calendar year.

(q-5) "State agency" means an agency directly responsible to the Governor, as defined in Section 3.1 of the Executive Reorganization Implementation Act, and the Illinois Commerce Commission, the Illinois Workers' Compensation Commission, the Civil Service Commission, the Pollution Control Board, the Illinois Racing Board, and the Department of State Police Merit Board.

(r) "Supervisor" is:

(1) An employee whose principal work is substantially different from that of his or her subordinates and who has authority, in the interest of the employer, to hire, transfer, suspend, lay off, recall, promote, discharge, direct, reward, or discipline employees, to adjust their grievances, or to effectively recommend any of those actions, if the exercise of that authority is not of a merely routine or clerical nature, but requires the consistent use of independent judgment. Except with respect to police employment, the term "supervisor" includes only those individuals who devote a preponderance of their employment time to exercising that authority, State supervisors notwithstanding.

Nothing in this definition prohibits an individual from also meeting the definition of "managerial employee" under subsection (j) of this Section. In addition, in determining supervisory status in police employment, rank shall not be determinative. The Board shall consider, as evidence of bargaining unit inclusion or exclusion, the common law enforcement policies and relationships between police officer ranks and certification under applicable civil service law, ordinances, personnel codes, or Division 2.1 of Article 10 of the Illinois Municipal Code, but these factors shall not be the sole or predominant factors considered by the Board in determining police supervisory status.

Notwithstanding the provisions of the preceding paragraph, in determining supervisory status in fire fighter employment, no fire fighter shall be excluded as a supervisor who has established representation rights under Section 9 of this Act. Further, in new fire fighter units, employees shall consist of fire fighters of the rank of company officer and below. If a company officer otherwise qualifies as a supervisor under the preceding paragraph, however, he or she shall not be included in the fire fighter unit. If there is no rank between that of chief and the highest company officer, the employer may designate a position on each shift as a Shift Commander, and the persons occupying those positions shall be supervisors. All other ranks above that of company officer shall be supervisors.

(2) With respect only to State employees in positions under the jurisdiction of the Attorney General, Secretary of State, Comptroller, or Treasurer (i) that were certified in a bargaining unit on or after December 2, 2008, (ii) for which a petition is filed with the Illinois Public Labor Relations Board on or after April 5, 2013 (the effective date of Public Act 97–1172), or (iii) for which a petition is pending before the Illinois Public Labor Relations Board on that date, an employee who qualifies as a supervisor under (A) Section 152 of the National Labor Relations Act and (B) orders of the National Labor Relations Board interpreting that provision or decisions of courts reviewing decisions of the National Labor Relations Board.

(s)(1) "Unit" means a class of jobs or positions that are held by employees whose collective interests may suitably be represented by a labor organization for collective bargaining. Except with respect to non-State fire fighters and paramedics employed by fire departments and fire protection districts, non-State peace officers, and peace officers in the Department of State Police, a bargaining unit determined by the Board shall not include both employees and supervisors, or supervisors only, except as provided in paragraph (2) of this subsection (s) and except for bargaining units in existence on July 1, 1984 (the effective date of this Act). With respect to non-State fire fighters and paramedics employed by fire departments and fire protection districts, non-State peace officers, and peace officers in the Department of State Police, a bargaining unit determined by the Board shall not include both supervisors and nonsupervisors, or supervisors only, except as provided in paragraph (2) of this subsection (s) and except for bargaining units in existence on January 1, 1986 (the effective date of this amendatory Act of 1985). A bargaining unit determined by the Board to contain peace officers shall contain no employees other than peace officers unless otherwise agreed to by the employer and the labor organization or labor organizations involved. Notwithstanding any other provision of this Act, a bargaining unit, including a historical bargaining unit, containing sworn peace officers of the Department of Natural Resources (formerly designated the Department of Conservation) shall contain no employees other than such sworn peace officers upon the effective date of this amendatory Act of 1990 or upon the expiration date of any collective bargaining agreement in effect upon the effective date of this amendatory Act of 1990 covering both such sworn peace officers and other employees.

(2) Notwithstanding the exclusion of supervisors from bargaining units as provided in paragraph (1) of this subsection (s), a public employer may agree to permit its supervisory employees to form bargaining units and may bargain with those units. This Act shall apply if the public employer chooses to bargain under this subsection.

(3) Public employees who are court reporters, as defined in the Court Reporters Act, shall be divided into 3 units for collective bargaining purposes. One unit shall be court reporters employed by the Cook County Judicial Circuit; one unit shall be court reporters employed by the 12th, 18th, 19th, and, on and after December 4, 2006, the 22nd judicial circuits; and one unit shall be court reporters employed by all other judicial circuits.

## § 4 (5 ILCS 315/4). Management Rights

Employers shall not be required to bargain over matters of inherent managerial policy, which shall include such areas of discretion or policy as the functions of the employer, standards of services, its overall budget, the organizational structure and selection of new employees, examination techniques and direction of employees. Employers, however, shall be required to bargain collectively with regard to policy matters directly affecting wages, hours and terms and conditions of employment as well as the impact thereon upon request by employee representatives, except as provided in Section 7.5.

To preserve the rights of employers and exclusive representatives which have established collective bargaining relationships or negotiated collective bargaining agreements prior to the effective date of this Act, employers shall be required to bargain collectively with regard to any matter concerning wages, hours or conditions of employment about which they have bargained for and agreed to in a collective bargaining agreement prior to the effective date of this Act, except as provided in Section 7.5.

The chief judge of the judicial circuit that employs a public employee who is a court reporter, as defined in the Court Reporters Act, has the authority to hire, appoint, promote, evaluate, discipline, and discharge court reporters within that judicial circuit.

Nothing in this amendatory Act of the 94th General Assembly shall be construed to intrude upon the judicial functions of any court. This amendatory Act of the 94th General Assembly applies only to nonjudicial administrative matters relating to the collective bargaining rights of court reporters.

## § 5  (5 ILCS 315/5). Illinois Labor Relations Board; State Panel; Local Panel

(a) There is created the Illinois Labor Relations Board. The Board shall be comprised of 2 panels, to be known as the State Panel and the Local Panel.

(a-5) The State Panel shall have jurisdiction over collective bargaining matters between employee organizations and the State of Illinois, excluding the General Assembly of the State of Illinois, between employee organizations and units of local government and school districts with a population not in excess of 2 million persons, and between employee organizations and the Regional Transportation Authority.

The State Panel shall consist of 5 members appointed by the Governor, with the advice and consent of the Senate. The Governor shall appoint to the State Panel only persons who have had a minimum of 5 years of experience directly related to labor and employment relations in representing public employers, private employers or labor organizations; or teaching labor or employment relations; or administering executive orders or regulations applicable to labor or employment relations. At the time of his or her appointment, each member of the State Panel shall be an Illinois resident. The Governor shall designate one member to serve as the Chairman of the State Panel and the Board.

Notwithstanding any other provision of this Section, the term of each member of the State Panel who was appointed by the Governor and is in office on June 30, 2003 shall terminate at the close of business on that date or when all of the successor members to be appointed pursuant to this amendatory Act of the 93rd General Assembly have been appointed by the Governor, whichever occurs later. As soon as possible, the

Governor shall appoint persons to fill the vacancies created by this amendatory Act.

The initial appointments under this amendatory Act of the 93rd General Assembly shall be for terms as follows: The Chairman shall initially be appointed for a term ending on the 4th Monday in January, 2007; 2 members shall be initially appointed for terms ending on the 4th Monday in January, 2006; one member shall be initially appointed for a term ending on the 4th Monday in January, 2005; and one member shall be initially appointed for a term ending on the 4th Monday in January, 2004. Each subsequent member shall be appointed for a term of 4 years, commencing on the 4th Monday in January. Upon expiration of the term of office of any appointive member, that member shall continue to serve until a successor shall be appointed and qualified. In case of a vacancy, a successor shall be appointed to serve for the unexpired portion of the term. If the Senate is not in session at the time the initial appointments are made, the Governor shall make temporary appointments in the same manner successors are appointed to fill vacancies. A temporary appointment shall remain in effect no longer than 20 calendar days after the commencement of the next Senate session.

(b) The Local Panel shall have jurisdiction over collective bargaining agreement matters between employee organizations and units of local government with a population in excess of 2 million persons, but excluding the Regional Transportation Authority.

The Local Panel shall consist of one person appointed by the Governor with the advice and consent of the Senate (or, if no such person is appointed, the Chairman of the State Panel) and two additional members, one appointed by the Mayor of the City of Chicago and one appointed by the President of the Cook County Board of Commissioners. Appointees to the Local Panel must have had a minimum of 5 years of experience directly related to labor and employment relations in representing public employers, private employers or labor organizations; or teaching labor or employment relations; or administering executive orders or regulations applicable to labor or employment relations. Each member of the Local Panel shall be an Illinois resident at the time of his or her appointment. The member appointed by the Governor (or, if no such person is appointed, the Chairman of the State Panel) shall serve as the Chairman of the Local Panel.

Notwithstanding any other provision of this Section, the term of the member of the Local Panel who was appointed by the Governor and is in office on June 30, 2003 shall terminate at the close of business on that date or when his or her successor has been appointed by the Governor, whichever occurs later. As soon as possible, the Governor shall appoint a person to fill the vacancy created by this amendatory Act. The initial appointment under this amendatory Act of the 93rd General Assembly shall be for a term ending on the 4th Monday in January, 2007.

The initial appointments under this amendatory Act of the 91st General Assembly shall be for terms as follows: The member appointed by the Governor shall initially be appointed for a term ending on the 4th Monday in January, 2001; the member appointed by the President of the Cook County Board shall be initially appointed for a term ending on the 4th Monday in January, 2003; and the member appointed by the Mayor of the City of Chicago shall be initially appointed for a term ending on the 4th Monday in January, 2004. Each subsequent member shall be appointed for a term of 4 years, commencing on the 4th Monday in January. Upon expiration of the term of office of any appointive member, the member shall continue to serve until a successor shall be appointed and qualified. In the case of a vacancy, a successor shall be appointed by the applicable appointive authority to serve for the unexpired portion of the term.

(c) Three members of the State Panel shall at all times constitute a quorum. Two members of the Local Panel shall at all times constitute a quorum. A vacancy on a panel does not impair the right of the remaining members to exercise all of the powers of that panel. Each panel shall adopt an official seal which shall be judicially noticed. The salary of the Chairman of the State Panel shall be $82,429 per year, or as set by the Compensation Review Board, whichever is greater, and that of the other members of the State and Local Panels shall be $74,188 per year, or as set by the Compensation Review Board, whichever is greater.

(d) Each member shall devote his or her entire time to the duties of the office, and shall hold no other office or position of profit, nor engage in any other business, employment, or vocation. No member shall hold any other public office or be employed as a labor or management representative by the State or any political subdivision of the State or of any department or agency thereof, or actively represent or act on behalf of an employer or an employee organization or an employer in labor relations matters. Any member of the State Panel may be removed from office by the Governor for inefficiency, neglect of duty, misconduct or malfeasance in office, and for no other cause, and only upon notice and hearing. Any member of the Local Panel may be removed from office by the applicable appointive authority for inefficiency, neglect of duty, misconduct or malfeasance in office, and for no other cause, and only upon notice and hearing.

(e) Each panel at the end of every State fiscal year shall make a report in writing to the Governor and the General Assembly, stating in detail the work it has done in hearing and deciding cases and otherwise.

(f) In order to accomplish the objectives and carry out the duties prescribed by this Act, a panel or its authorized designees may hold elections to determine whether a labor organization has majority status; investigate and attempt to resolve or settle charges of unfair labor practices; hold hearings in order to carry out its functions; develop and effectuate appropriate impasse resolution procedures for purposes of resolving labor disputes; require the appearance of witnesses and the production of evidence on any matter under inquiry; and administer oaths and affirmations. The panels shall sign and report in full an opinion in every case which they decide.

(g) Each panel may appoint or employ an executive director, attorneys, hearing officers, mediators, fact-finders, arbitrators, and such other employees as it may deem necessary to perform its functions. The governing boards shall prescribe the duties and qualifications of such persons appointed and, subject to the annual appropriation, fix their compensation and provide for reimbursement of actual and necessary expenses incurred in the performance of their duties. The Board shall employ a minimum of 16 attorneys and 6 investigators.

(h) Each panel shall exercise general supervision over all attorneys which it employs and over the other persons employed to provide necessary support services for such attorneys. The panels shall have final authority in respect to complaints brought pursuant to this Act.

(i) The following rules and regulations shall be adopted by the panels meeting in joint session: (1) procedural rules and regulations which shall govern all Board proceedings; (2) procedures for election of exclusive bargaining representatives pursuant to Section 9, except for the determination of appropriate bargaining units; and (3) appointment of counsel pursuant to subsection (k) of this Section.

(j) Rules and regulations may be adopted, amended or rescinded only upon a vote of 5 of the members of the State and Local Panels meeting in joint session. The adoption, amendment or rescission of rules and regulations shall be in conformity with the requirements of the Illinois Administrative Procedure Act.

(k) The panels in joint session shall promulgate rules and regulations providing for the appointment of attorneys or other Board representatives to represent persons in unfair labor practice proceedings before a panel. The regulations governing appointment shall require the applicant to demonstrate an inability to pay for or inability to otherwise provide for adequate representation before a panel. Such rules must also provide: (1) that an attorney may not be appointed in cases which, in the opinion of a panel, are clearly without merit; (2) the stage of the unfair labor proceeding at which counsel will be appointed; and (3) the circumstances under which a client will be allowed to select counsel.

(l) The panels in joint session may promulgate rules and regulations which allow parties in proceedings before a panel to be represented by counsel or any other representative of the party's choice.

(m) The Chairman of the State Panel shall serve as Chairman of a joint session of the panels. Attendance of at least 2 members of the State Panel and at least one member of the Local Panel, in addition to the Chairman, shall constitute a quorum at a joint session. The panels shall meet in joint session at least annually.

## § 5.1 (5 ILCS 315/5.1). Dissolution of Illinois State Labor Relations Board and Illinois Local Labor Relations Board; Transfer and Savings Provisions.

(a) The Illinois State Labor Relations Board is dissolved. The State Panel of the Illinois Labor Relations Board, created by this amendatory Act of the 91st General Assembly, shall succeed to all of the powers, duties, rights, and property, including contractual rights and obligations, of the Illinois State Labor Relations Board. Rules, procedures, and decisions of the Illinois State Labor Relations Board in effect at the time of its dissolution shall be deemed to be those of the State Panel of the Illinois Labor Relations Board. Matters pending before the Illinois State Labor Relations Board at the time of its dissolution shall continue as matters before the State Panel of the Illinois Labor Relations Board. The State Panel of the Illinois Labor Relations Board shall be deemed successor in interest to the Illinois State Labor Relations Board for the purposes of any pending litigation.

(b) The Illinois Local Labor Relations Board is dissolved. The Local Panel of the Illinois Labor Relations Board, created by this amendatory Act of the 91st General Assembly, shall succeed to all of the powers, duties, rights, and property, including contractual rights and obligations, of the Illinois Local Labor Relations Board. Rules, procedures, and decisions of the Illinois Local Labor Relations Board in effect at the time of its dissolution shall be deemed to be those of the Local Panel of the Illinois Labor Relations Board. Matters pending before the Illinois Local Labor Relations Board at the time of its dissolution shall continue as matters before the Local Panel of the Illinois Labor Relations Board. The Local Panel of the Illinois Labor Relations Board shall be deemed successor in interest to the Illinois Local Labor Relations Board for the purposes of any pending litigation.

(c) Rules and procedures adopted jointly by the Illinois State Labor Relations Board and the Illinois Local Labor Relations Board that are in effect at the time of the dissolution of those Boards shall be deemed to have been adopted jointly by the State and Local Panels of the Illinois Labor Relations Board.

(d) Fiscal Year 2000 appropriations to the Illinois State Labor Relations Board and the Illinois Local Labor Relations Board may be expended by the Illinois Labor Relations Board.

(e) Persons employed by the Illinois State Labor Relations Board or the Illinois Local Labor Relations Board on the date of the dissolution of those Boards shall thereupon become employees, respectively, of the State Panel or the Local Panel of the Illinois Labor Relations Board, without loss of seniority or accrued benefits.

## § 6 (5 ILCS 315/6). Right to Organize and Bargain Collectively; Exclusive Representation; and Fair Share Arrangements

(a) Employees of the State and any political subdivision of the State, excluding employees of the General Assembly of the State of Illinois and employees excluded from the definition of "public employee" under subsection (n) of Section 3 of this Act, have, and are protected in the exercise of, the right of self-organization, and may form, join or assist any labor organization, to bargain collectively through representatives of their own choosing on questions of wages, hours and other conditions of employment, not excluded by Section 4 of this Act, and to engage in other concerted activities not otherwise prohibited by law for the purposes of collective bargaining or other mutual aid or protection, free from interference, restraint or coercion. Employees also have, and are protected in the exercise of, the right to refrain from participating in any such concerted activities. Employees may be required, pursuant to the terms of a lawful fair share agreement, to pay a fee which shall be their proportionate share of the costs of the collective bargaining process, contract administration and pursuing matters affecting wages, hours and other conditions of employment as defined in Section 3(g).

(b) Nothing in this Act prevents an employee from presenting a grievance to the employer and having the grievance heard and settled without the intervention of an employee organization; provided that the exclusive bargaining representative is afforded the opportunity to be present at such conference and that any settlement made shall not be inconsistent with the terms of any agreement in effect between the employer and the exclusive bargaining representative.

(c) A labor organization designated by the Board as the representative of the majority of public employees in an appropriate unit in accordance with the procedures herein or recognized by a public employer as the representative of the majority of public employees in an appropriate unit is the exclusive representative for the employees of such unit for the purpose of collective bargaining with respect to rates of pay, wages, hours and other conditions of employment not excluded by Section 4 of this Act. A public employer is required upon request to furnish the exclusive bargaining representative with a complete list of the names and addresses of the public employees in the bargaining unit, provided that a public employer shall not be required to furnish such a list more than once per payroll period. The exclusive bargaining representative shall use the list exclusively for bargaining representation purposes and shall not disclose any information contained in the list for any other purpose. Nothing in this Section, however, shall prohibit a bargaining representative from disseminating a list of its union members.

(d) Labor organizations recognized by a public employer as the exclusive representative or so designated in accordance with the provisions of this Act are responsible for representing the interests of all public employees in the unit. Nothing herein shall be construed to limit an exclusive representative's right to exercise its discretion to refuse to process grievances of employees that are unmeritorious.

(e) When a collective bargaining agreement is entered into with an exclusive representative, it may include in the agreement a provision requiring employees covered by the agreement who are not members of the organization to pay their proportionate share of the costs of the collective bargaining process, contract administration and pursuing matters affecting wages, hours and conditions of employment, as defined in Section 3 (g), but not to exceed the amount of dues uniformly required of members. The organization shall certify to the employer the amount constituting each nonmember employee's proportionate share which shall not exceed dues uniformly required of members. In such case, the proportionate share payment in this Section shall be deducted by the employer from the earnings of the nonmember employees and paid to the employee organization.

(f) Only the exclusive representative may negotiate provisions in a collective bargaining agreement providing for the payroll deduction of labor organization dues, fair share payment, initiation fees and assessments. Except as provided in subsection (e) of this Section, any such deductions shall only be made upon an employee's written authorization, and continued until revoked in writing in the same manner or until the termination date of an applicable collective bargaining agreement. Such payments shall be paid to the exclusive representative.

Where a collective bargaining agreement is terminated, or continues in effect beyond its scheduled expiration date pending the negotiation of a successor agreement or the resolution of an impasse under Section 14, the employer shall continue to honor and abide by any dues deduction or fair share clause contained therein until a new agreement is reached including dues deduction or a fair share clause. For the benefit of any successor exclusive representative certified under this Act, this provision shall be applicable, provided the successor exclusive representative:

(i) certifies to the employer the amount constituting each non-member's proportionate share under subsection (e); or

(ii) presents the employer with employee written authorizations for the deduction of dues, assessments, and fees under this subsection.

Failure to so honor and abide by dues deduction or fair share clauses for the benefit of any exclusive representative, including a successor, shall be a violation of the duty to bargain and an unfair labor practice.

(g) Agreements containing a fair share agreement must safeguard the right of nonassociation of employees based upon bona fide religious tenets or teachings of a church or religious body of which such employees are members. Such employees may be required to pay an amount equal to their fair share, determined under a lawful fair share agreement, to a nonreligious charitable organization mutually agreed upon by the employees affected and the exclusive bargaining representative to which such employees would otherwise pay such service fee. If the affected employees and the bargaining representative are unable to reach an agreement on the matter, the Board may establish an approved list of charitable organizations to which such payments may be made.

## § 6.1    (5 ILCS 315/6.1).    Gubernatorial    Designation    of Certain Public Employment Positions as Excluded From Collective Bargaining

(a) Notwithstanding any provision of this Act to the contrary, except subsections (e) and (f) of this Section, the Governor is authorized to designate up to 3,580 State employment positions collectively within State agencies directly responsible to the Governor, and, upon designation, those positions and employees in those positions, if any, are hereby excluded from the self-organization and collective bargaining provisions of Section 6 of this Act. Only those employment positions that have been certified in a bargaining unit on or after December 2, 2008, that have a pending petition for certification in a bargaining unit on April 5, 2013 (the effective date of Public Act 97–1172), or that neither have been certified in a bargaining unit on or after December 2, 2008 nor have a pending petition for certification in a bargaining unit on the effective date of this amendatory Act of the 97th General Assembly are eligible to be designated by the Governor under this Section. The Governor may not designate under this Section, however, more than 1,900 employment positions that have been certified in a bargaining unit on or after December 2, 2008.

(b) In order to properly designate a State employment position under this Section, the Governor shall provide in writing to the Board: the job title and job duties of the employment position; the name of the State employee currently in the employment position, if any; the name of the

State agency employing the public employee; and the category under which the position qualifies for designation under this Section.

To qualify for designation under this Section, the employment position must meet one or more of the following requirements:

(1) it must authorize an employee in that position to act as a legislative liaison;

(2) it must have a title of, or authorize a person who holds that position to exercise substantially similar duties as an, Agency General Counsel, Agency Chief of Staff, Agency Executive Director, Agency Deputy Director, Agency Chief Fiscal Officer, Agency Human Resources Director, Senior Public Service Administrator, Public Information Officer, or Chief Information Officer;

(3) it must be a Rutan-exempt, as designated by the employer, position and completely exempt from jurisdiction B of the Personnel Code;

(4) it must be a term appointed position pursuant to Section 8b.18 or 8b.19 of the Personnel Code; or

(5) it must authorize an employee in that position to have significant and independent discretionary authority as an employee.

Within 60 days after the Governor makes a designation under this Section, the Board shall determine, in a manner that is consistent with the requirements of due process, whether the designation comports with the requirements of this Section.

(c) For the purposes of this Section, a person has significant and independent discretionary authority as an employee if he or she (i) is engaged in executive and management functions of a State agency and charged with the effectuation of management policies and practices of a State agency or represents management interests by taking or recommending discretionary actions that effectively control or implement the policy of a State agency or (ii) qualifies as a supervisor of a State agency as that term is defined under Section 152 of the National Labor Relations Act or any orders of the National Labor Relations Board interpreting that provision or decisions of courts reviewing decisions of the National Labor Relations Board.

(d) The Governor must exercise the authority afforded under this Section within 365 calendar days after April 5, 2013 (the effective date of Public Act 97–1172). Any designation made by the Governor under this Section shall be presumed to have been properly made.

If the Governor chooses not to designate a position under this Section, then that decision does not preclude a State agency from otherwise challenging the certification of that position under this Act.

The qualifying categories set forth in paragraphs (1) through (5) of subsection (b) of this Section are operative and function solely within this Section and do not expand or restrict the scope of any other provision contained in this Act.

(e) The provisions of this Section do not apply to any employee who is employed by a public employer and who is classified as, or holds the employment title of, Chief Stationary Engineer, Assistant Chief Stationary Engineer, Sewage Plant Operator, Water Plant Operator, Stationary Engineer, Plant Operating Engineer, and any employee who holds the position of: Civil Engineer V, Civil Engineer VI, Civil Engineer VII, Technical Manager I, Technical Manager II, Technical Manager III, Technical Manager IV, Technical Manager V, Technical Manager VI, Realty Specialist III, Realty Specialist IV, Realty Specialist V, Technical Advisor I, Technical Advisor II, Technical Advisor III, Technical Advisor IV, or Technical Advisor V employed by the Department of Transportation who is in a position which is certified in a bargaining unit on or before the effective date of this amendatory Act of the 98th General Assembly.

(f) The provisions of this Section also do not apply to any mental health administrator in the Department of Corrections who is classified as or who holds the position of Public Service Administrator (Option 8K), any employee of the Office of the Inspector General in the Department of Human Services who is classified as or who holds the position of Public Service Administrator (Option 7), any Deputy of Intelligence in the Department of Corrections who is classified as or who holds the position of Public Service Administrator (Option 7), or any employee of the Department of State Police who handles issues concerning the Illinois State Police Sex Offender Registry and who is classified as or holds the position of Public Service Administrator (Option 7).

## § 7 (5 ILCS 315/7).  Duty to Bargain

A public employer and the exclusive representative have the authority and the duty to bargain collectively set forth in this Section.

For the purposes of this Act, "to bargain collectively" means the performance of the mutual obligation of the public employer or his designated representative and the representative of the public employees to meet at reasonable times, including meetings in advance of the budget-making process, and to negotiate in good faith with respect to wages, hours, and other conditions of employment, not excluded by Section 4 of this Act, or the negotiation of an agreement, or any question arising thereunder and the execution of a written contract incorporating any agreement reached if requested by either party, but such obligation does not compel either party to agree to a proposal or require the making of a concession.

The duty "to bargain collectively" shall also include an obligation to negotiate over any matter with respect to wages, hours and other conditions of employment, not specifically provided for in any other law or not specifically in violation of the provisions of any law. If any other law pertains, in part, to a matter affecting the wages, hours and other conditions of employment, such other law shall not be construed as limiting the duty "to bargain collectively" and to enter into collective bargaining agreements containing clauses which either supplement, implement, or relate to the effect of such provisions in other laws.

The duty "to bargain collectively" shall also include negotiations as to the terms of a collective bargaining agreement. The parties may, by mutual agreement, provide for arbitration of impasses resulting from their inability to agree upon wages, hours and terms and conditions of employment to be included in a collective bargaining agreement. Such arbitration provisions shall be subject to the Illinois "Uniform Arbitration Act" unless agreed by the parties.

The duty "to bargain collectively" shall also mean that no party to a collective bargaining contract shall terminate or modify such contract, unless the party desiring such termination or modification:

(1) serves a written notice upon the other party to the contract of the proposed termination or modification 60 days prior to the expiration date thereof, or in the event such contract contains no expiration date, 60 days prior to the time it is proposed to make such termination or modification;

(2) offers to meet and confer with the other party for the purpose of negotiating a new contract or a contract containing the proposed modifications;

(3) notifies the Board within 30 days after such notice of the existence of a dispute, provided no agreement has been reached by that time; and

(4) continues in full force and effect, without resorting to strike or lockout, all the terms and conditions of the existing contract for a period of 60 days after such notice is given to the other party or until the expiration date of such contract, whichever occurs later.

The duties imposed upon employers, employees and labor organizations by paragraphs (2), (3) and (4) shall become inapplicable upon an intervening certification of the Board, under which the labor organization, which is a party to the contract, has been superseded as or ceased to be the exclusive representative of the employees pursuant to the provisions of subsection (a) of Section 9, and the duties so imposed shall not be construed as requiring either party to discuss or agree to any modification of the terms and conditions contained in a contract for a fixed period, if such modification is to become effective before such terms and conditions can be reopened under the provisions of the contract.

Collective bargaining for home care and home health workers who function as personal care attendants, personal assistants, and individual maintenance home health workers under the Home Services Program shall be limited to the terms and conditions of employment under the State's control, as defined in Public Act 93–204 or this amendatory Act of the 97th General Assembly, as applicable.

Collective bargaining for child and day care home providers under the child care assistance program shall be limited to the terms and conditions of employment under the State's control, as defined in this amendatory Act of the 94th General Assembly.

Notwithstanding any other provision of this Section, whenever collective bargaining is for the purpose of establishing an initial agreement following original certification of units with fewer than 35 employees, with respect to public employees other than peace officers, fire fighters, and security employees, the following apply:

(1) Not later than 10 days after receiving a written request for collective bargaining from a labor organization that has been newly certified as a representative as defined in Section 6(c), or within such further period as the parties agree upon, the parties shall meet and commence to bargain collectively and shall make every reasonable effort to conclude and sign a collective bargaining agreement.

(2) If anytime after the expiration of the 90-day period beginning on the date on which bargaining is commenced the parties have failed to reach an agreement, either party may notify the Illinois Public Labor Relations Board of the existence of a dispute and request mediation in accordance with the provisions of Section 14 of this Act.

(3) If after the expiration of the 30-day period beginning on the date on which mediation commenced, or such additional period as the parties may agree upon, the mediator is not able to bring the parties to agreement by conciliation, either the exclusive representative of the employees or the employer may request of the other, in writing, arbitration and shall submit a copy of the request to the board. Upon submission of the request for arbitration, the parties shall be required to participate in the impasse arbitration procedures set forth in Section 14 of this Act, except the right to strike shall not be considered waived pursuant to Section 17 of this Act, until the actual convening of the arbitration hearing.

## § 7.5 (5 ILCS 315/7.5). Duty to Bargain Regarding Pension Amendments

(a) Notwithstanding any provision of this Act, employers shall not be required to bargain over matters affected by the changes, the impact of changes, and the implementation of changes made to Article 14, 15, or 16 of the Illinois Pension Code, or Article 1 of that Code as it applies to those Articles, made by this amendatory Act of the 98th General Assembly, or over any other provision of Article 14, 15, or 16 of the Illinois Pension Code, or of Article 1 of that Code as it applies to those Articles, which are prohibited subjects of bargaining; nor shall the changes, the impact of changes, or the implementation of changes made to Article 14, 15, or 16 of the Illinois Pension Code, or to Article 1 of that Code as it applies to those Articles, by this amendatory Act of the 98th General Assembly or any other provision of Article 14, 15, or 16 of the Illinois Pension Code, or of Article 1 of that Code as it applies to those Articles, be subject to interest arbitration or any award issued pursuant to interest arbitration. The provisions of this Section shall not apply to an employment contract or collective bargaining agreement that is in effect on the effective date of this amendatory Act of the 98th General Assembly. However, any such contract or agreement that is subsequently modified, amended, or renewed shall be subject to the provisions of this Section. The provisions of this Section shall also not apply to the ability of an employer and employee representative to bargain collectively with regard to the pick up of employee contributions pursuant to Section 14–133.1, 15–157.1, or 16–152.1 of the Illinois Pension Code.

(b) Nothing in this Section, however, shall be construed as otherwise limiting any of the obligations and requirements applicable to each employer under any of the provisions of this Act, including, but not limited to, the requirement to bargain collectively with regard to policy matters directly affecting wages, hours and terms and conditions of employment as well as the impact thereon upon request by employee representatives, except for the matters deemed prohibited subjects of bargaining under subsection (a) of this Section. Nothing in this Section shall further be construed as otherwise limiting any of the rights of employees or employee representatives under the provisions of this Act, except for matters deemed prohibited subjects of bargaining under subsection (a) of this Section.

(c) In case of any conflict between this Section and any other provisions of this Act or any other law, the provisions of this Section shall control.

## § 8 (5 ILCS 315/8). Grievance Procedure

The collective bargaining agreement negotiated between the employer and the exclusive representative shall contain a grievance resolution procedure which shall apply to all employees in the bargaining unit and shall provide for final and binding arbitration of disputes concerning the administration or interpretation of the agreement unless mutually agreed otherwise. Any agreement containing a final and binding arbitration provision shall also contain a provision prohibiting strikes for the duration of the agreement. The grievance and arbitration provisions of any collective bargaining agreement shall be subject to the Illinois "Uniform Arbitration Act". The costs of such arbitration shall be borne equally by the employer and the employee organization.

## § 9 (5 ILCS 315/9). Elections; Recognition

(a) Whenever in accordance with such regulations as may be prescribed by the Board a petition has been filed:

> (1) by a public employee or group of public employees or any labor organization acting in their behalf demonstrating that 30% of the public employees in an appropriate unit (A) wish to be represented for the purposes of collective bargaining by a labor organization as exclusive representative, or (B) asserting that the labor organization which has been certified or is currently recognized by the public employer as bargaining representative is no longer the representative of the majority of public employees in the unit; or

> (2) by a public employer alleging that one or more labor organizations have presented to it a claim that they be recognized as the representative of a majority of the public employees in an appropriate unit,

the Board shall investigate such petition, and if it has reasonable cause to believe that a question of representation exists, shall provide for an appropriate hearing upon due notice. Such hearing shall be held at the offices of the Board or such other location as the Board deems appropriate. If it finds upon the record of the hearing that a question of representation exists, it shall direct an election in accordance with subsection (d) of this Section, which election shall be held not later than 120 days after the date the petition was filed regardless of whether that petition was filed before or after the effective date of this amendatory Act of 1987; provided, however, the Board may extend the time for holding an election by an additional 60 days if, upon motion by a person who has filed a petition under this Section or is the subject of a petition filed under this Section and is a party to such hearing, or upon the Board's own motion, the Board finds that good cause has been shown for extending the election date; provided further, that nothing in this Section shall prohibit the Board, in its discretion, from extending the time for holding an election for so long as may be necessary under the circumstances, where the purpose for such extension is to permit resolution by the Board of an unfair labor practice charge filed by one of the parties to a representational proceeding against the other based upon conduct which may either affect the existence of a question concerning representation or have a tendency to interfere with a fair and free election, where the party filing the charge has not filed a request to proceed with the election; and provided further that prior to the expiration of the total time allotted for holding an election, a person who has filed a petition under this Section or is the subject of a petition filed under this Section and is a party to such hearing or the Board, may move for and obtain the entry of an order in the circuit court of the county in which the majority of the public employees sought to be represented by such person reside, such order extending the date upon which the election shall be held. Such order shall be issued by the circuit court only upon a judicial finding that there has been a sufficient showing that there is good cause to extend the election date beyond such period and shall require the Board to hold the election as soon as is feasible given the totality of the circumstances. Such 120 day period may be extended one or more times by the agreement of all parties to the hearing to a date certain without the necessity of obtaining a court order. Nothing in this Section prohibits the waiving of hearings by stipulation for the purpose of a consent election in conformity with the rules and regulations of the Board or an election in a unit agreed upon by the parties. Other interested employee organizations may intervene in the proceedings in the manner and within the time period specified by rules and regulations of the Board. Interested parties who are necessary to the proceedings may also intervene in the proceedings in the manner and within the time period specified by the rules and regulations of the Board.

(a-5) The Board shall designate an exclusive representative for purposes of collective bargaining when the representative demonstrates a showing of majority interest by employees in the unit. If the parties to a dispute are without agreement on the means to ascertain the choice, if any, of employee organization as their representative, the Board shall ascertain the employees' choice of employee organization, on the basis of dues deduction authorization or other evidence, or, if necessary, by conducting an election. All evidence submitted by an employee organization to the Board to ascertain an employee's choice of an employee organization is confidential and shall not be submitted to the employer for review. The Board shall ascertain the employee's choice of employee organization within 120 days after the filing of the majority interest petition; however, the Board may extend time by an additional 60 days, upon its own motion or upon the motion of a party to the proceeding. If either party provides to the Board, before the designation of a representative, clear and convincing evidence that the dues deduction authorizations, and other evidence upon which the Board would otherwise rely to ascertain the employees' choice of representative, are fraudulent or were obtained through coercion, the Board shall promptly thereafter conduct an election.

The Board shall also investigate and consider a party's allegations that the dues deduction authorizations and other evidence submitted in support of a designation of representative without an election were subsequently changed, altered, withdrawn, or withheld as a result of employer fraud, coercion, or any other unfair labor practice by the employer. If the Board determines that a labor organization would have had a majority interest but for an employer's fraud, coercion, or unfair labor practice, it shall designate the labor organization as an exclusive representative without conducting an election. If a hearing is necessary to resolve any issues of representation under this Section, the Board shall conclude its hearing process and issue a certification of the entire appropriate unit not later than 120 days after the date the petition was filed. The 120-day period may be extended one or more times by the agreement of all parties to a hearing to a date certain.

(a-6) A labor organization or an employer may file a unit clarification petition seeking to clarify an existing bargaining unit. The Board shall conclude its investigation, including any hearing process deemed necessary, and issue a certification of clarified unit or dismiss the petition not later than 120 days after the date the petition was filed. The 120-day period may be extended one or more times by the agreement of all parties to a hearing to a date certain.

(b) The Board shall decide in each case, in order to assure public employees the fullest freedom in exercising the rights guaranteed by this Act, a unit appropriate for the purpose of collective bargaining, based upon but not limited to such factors as: historical pattern of recognition; community of interest including employee skills and functions; degree of functional integration; interchangeability and contact among employees; fragmentation of employee groups; common supervision, wages, hours and other working conditions of the employees involved; and the desires of the employees. For purposes of this subsection, fragmentation shall not be the sole or predominant factor used by the Board in determining an appropriate bargaining unit. Except with respect to non-State fire fighters and paramedics employed by fire departments and fire protection districts, non-State peace officers and peace officers in the State Department of State Police, a single bargaining unit determined by the Board may not include both supervisors and nonsupervisors, except for bargaining units in existence on the effective date of this Act. With respect to non-State fire fighters and paramedics employed by fire departments and fire protection districts, non-State peace officers and peace officers in the State Department of State Police, a single bargaining unit determined by the Board may not include both supervisors and nonsupervisors, except for bargaining units in existence on the effective date of this amendatory Act of 1985.

In cases involving an historical pattern of recognition, and in cases where the employer has recognized the union as the sole and exclusive bargaining agent for a specified existing unit, the Board shall find the employees in the unit then represented by the union pursuant to the recognition to be the appropriate unit.

Notwithstanding the above factors, where the majority of public employees of a craft so decide, the Board shall designate such craft as a unit appropriate for the purposes of collective bargaining.

The Board shall not decide that any unit is appropriate if such unit includes both professional and nonprofessional employees, unless a majority of each group votes for inclusion in such unit.

(c) Nothing in this Act shall interfere with or negate the current representation rights or patterns and practices of labor organizations which have historically represented public employees for the purpose of collective bargaining, including but not limited to the negotiations of wages, hours and working conditions, discussions of employees' grievances, resolution of jurisdictional disputes, or the establishment and maintenance of prevailing wage rates, unless a majority of employees so represented express a contrary desire pursuant to the procedures set forth in this Act.

(d) In instances where the employer does not voluntarily recognize a labor organization as the exclusive bargaining representative for a unit of employees, the Board shall determine the majority representative of the public employees in an appropriate collective bargaining unit by conducting a secret ballot election, except as otherwise provided in subsection (a-5). Within 7 days after the Board issues its bargaining unit determination and direction of election or the execution of a stipulation for the purpose of a consent election, the public employer shall submit to the labor organization the complete names and addresses of those employees who are determined by the Board to be eligible to participate in the election. When the Board has determined that a labor organization has been fairly and freely chosen by a majority of employees in an appropriate unit, it shall certify such organization as the exclusive representative. If the Board determines that a majority of employees in an appropriate unit has fairly and freely chosen not to be represented by a labor organization, it shall so certify. The Board may also revoke the certification of the public employee organizations as exclusive bargaining representatives which have been found by a secret ballot election to be no longer the majority representative.

(e) The Board shall not conduct an election in any bargaining unit or any subdivision thereof within which a valid election has been held in the preceding 12–month period. The Board shall determine who is eligible to vote in an election and shall establish rules governing the conduct of the election or conduct affecting the results of the election. The Board shall include on a ballot in a representation election a choice of "no representation". A labor organization currently representing the bargaining unit of employees shall be placed on the ballot in any representation election. In any election where none of the choices on the ballot receives a majority, a runoff election shall be conducted between the 2 choices receiving the largest number of valid votes cast in the election. A labor organization which receives a majority of the votes cast in an election shall be certified by the Board as exclusive representative of all public employees in the unit.

(f) A labor organization shall be designated as the exclusive representative by a public employer, provided that the labor organization represents a majority of the public employees in an appropriate unit. Any employee organization which is designated or selected by the majority of public employees, in a unit of the public employer having no other recognized or certified representative, as their representative for purposes of collective bargaining may request recognition by the public employer in writing. The public employer shall post such request for a period of at least 20 days following its receipt thereof on bulletin boards or other places used or reserved for employee notices.

(g) Within the 20-day period any other interested employee organization may petition the Board in the manner specified by rules and regulations of the Board, provided that such interested employee organization has been designated by at least 10% of the employees in an appropriate bargaining unit which includes all or some of the employees in the unit recognized by the employer. In such event, the Board shall proceed with the petition in the same manner as provided by paragraph (1) of subsection (a) of this Section.

(h) No election shall be directed by the Board in any bargaining unit where there is in force a valid collective bargaining agreement. The Board, however, may process an election petition filed between 90 and 60 days prior to the expiration of the date of an agreement, and may further refine, by rule or decision, the implementation of this provision. Where more than 4 years have elapsed since the effective date of the agreement, the agreement shall continue to bar an election, except that the Board may process an election petition filed between 90 and 60 days prior to the end of the fifth year of such an agreement, and between 90 and 60 days prior to the end of each successive year of such agreement.

(i) An order of the Board dismissing a representation petition, determining and certifying that a labor organization has been fairly and freely chosen by a majority of employees in an appropriate bargaining unit, determining and certifying that a labor organization has not been fairly and freely chosen by a majority of employees in the bargaining unit or certifying a labor organization as the exclusive representative of employees in an appropriate bargaining unit because of a determination by the Board that the labor organization is the historical bargaining representative of employees in the bargaining unit, is a final order. Any person aggrieved by any such order issued on or after the effective date of this amendatory Act of 1987 may apply for and obtain judicial review in accordance with provisions of the Administrative Review Law, as now or hereafter amended, except that such review shall be afforded directly in the Appellate Court for the district in which the aggrieved party resides or transacts business. Any direct appeal to the Appellate Court shall be filed within 35 days from the date that a copy of the decision sought to be reviewed was served upon the party affected by the decision.

## § 10 (5 ILCS 315/10). Unfair Labor Practices

(a) It shall be an unfair labor practice for an employer or its agents:

(1) to interfere with, restrain or coerce public employees in the exercise of the rights guaranteed in this Act or to dominate or interfere with the formation, existence or administration of any labor organization or contribute financial or other support to it; provided, an employer shall not be prohibited from permitting employees to confer with him during working hours without loss of time or pay;

(2) to discriminate in regard to hire or tenure of employment or any term or condition of employment in order to encourage or discourage membership in or other support for any labor organization. Nothing in this Act or any other law precludes a public employer from making an agreement with a labor organization to require as a condition of employment the payment of a fair share under paragraph (e) of Section 6;

(3) to discharge or otherwise discriminate against a public employee because he has signed or filed an affidavit, petition or charge or provided any information or testimony under this Act;

(4) to refuse to bargain collectively in good faith with a labor organization which is the exclusive representative of public employees in an appropriate unit, including, but not limited to, the discussing of grievances with the exclusive representative;

(5) to violate any of the rules and regulations established by the Board with jurisdiction over them relating to the conduct of representation elections or the conduct affecting the representation elections;

(6) to expend or cause the expenditure of public funds to any external agent, individual, firm, agency, partnership or association in any attempt to influence the outcome of representational elections held pursuant to Section 9 of this Act; provided, that nothing in this subsection shall be construed to limit an employer's right to

internally communicate with its employees as provided in subsection (c) of this Section, to be represented on any matter pertaining to unit determinations, unfair labor practice charges or pre-election conferences in any formal or informal proceeding before the Board, or to seek or obtain advice from legal counsel. Nothing in this paragraph shall be construed to prohibit an employer from expending or causing the expenditure of public funds on, or seeking or obtaining services or advice from, any organization, group, or association established by and including public or educational employers, whether covered by this Act, the Illinois Educational Labor Relations Act or the public employment labor relations law of any other state or the federal government, provided that such services or advice are generally available to the membership of the organization, group or association, and are not offered solely in an attempt to influence the outcome of a particular representational election; or

(7) to refuse to reduce a collective bargaining agreement to writing or to refuse to sign such agreement.

(b) It shall be an unfair labor practice for a labor organization or its agents:

(1) to restrain or coerce public employees in the exercise of the rights guaranteed in this Act, provided, (i) that this paragraph shall not impair the right of a labor organization to prescribe its own rules with respect to the acquisition or retention of membership therein or the determination of fair share payments and (ii) that a labor organization or its agents shall commit an unfair labor practice under this paragraph in duty of fair representation cases only by intentional misconduct in representing employees under this Act;

(2) to restrain or coerce a public employer in the selection of his representatives for the purposes of collective bargaining or the settlement of grievances; or

(3) to cause, or attempt to cause, an employer to discriminate against an employee in violation of subsection (a)(2);

(4) to refuse to bargain collectively in good faith with a public employer, if it has been designated in accordance with the provisions of this Act as the exclusive representative of public employees in an appropriate unit;

(5) to violate any of the rules and regulations established by the boards with jurisdiction over them relating to the conduct of representation elections or the conduct affecting the representation elections;

(6) to discriminate against any employee because he has signed or filed an affidavit, petition or charge or provided any information or testimony under this Act;

(7) to picket or cause to be picketed, or threaten to picket or cause to be picketed, any public employer where an object thereof is forcing or requiring an employer to recognize or bargain with a labor organization of the representative of its employees, or forcing or requiring the employees of an employer to accept or select such labor organization as their collective bargaining representative, unless such labor organization is currently certified as the representative of such employees:

(A) where the employer has lawfully recognized in accordance with this Act any labor organization and a question concerning representation may not appropriately be raised under Section 9 of this Act;

(B) where within the preceding 12 months a valid election under Section 9 of this Act has been conducted; or

(C) where such picketing has been conducted without a petition under Section 9 being filed within a reasonable period of time not to exceed 30 days from the commencement of such picketing; provided that when such a petition has been filed the Board shall forthwith, without regard to the provisions of subsection (a) of Section 9 or the absence of a showing of a substantial interest on the part of the labor organization, direct an election in such unit as the Board finds to be appropriate and shall certify the results thereof; provided further, that nothing in this subparagraph shall be construed to prohibit any picketing or other publicity for the purpose of truthfully advising the public that an employer does not employ members of, or have a contract with, a labor organization unless an effect of such picketing is to induce any individual employed by any other person in the course of his employment, not to pick up, deliver, or transport any goods or not to perform any services; or

(8) to refuse to reduce a collective bargaining agreement to writing or to refuse to sign such agreement.

(c) The expressing of any views, argument, or opinion or the dissemination thereof, whether in written, printed, graphic, or visual form, shall not constitute or be evidence of an unfair labor practice under any of the provisions of this Act, if such expression contains no threat of reprisal or force or promise of benefit.

## § 11 (5 ILCS 315/11).   Unfair Labor Practice Procedures

Unfair labor practices may be dealt with by the Board in the following manner:

(a) Whenever it is charged that any person has engaged in or is engaging in any unfair labor practice, the Board or any agent designated by the

Board for such purposes, shall conduct an investigation of the charge. If after such investigation the Board finds that the charge involves a dispositive issue of law or fact the Board shall issue a complaint and cause to be served upon the person a complaint stating the charges, accompanied by a notice of hearing before the Board or a member thereof designated by the Board, or before a qualified hearing officer designated by the Board at the offices of the Board or such other location as the Board deems appropriate, not less than 5 days after serving of such complaint provided that no complaint shall issue based upon any unfair labor practice occurring more than six months prior to the filing of a charge with the Board and the service of a copy thereof upon the person against whom the charge is made, unless the person aggrieved thereby did not reasonably have knowledge of the alleged unfair labor practice or was prevented from filing such a charge by reason of service in the armed forces, in which event the six month period shall be computed from the date of his discharge. Any such complaint may be amended by the member or hearing officer conducting the hearing for the Board in his discretion at any time prior to the issuance of an order based thereon. The person who is the subject of the complaint has the right to file an answer to the original or amended complaint and to appear in person or by a representative and give testimony at the place and time fixed in the complaint. In the discretion of the member or hearing officer conducting the hearing or the Board, any other person may be allowed to intervene in the proceeding and to present testimony. In any hearing conducted by the Board, neither the Board nor the member or agent conducting the hearing shall be bound by the rules of evidence applicable to courts, except as to the rules of privilege recognized by law.

(b) The Board shall have the power to issue subpoenas and administer oaths. If any party wilfully fails or neglects to appear or testify or to produce books, papers and records pursuant to the issuance of a subpoena by the Board, the Board may apply to a court of competent jurisdiction to request that such party be ordered to appear before the Board to testify or produce the requested evidence.

(c) Any testimony taken by the Board, or a member designated by the Board or a hearing officer thereof, must be reduced to writing and filed with the Board. A full and complete record shall be kept of all proceedings before the Board, and all proceedings shall be transcribed by a reporter appointed by the Board. The party on whom the burden of proof rests shall be required to sustain such burden by a preponderance of the evidence. If, upon a preponderance of the evidence taken, the Board is of the opinion that any person named in the charge has engaged in or is engaging in an unfair labor practice, then it shall state its findings of fact and shall issue and cause to be served upon the person an order requiring him to cease and desist from the unfair labor practice, and to take such affirmative action, including reinstatement of public employees with or without back pay, as will effectuate the policies of this Act. If the Board awards back pay, it shall also award interest at the rate of 7% per annum. The Board's order may further require the person to make reports from time to time, and demonstrate the extent to which he has complied with the order. If there is no preponderance of evidence to indicate to the Board that the person named in the charge has engaged in or is engaging in the unfair labor practice, then the Board shall state its findings of fact and shall issue an order dismissing the complaint. The Board's order may in its discretion also include an appropriate sanction, based on the Board's rules and regulations, and the sanction may include an order to pay the other party or parties' reasonable expenses including costs and reasonable attorney's fee, if the other party has made allegations or denials without reasonable cause and found to be untrue or has engaged in frivolous litigation for the purpose of delay or needless increase in the cost of litigation; the State of Illinois or any agency thereof shall be subject to the provisions of this sentence in the same manner as any other party.

(d) Until the record in a case has been filed in court, the Board at any time, upon reasonable notice and in such manner as it deems proper, may modify or set aside, in whole or in part, any finding or order made or issued by it.

(e) A charging party or any person aggrieved by a final order of the Board granting or denying in whole or in part the relief sought may apply for and obtain judicial review of an order of the Board entered under this Act, in accordance with the provisions of the Administrative Review Law, as now or hereafter amended, except that such judicial review shall be afforded directly in the appellate court for the district in which the aggrieved party resides or transacts business, and provided, that such judicial review shall not be available for the purpose of challenging a final order issued by the Board pursuant to Section 9 of this Act for which judicial review has been petitioned pursuant to subsection (i) of Section 9. Any direct appeal to the Appellate Court shall be filed within 35 days from the date that a copy of the decision sought to be reviewed was served upon the party affected by the decision. The Board in proceedings under this Section may obtain an order of the court for the enforcement of its order.

(f) Whenever it appears that any person has violated a final order of the Board issued pursuant to this Section, the Board must commence an action in the name of the People of the State of Illinois by petition, alleging the violation, attaching a copy of the order of the Board, and praying for the issuance of an order directing the person, his officers, agents, servants, successors, and assigns to comply with the order of the Board. The Board shall be represented in this action by the Attorney

General in accordance with the Attorney General Act. The court may grant or refuse, in whole or in part, the relief sought, provided that the court may stay an order of the Board in accordance with the Administrative Review Law, pending disposition of the proceedings. The court may punish a violation of its order as in civil contempt.

(g) The proceedings provided in paragraph (f) of this Section shall be commenced in the Appellate Court for the district where the unfair labor practice which is the subject of the Board's order was committed, or where a person required to cease and desist by such order resides or transacts business.

(h) The Board through the Attorney General, shall have power, upon issuance of an unfair labor practice complaint alleging that a person has engaged in or is engaging in an unfair labor practice, to petition the circuit court where the alleged unfair labor practice which is the subject of the Board's complaint was allegedly committed, or where a person required to cease and desist from such alleged unfair labor practice resides or transacts business, for appropriate temporary relief or restraining order. Upon the filing of any such petition, the court shall cause notice thereof to be served upon such persons, and thereupon shall have jurisdiction to grant to the Board such temporary relief or restraining order as it deems just and proper.

(i) If an unfair labor practice charge involves the interpretation or application of a collective bargaining agreement and said agreement contains a grievance procedure with binding arbitration as its terminal step, the Board may defer the resolution of such dispute to the grievance and arbitration procedure contained in said agreement.

## § 12 (5 ILCS 315/12).   Mediation

(a) The State and Local Panels in joint session shall establish a Public Employees Mediation Roster, the services of which shall be available to public employers and to labor organizations upon request of the parties for the purposes of mediation of grievances or contract disputes. Upon the request of either party, services of the Public Employees Mediation Roster shall be available for purposes of arbitrating disputes over interpretation or application of the terms of an agreement pursuant to Section 8. The members of the Roster shall be appointed by majority vote of the members of both panels. Members shall be impartial, competent, and reputable citizens of the United States, residents of the State of Illinois, and shall qualify by taking and subscribing to the constitutional oath or affirmation of office. The function of the mediator shall be to communicate with the employer and exclusive representative or their representatives and to endeavor to bring about an amicable and voluntary settlement. Compensation of Roster members for services performed as mediators shall be paid equally by the parties to a mediated labor dispute. The

Board shall have authority but not the obligation to promulgate regulations setting compensation levels for members of the Roster, and establishing procedures for suspension or dismissal of mediators for good cause shown following hearing.

(b) A mediator in a mediated labor dispute shall be selected by the Board from among the members of the Roster.

(c) Nothing in this Act or any other law prohibits the use of other mediators selected by the parties for the resolution of disputes over interpretation or application of the terms or conditions of the collective bargaining agreements between a public employer and a labor organization.

(d) If requested by the parties to a labor dispute, a mediator may perform fact-finding as set forth in Section 13.

## § 13 (5 ILCS 315/13).    Fact-finding

(a) If, after a reasonable period of negotiation over the terms of the agreement, or upon expiration of an existing collective bargaining agreement and the parties have not been able to mutually resolve the dispute, the parties may, by mutual consent initiate a fact-finding.

(b) Within three days of such request the Board must submit to the parties a panel of 7 qualified, disinterested persons from the Illinois Public Employees Mediation Roster to serve as a fact-finder. The parties to the dispute shall designate one of the 7 persons to serve as fact-finder. The fact-finder must act independently of the Board and may be the same person who participated in the mediation of the labor dispute if both parties consent. The person selected or appointed as fact-finder shall immediately establish the dates and place of hearings. Upon request, the Board shall issue subpoenas for hearings conducted by the fact-finder. The fact-finder may administer oaths. The fact-finder shall initially determine what issues are in dispute and therefore properly before the fact-finder. Upon completion of the hearings, but no later than 45 days from the date of appointment, the fact-finder must make written findings of facts and recommendations for resolution of the dispute, must serve findings on the public employer and the labor organization involved, and must publicize such findings by mailing them to all newspapers of general circulation in the community. The fact-finder's findings shall be advisory only and shall not be binding upon the parties. If the parties do not accept the recommendations of the fact-finder as the basis for settlement, or if the fact-finder does not make written findings of facts and recommendations for the resolution of the dispute and serve and publicize such findings within 45 days of the date of appointment, the parties may resume negotiations.

(c) The public employer and the labor organization which is certified as exclusive representative or which is recognized as exclusive representative in any particular bargaining unit by the state or political subdivision are the only proper parties to the fact-finding proceedings.

## § 14 (5 ILCS 315/14).   Security Employee, Peace Officer and Fire Fighter Disputes

(a) In the case of collective bargaining agreements involving units of security employees of a public employer, Peace Officer Units, or units of fire fighters or paramedics, and in the case of disputes under Section 18, unless the parties mutually agree to some other time limit, mediation shall commence 30 days prior to the expiration date of such agreement or at such later time as the mediation services chosen under subsection (b) of Section 12 can be provided to the parties. In the case of negotiations for an initial collective bargaining agreement, mediation shall commence upon 15 days notice from either party or at such later time as the mediation services chosen pursuant to subsection (b) of Section 12 can be provided to the parties. In mediation under this Section, if either party requests the use of mediation services from the Federal Mediation and Conciliation Service, the other party shall either join in such request or bear the additional cost of mediation services from another source. The mediator shall have a duty to keep the Board informed on the progress of the mediation. If any dispute has not been resolved within 15 days after the first meeting of the parties and the mediator, or within such other time limit as may be mutually agreed upon by the parties, either the exclusive representative or employer may request of the other, in writing, arbitration, and shall submit a copy of the request to the Board.

(b) Within 10 days after such a request for arbitration has been made, the employer shall choose a delegate and the employees' exclusive representative shall choose a delegate to a panel of arbitration as provided in this Section. The employer and employees shall forthwith advise the other and the Board of their selections.

(c) Within 7 days after the request of either party, the parties shall request a panel of impartial arbitrators from which they shall select the neutral chairman according to the procedures provided in this Section. If the parties have agreed to a contract that contains a grievance resolution procedure as provided in Section 8, the chairman shall be selected using their agreed contract procedure unless they mutually agree to another procedure. If the parties fail to notify the Board of their selection of neutral chairman within 7 days after receipt of the list of impartial arbitrators, the Board shall appoint, at random, a neutral chairman from the list. In the absence of an agreed contract procedure for selecting an impartial arbitrator, either party may request a panel from the Board. Within 7 days of the request of either party, the Board shall select from the Public Employees Labor Mediation Roster 7 persons who are on the labor arbitration panels of either the American Arbitration Association or the Federal Mediation and Conciliation Service, or who are members of the National Academy of Arbitrators, as nominees for impartial arbitrator of the arbitration panel. The parties may select an individual on the list provided by the Board or any other individual mutually agreed upon by the parties. Within 7 days following the receipt of the list, the parties shall notify the Board of the person they have selected. Unless the parties agree on an alternate selection procedure, they shall alternatively strike one name from the list provided by the Board until only one name remains. A coin toss shall determine which party shall strike the first name. If the parties fail to notify the Board in a timely manner of their selection for neutral chairman, the Board shall appoint a neutral chairman from the Illinois Public Employees Mediation/Arbitration Roster.

(d) The chairman shall call a hearing to begin within 15 days and give reasonable notice of the time and place of the hearing. The hearing shall be held at the offices of the Board or at such other location as the Board deems appropriate. The chairman shall preside over the hearing and shall take testimony. Any oral or documentary evidence and other data deemed relevant by the arbitration panel may be received in evidence. The proceedings shall be informal. Technical rules of evidence shall not apply and the competency of the evidence shall not thereby be deemed impaired. A verbatim record of the proceedings shall be made and the arbitrator shall arrange for the necessary recording service. Transcripts may be ordered at the expense of the party ordering them, but the transcripts shall not be necessary for a decision by the arbitration panel. The expense of the proceedings, including a fee for the chairman, shall be borne equally by each of the parties to the dispute. The delegates, if public officers or employees, shall continue on the payroll of the public employer without loss of pay. The hearing conducted by the arbitration panel may be adjourned from time to time, but unless otherwise agreed by the parties, shall be concluded within 30 days of the time of its commencement. Majority actions and rulings shall constitute the actions and rulings of the arbitration panel. Arbitration proceedings under this Section shall not be interrupted or terminated by reason of any unfair labor practice charge filed by either party at any time.

(e) The arbitration panel may administer oaths, require the attendance of witnesses, and the production of such books, papers, contracts, agreements and documents as may be deemed by it material to a just determination of the issues in dispute, and for such purpose may issue subpoenas. If any person refuses to obey a subpoena, or refuses to be sworn or to testify, or if any witness, party or attorney is guilty of any contempt while in attendance at any hearing, the arbitration panel may, or the attorney general if requested shall, invoke the aid of any circuit court within the jurisdiction in which the hearing is being held, which court shall issue an appropriate order. Any failure to obey the order may be punished by the court as contempt.

(f) At any time before the rendering of an award, the chairman of the arbitration panel, if he is of the opinion that it would be useful or beneficial to do so, may remand the dispute to the parties for further collective bargaining for a period not to exceed 2 weeks. If the dispute is remanded for further collective bargaining the time provisions of this Act shall be extended for a time period equal to that of the remand. The chairman of the panel of arbitration shall notify the Board of the remand.

(g) At or before the conclusion of the hearing held pursuant to subsection (d), the arbitration panel shall identify the economic issues in dispute, and direct each of the parties to submit, within such time limit as the panel shall prescribe, to the arbitration panel and to each other its last offer of settlement on each economic issue. The determination of the arbitration panel as to the issues in dispute and as to which of these issues are economic shall be conclusive. The arbitration panel, within 30 days after the conclusion of the hearing, or such further additional periods to which the parties may agree, shall make written findings of fact and promulgate a written opinion and shall mail or otherwise deliver a true copy thereof to the parties and their representatives and to the Board. As to each economic issue, the arbitration panel shall adopt the last offer of settlement which, in the opinion of the arbitration panel, more nearly complies with the applicable factors prescribed in subsection (h). The findings, opinions and order as to all other issues shall be based upon the applicable factors prescribed in subsection (h).

(h) Where there is no agreement between the parties, or where there is an agreement but the parties have begun negotiations or discussions looking to a new agreement or amendment of the existing agreement, and wage rates or other conditions of employment under the proposed new or amended agreement are in dispute, the arbitration panel shall base its findings, opinions and order upon the following factors, as applicable:

(1) The lawful authority of the employer.

(2) Stipulations of the parties.

(3) The interests and welfare of the public and the financial ability of the unit of government to meet those costs.

(4) Comparison of the wages, hours and conditions of employment of the employees involved in the arbitration proceeding with the wages, hours and conditions of employment of other employees performing similar services and with other employees generally:

(A) In public employment in comparable communities.

(B) In private employment in comparable communities.

(5) The average consumer prices for goods and services, commonly known as the cost of living.

(6) The overall compensation presently received by the employees, including direct wage compensation, vacations, holidays and other excused time, insurance and pensions, medical and hospitalization benefits, the continuity and stability of employment and all other benefits received.

(7) Changes in any of the foregoing circumstances during the pendency of the arbitration proceedings.

(8) Such other factors, not confined to the foregoing, which are normally or traditionally taken into consideration in the determination of wages, hours and conditions of employment through voluntary collective bargaining, mediation, fact-finding, arbitration or otherwise between the parties, in the public service or in private employment.

(i) In the case of peace officers, the arbitration decision shall be limited to wages, hours, and conditions of employment (which may include residency requirements in municipalities with a population under 1,000,000, but those residency requirements shall not allow residency outside of Illinois) and shall not include the following: i) residency requirements in municipalities with a population of at least 1,000,000; ii) the type of equipment, other than uniforms, issued or used; iii) manning; iv) the total number of employees employed by the department; v) mutual aid and assistance agreements to other units of government; and vi) the criterion pursuant to which force, including deadly force, can be used; provided, nothing herein shall preclude an arbitration decision regarding equipment or manning levels if such decision is based on a finding that the equipment or manning considerations in a specific work assignment involve a serious risk to the safety of a peace officer beyond that which is inherent in the normal performance of police duties. Limitation of the terms of the arbitration decision pursuant to this subsection shall not be construed to limit the factors upon which the decision may be based, as set forth in subsection (h).

In the case of fire fighter, and fire department or fire district paramedic matters, the arbitration decision shall be limited to wages, hours, and conditions of employment (which may include residency requirements in municipalities with a population under 1,000,000, but those residency requirements shall not allow residency outside of Illinois) and shall not include the following matters: i) residency requirements in municipalities with a population of at least 1,000,000; ii) the type of equipment (other than uniforms and fire fighter turnout gear) issued or used; iii) the total number of employees employed by the department; iv) mutual aid and assistance agreements to other units of government; and v) the criterion pursuant to which force, including deadly force, can be used; provided, however, nothing herein shall preclude an arbitration decision regarding equipment levels if such decision is based on a finding that the equipment considerations in a specific work assignment involve a serious risk to the safety of a fire fighter beyond that which is inherent in the normal performance of fire fighter duties. Limitation of the terms of the arbitration decision pursuant to this subsection shall not be construed to limit the facts upon which the decision may be based, as set forth in subsection (h).

The changes to this subsection (i) made by Public Act 90–385 (relating to residency requirements) do not apply to persons who are employed by a combined department that performs both police and firefighting services; these persons shall be governed by the provisions of this subsection (i) relating to peace officers, as they existed before the amendment by Public Act 90–385.

To preserve historical bargaining rights, this subsection shall not apply to any provision of a fire fighter collective bargaining agreement in effect and applicable on the effective date of this Act; provided, however, nothing herein shall preclude arbitration with respect to any such provision.

(j) Arbitration procedures shall be deemed to be initiated by the filing of a letter requesting mediation as required under subsection (a) of this Section. The commencement of a new municipal fiscal year after the initiation of arbitration procedures under this Act, but before the arbitration decision, or its enforcement, shall not be deemed to render a dispute moot, or to otherwise impair the jurisdiction or authority of the arbitration panel or its decision. Increases in rates of compensation awarded by the arbitration panel may be effective only at the start of the fiscal year next commencing after the date of the arbitration award. If a new fiscal year has commenced either since the initiation of arbitration procedures under this Act or since any mutually agreed extension of the statutorily required period of mediation under this Act by the parties to the labor dispute causing a delay in the initiation of arbitration, the foregoing limitations shall be inapplicable, and such awarded increases may be retroactive to the commencement of the fiscal year, any other statute or charter provisions to the contrary, notwithstanding. At any time the parties, by stipulation, may amend or modify an award of arbitration.

(k) Orders of the arbitration panel shall be reviewable, upon appropriate petition by either the public employer or the exclusive bargaining representative, by the circuit court for the county in which the dispute arose or in which a majority of the affected employees reside, but only for reasons that the arbitration panel was without or exceeded its statutory authority; the order is arbitrary, or capricious; or the order was procured by fraud, collusion or other similar and unlawful means. Such petitions for review must be filed with the appropriate circuit court within 90 days following the issuance of the arbitration order. The pendency of such proceeding for review shall not automatically stay the order of the arbitration panel. The party against whom the final decision of any such court shall be adverse, if such court finds such appeal or petition to be frivolous, shall pay reasonable attorneys' fees and costs to the successful party as determined by said court in its discretion. If said court's decision affirms the award of money, such award, if retroactive, shall bear interest at the rate of 12 percent per annum from the effective retroactive date.

(l) During the pendency of proceedings before the arbitration panel, existing wages, hours, and other conditions of employment shall not be changed by action of either party without the consent of the other but a party may so consent without prejudice to his rights or position under this Act. The proceedings are deemed to be pending before the arbitration panel upon the initiation of arbitration procedures under this Act.

(m) Security officers of public employers, and Peace Officers, Fire Fighters and fire department and fire protection district paramedics, covered by this Section may not withhold services, nor may public employers lock out or prevent such employees from performing services at any time.

(n) All of the terms decided upon by the arbitration panel shall be included in an agreement to be submitted to the public employer's governing body for ratification and adoption by law, ordinance or the equivalent appropriate means.

The governing body shall review each term decided by the arbitration panel. If the governing body fails to reject one or more terms of the arbitration panel's decision by a 3/5 vote of those duly elected and qualified members of the governing body, within 20 days of issuance, or in the case of firefighters employed by a state university, at the next regularly scheduled meeting of the governing body after issuance, such term or terms shall become a part of the collective bargaining agreement of the parties. If the governing body affirmatively rejects one or more terms of the arbitration panel's decision, it must provide reasons for such rejection with respect to each term so rejected, within 20 days of such rejection and the parties shall return to the arbitration panel for further proceedings and issuance of a supplemental decision with respect to the rejected terms. Any supplemental decision by an arbitration panel or other decision maker agreed to by the parties shall be submitted to the governing body for ratification and adoption in accordance with the procedures and voting requirements set forth in this Section. The voting requirements of this subsection shall apply to all disputes submitted to arbitration pursuant to this Section notwithstanding any contrary voting requirements contained in any existing collective bargaining agreement between the parties.

(o) If the governing body of the employer votes to reject the panel's decision, the parties shall return to the panel within 30 days from the issuance of the reasons for rejection for further proceedings and issuance of a supplemental decision. All reasonable costs of such supplemental proceeding including the exclusive representative's reasonable attorney's fees, as established by the Board, shall be paid by the employer.

(p) Notwithstanding the provisions of this Section the employer and exclusive representative may agree to submit unresolved disputes concerning wages, hours, terms and conditions of employment to an alternative form of impasse resolution.

## § 15  (5 ILCS 315/15).    Act Takes Precedence

(a) In case of any conflict between the provisions of this Act and any other law (other than Section 5 of the State Employees Group Insurance Act of 1971 and other than the changes made to the Illinois Pension Code by Public Act 96–889 and other than as provided in Section 7.5), executive order or administrative regulation relating to wages, hours and conditions of employment and employment relations, the provisions of this Act or any collective bargaining agreement negotiated thereunder shall prevail and control. Nothing in this Act shall be construed to replace or diminish the rights of employees established by Sections 28 and 28a of the Metropolitan Transit Authority Act, Sections 2.15 through 2.19 of the Regional Transportation Authority Act. The provisions of this Act are subject to Section 7.5 of this Act and Section 5 of the State Employees Group Insurance Act of 1971. Nothing in this Act shall be construed to replace the necessity of complaints against a sworn peace officer, as defined in Section 2(a) of the Uniform Peace Officer Disciplinary Act, from having a complaint supported by a sworn affidavit.

(b) Except as provided in subsection (a) above, any collective bargaining contract between a public employer and a labor organization executed pursuant to this Act shall supersede any contrary statutes, charters, ordinances, rules or regulations relating to wages, hours and conditions of employment and employment relations adopted by the public employer or its agents. Any collective bargaining agreement entered into prior to the effective date of this Act shall remain in full force during its duration.

(c) It is the public policy of this State, pursuant to paragraphs (h) and (i) of Section 6 of Article VII of the Illinois Constitution, that the provisions of this Act are the exclusive exercise by the State of powers and functions which might otherwise be exercised by home rule units. Such powers and functions may not be exercised concurrently, either directly or indirectly, by any unit of local government, including any home rule unit, except as otherwise authorized by this Act.

## § 17 (5 ILCS 315/17).    Right to Strike

(a) Nothing in this Act shall make it unlawful or make it an unfair labor practice for public employees, other than security employees, as defined in Section 3(p), Peace Officers, Fire Fighters, and paramedics employed by fire departments and fire protection districts, to strike except as otherwise provided in this Act. Public employees who are permitted to strike may strike only if:

(1) the employees are represented by an exclusive bargaining representative;

(2) the collective bargaining agreement between the public employer and the public employees, if any, has expired, or such collective bargaining agreement does not prohibit the strike;

(3) the public employer and the labor organization have not mutually agreed to submit the disputed issues to final and binding arbitration;

(4) the exclusive representative has requested a mediator pursuant to Section 12 for the purpose of mediation or conciliation of a dispute between the public employer and the exclusive representative and mediation has been used; and

(5) at least 5 days have elapsed after a notice of intent to strike has been given by the exclusive bargaining representative to the public employer.

In mediation under this Section, if either party requests the use of mediation services from the Federal Mediation and Conciliation Service, the other party shall either join in such request or bear the additional cost of mediation services from another source.

(b) An employee who participates in a strike, work stoppage or slowdown, in violation of this Act shall be subject to discipline by the employer. No employer may pay or cause such employee to be paid any wages or other compensation for such periods of participation, except for wages or compensation earned before participation in such strike.

## § 18 (5 ILCS 315/18). Strikes Presenting Clear and Present Danger to Public; Procedure

(a) If a strike, which may constitute a clear and present danger to the health and safety of the public is about to occur or is in progress, the public employer concerned may petition the board to make an investigation and conduct a hearing. Unfair labor practices committed by the employer shall be a defense to such petition. If the board finds that within 72 hours there is a clear and present danger to the health and safety of the public the employer shall petition the circuit court where the strike is about to occur or is in progress for appropriate judicial relief to stop the strike or to set conditions and requirements which must be complied with by the exclusive representative, to avoid or remove any such clear and present danger. No injunctive relief shall be granted except upon a showing that the strike constitutes a clear and present danger to the health and safety of the public. The court may allow the strike to occur or continue under conditions which it finds will avoid or remove any such clear and present danger. The court shall designate the essential employees within the affected unit whose services are necessary to avoid or remove any such clear and present danger. Such employees may be ordered to return to work under conditions and requirements which the court finds to be appropriate and such order may be only for a limited duration, and may be extended only upon demonstration that such extension is necessary to protect the public health and safety from a clear and present danger.

If the court orders any of the employees in the affected unit to return to work it shall require the employer and exclusive representative to participate in the impasse arbitration procedures set forth in Section 14 of this Act. The Court shall determine for which employees such procedures in Section 14 shall apply.

(b) Equitable defenses such as unclean hands and any unfair labor practices committed by the employer shall be considered as defenses by the court. Failure to agree to a proposal or to make a concession is not per se a violation of the unclean hands doctrine.

(c) If any employee or employee organization fails to comply with any order of the Court issued pursuant to this Section, the employer may institute judicial proceedings to enforce the order of the court.

## § 20 (5 ILCS 315/20).   Prohibitions

(a) Nothing in this Act shall be construed to require an individual employee to render labor or service without his consent, nor shall anything in this Act be construed to make the quitting of his labor by an individual employee an illegal act; nor shall any court issue any process to compel the performance by an individual employee of such labor or service, without his consent; nor shall the quitting of labor by an employee or employees in good faith because of abnormally dangerous conditions for work at the place of employment of such employee be deemed a strike under this Act.

(b) This Act shall not be applicable to units of local government employing less than 5 employees at the time the Petition for Certification or Representation is filed with the Board. This prohibition shall not apply to bargaining units in existence on the effective date of this Act and units of local government employing more than 5 employees where the total number of employees falls below 5 after the Board has certified a bargaining unit.

# THE TAYLOR LAW
# (PUBLIC EMPLOYEES' FAIR
# EMPLOYMENT ACT)

∎ ∎ ∎

N.Y. Civ. Serv. §§ 200–214
(selections)

## § 200.   Statement of Policy

The legislature of the state of New York declares that it is the public policy of the state and the purpose of this act to promote harmonious and cooperative relationships between government and its employees and to protect the public by assuring, at all times, the orderly and uninterrupted operations and functions of government. These policies are best effectuated by (a) granting to public employees the right of organization and representation, (b) requiring the state, local governments and other political subdivisions to negotiate with, and enter into written agreements with employee organizations representing public employees which have been certified or recognized, (c) encouraging such public employers and such employee organizations to agree upon procedures for resolving disputes, (d) creating a public employment relations board to assist in resolving disputes between public employees and public employers, and (e) continuing the prohibition against strikes by public employees and providing remedies for violations of such prohibition.

## § 201.   Definitions

As used in this article:

4. The term "terms and conditions of employment" means salaries, wages, hours and other terms and conditions of employment provided, however, that such term shall not include any benefits provided by or to be provided by a public retirement system, or payments to a fund or insurer to provide an income for retirees, or payment to retirees or their beneficiaries. No such retirement benefits shall be negotiated pursuant to this article, and any benefits so negotiated shall be void.

6. (a) The term "government" or "public employer" means (i) the state of New York, (ii) a county, city, town, village or any other political subdivision or civil division of the state, (iii) a school district or any governmental entity operating a public school, college or university, (iv) a public improvement or special district, (v) a public authority, commission,

or public benefit corporation, (vi) any other public corporation, agency or instrumentality or unit of government which exercises governmental powers under the laws of the state, or (vii) in the case of a county sheriff's office in those counties where the office of sheriff is an elected position, both the county and the sheriff, shall be designated as a joint employer for all purposes of this article.

(b) Upon the application of any government, the board may determine that the applicant shall be deemed to be a joint public employer of public employees in an employer-employee negotiating unit determined pursuant to section two hundred seven of this chapter when such determination would best effectuate the purposes of this chapter.

7. (a) The term "public employee" means any person holding a position by appointment or employment in the service of a public employer, except that such term shall not include for the purposes of any provision of this article other than sections two hundred ten and two hundred eleven of this article, judges and justices of the unified court system, persons holding positions by appointment or employment in the organized militia of the state and persons who may reasonably be designated from time to time as managerial or confidential upon application of the public employer to the appropriate board in accordance with procedures established pursuant to section two hundred five or two hundred twelve of this article, which procedures shall provide that any such designations made during a period of unchallenged representation pursuant to subdivision two of section two hundred eight of this chapter shall only become effective upon the termination of such period of unchallenged representation. Employees may be designated as managerial only if they are persons (i) who formulate policy or (ii) who may reasonably be required on behalf of the public employer to assist directly in the preparation for and conduct of collective negotiations or to have a major role in the administration of agreements or in personnel administration provided that such role is not of a routine or clerical nature and requires the exercise of independent judgment. Employees may be designated as confidential only if they are persons who assist and act in a confidential capacity to managerial employees described in clause (ii).

(b) For the purposes of this article, assistant attorneys general, assistant district attorneys, and law school graduates employed in titles which promote to assistant district attorney upon admission to the bar of the state of New York shall be designated managerial employees, and confidential investigators employed in the department of law shall be designated confidential employees.

(c) Notwithstanding the provisions of any general, special or local law or code to the contrary, for the purposes of this article and with respect to the officers of a paid city fire department in a city of one million or more inhabitants, members in the rank of deputy chief designated as deputy assistant chief and higher shall be designated as managerial and confidential employees and members in the rank of deputy chief or lower shall not be so designated.

(d) A substitute teacher or a person employed in a nonpedagogical position who has received a reasonable assurance of continuing employment in accordance with subdivision ten or eleven of section five hundred ninety of the labor law which is sufficient to disqualify the substitute teacher or person employed in a nonpedagogical position from receiving unemployment insurance benefits shall be deemed to be an employee of the school district or board of cooperative educational services that has furnished such reasonable assurance of continuing employment; provided however that for the purposes of this article only, the determination of whether such reasonable assurance was furnished shall be made as if such determination were made prior to the promulgation by the United States department of labor of program letter number 4-87, dated December twenty-fourth, nineteen hundred eighty-six.

(e) Notwithstanding the provisions of any general, special or local law or code to the contrary, for the purposes of this article and with respect to the officers of a paid city police department, in a city of one million or more inhabitants, members in the rank of captain designated as assistant chief and higher shall be designated as managerial and confidential employees; members in the rank of captain, deputy inspector, inspector and deputy chief or lower shall not be so designated, unless a final determination to the contrary results from a petition to decertify (or from an action to otherwise designate any or all such members as managerial or confidential employees), which petition or action is or was initiated at any time prior to October first, nineteen hundred eighty-four and such petition or action is not withdrawn or otherwise discontinued.

(f) The term "public employee" means any person employed by a school district or board of cooperative educational services not otherwise deemed to be a public employee pursuant to the provisions of this subdivision, but who would be deemed a public employee under precedents or standards utilized or promulgated by the board for determining whether a person employed in a part-time, seasonal or casual position by a public employer other than a school district or board of cooperative educational services would be a public employee under paragraph (a) of this subdivision, taking into account the length of the school day and school year.

(g) Notwithstanding the provisions of any general, special or local law or code to the contrary, for the purposes of this article and with respect to employees of a city school district having a population of one million or more inhabitants, members in a title of school plant manager shall be designated as managerial and confidential employees in the noncompetitive classification.

9. The term "strike" means any strike or other concerted stoppage of work or slowdown by public employees.

## § 202. Right of Organization

Public employees shall have the right to form, join and participate in, or to refrain from forming, joining, or participating in, any employee organization of their own choosing.

## § 203. Right of Representation

Public employees shall have the right to be represented by employee organizations to negotiate collectively with their public employers in the determination of their terms and conditions of employment, and the administration of grievances arising thereunder.

## § 204. Recognition and Certification of Employee Organizations

1. Public employers are hereby empowered to recognize employee organizations for the purpose of negotiating collectively in the determination of, and administration of grievances arising under, the terms and conditions of employment of their public employees as provided in this article, and to negotiate and enter into written agreements with such employee organizations in determining such terms and conditions of employment.

2. Where an employee organization has been certified or recognized pursuant to the provisions of this article, it shall be the exclusive representative, for the purposes of this article, of all the employees in the appropriate negotiating unit, and the appropriate public employer shall be, and hereby is, required to negotiate collectively with such employee organization in the determination of, and administration of grievances arising under, the terms and conditions of employment of the public employees as provided in this article, and to negotiate and enter into written agreements with such employee organizations in determining such terms and conditions of employment.

3. For the purpose of this article, to negotiate collectively is the performance of the mutual obligation of the public employer and a recognized or certified employee organization to meet at reasonable times and confer in good faith with respect to wages, hours, and other terms and conditions of employment, or the negotiation of an agreement, or any question arising thereunder, and the execution of a written agreement incorporating any agreement reached if requested by either party, but

such obligation does not compel either party to agree to a proposal or require the making of a concession.

## § 204–a.    Agreements Between Public Employers and Employee Organizations

1. Any written agreement between a public employer and employee organization determining the terms and conditions of employment of public employees shall contain the following notice in type not smaller than the largest type used elsewhere in such agreement:

> "It is agreed by and between the parties that any provision of this agreement requiring legislative action to permit its implementation by amendment of law or by providing the additional funds therefor, shall not become effective until the appropriate legislative body has given approval."

2. Every employee organization submitting such a written agreement to its members for ratification shall publish such notice, include such notice in the documents accompanying such submission and shall read it aloud at any membership meeting called to consider such ratification.

3. Within sixty days after the effective date of this act, a copy of this section shall be furnished by the chief fiscal officer of each public employer to each public employee. Each public employee employed thereafter shall, upon such employment, be furnished with a copy of the provisions of this section.

## § 207.    Determination of Representation Status

> For purposes of resolving disputes concerning representation status, pursuant to section two hundred five or two hundred six of this article, the board or government, as the case may be, shall
>
> 1. define the appropriate employer-employee negotiating unit taking into account the following standards:
>
> (a) the definition of the unit shall correspond to a community of interest among the employees to be included in the unit;
>
> (b) the officials of government at the level of the unit shall have the power to agree, or to make effective recommendations to other administrative authority or the legislative body with respect to, the terms and conditions of employment upon which the employees desire to negotiate; and
>
> (c) the unit shall be compatible with the joint responsibilities of the public employer and public employees to serve the public.
>
> 2. ascertain the public employees' choice of employee organization as their representative (in cases where the parties to a dispute have not agreed on the means to ascertain the choice, if any, of the employees

in the unit) on the basis of dues deduction authorization and other evidences, or, if necessary, by conducting an election.

3. certify or recognize an employee organization upon (a) the determination that such organization represents that group of public employees it claims to represent, and (b) the affirmation by such organization that it does not assert the right to strike against any government, to assist or participate in any such strike, or to impose an obligation to conduct, assist or participate in such a strike.

## § 208. Rights Accompanying Certification or Recognition

1. A public employer shall extend to an employee organization certified or recognized pursuant to this article the following rights:

(a) to represent the employees in negotiations notwithstanding the existence of an agreement with an employee organization that is no longer certified or recognized, and in the settlement of grievances; and

(b) to membership dues deduction, upon presentation of dues deduction authorization cards signed by individual employees.

## § 209. Resolution of Disputes in the Course of Collective Negotiations

1. For purposes of this section, an impasse may be deemed exist if the parties fail to achieve agreement at least one hundred twenty days prior to the end of the fiscal year of the public employer.

2. Public employers are hereby empowered to enter into written agreements with recognized or certified employee organizations setting forth procedures to be invoked in the event of disputes which reach an impasse in the course of collective negotiations. Such agreements may include the undertaking by each party to submit unresolved issues to impartial arbitration. In the absence or upon the failure of such procedures, public employers and employee organizations may request the board to render assistance as provided in this section, or the board may render such assistance on its own motion, as provided in subdivision three of this section, or, in regard to officers or members of any organized fire department, or any unit of the public employer which previously was a part of an organized fire department whose primary mission includes the prevention and control of aircraft fires, police force or police department of any county, city, town, village or fire or police district, or detective-investigators, or rackets investigators employed in the office of a district attorney of a county, or in regard to any organized unit of troopers, commissioned or noncommissioned officers of the division of state police, or in regard to investigators, senior investigators and

investigator specialists of the division of state police, or in regard to members of collective negotiating units designated as security services and security supervisors who are police officers, who are forest ranger captains or who are employed by the state department of correctional services and are designated as peace officers pursuant to subdivision twenty-five of section 2.10 of the criminal procedure law, or in regard to members of the collective negotiating unit designated as the agency law enforcement services unit who are police officers pursuant to subdivision thirty-four of section 1.20 of the criminal procedure law or who are forest rangers, or in regard to organized units of deputy sheriffs who are engaged directly in criminal law enforcement activities that aggregate more than fifty per centum of their service as certified by the county sheriff and are police officers pursuant to subdivision thirty-four of section 1.20 of the criminal procedure law as certified by the municipal police training council or Suffolk county correction officers or Suffolk county park police, as provided in subdivision four of this section.

3.  On request of either party or upon its own motion, as provided in subdivision two of this section, and in the event the board determines that an impasse exists in collective negotiations between such employee organization and a public employer as to the conditions of employment of public employees, the board shall render assistance as follows:

(a)  to assist the parties to effect a voluntary resolution of the dispute, the board shall appoint a mediator or mediators representative of the public from a list of qualified persons maintained by the board;

(b)  if the impasse continues, the board shall appoint a fact-finding board of not more than three members, each representative of the public, from a list of qualified persons maintained by the board, which fact-finding board shall have, in addition to the powers delegated to it by the board, the power to make public recommendations for the resolution of the dispute;

(c)  if the dispute is not resolved at least eighty days prior to the end of the fiscal year of the public employer or by such other date determined by the board to be appropriate, the fact-finding board, acting by a majority of its members, (i) shall immediately transmit its findings of fact and recommendations for resolution of the dispute to the chief executive officer of the government involved and to the employee organization involved, (ii) may thereafter assist the parties to effect a voluntary resolution of the dispute, and (iii) shall within five days of such transmission make public such findings and recommendations;

(d) in the event that the findings of fact and recommendations are made public by a fact-finding board appointed by the board or established pursuant to procedures agreed upon by the parties under subdivision two of this section, and the impasse continues, the public employment relations board shall have the power to take whatever steps it deems appropriate to resolve the dispute, including (i) the making of recommendations after giving due consideration to the findings of fact and recommendations of such fact-finding board, but no further fact-finding board shall be appointed and (ii) upon the request of the parties, assistance in providing for voluntary arbitration;

(e) should either the public employer or the employee organization not accept in whole or in part the recommendations of the fact-finding board, (i), the chief executive officer of the government involved shall, within ten days after receipt of the findings of fact and recommendations of the fact-finding board, submit to the legislative body of the government involved a copy of the findings of fact and recommendations of the fact-finding board, together with his recommendations for settling the dispute; (ii) the employee organization may submit to such legislative body its recommendations for settling the dispute; (iii) the legislative body or a duly authorized committee thereof shall forthwith conduct a public hearing at which the parties shall be required to explain their positions with respect to the report of the fact-finding board; and (iv) thereafter, the legislative body shall take such action as it deems to be in the public interest, including the interest of the public employees involved.

(f) where the public employer is a school district, a board of cooperative educational services, a community college, the state university of New York, or the city university of New York, the provisions of subparagraphs (iii) and (iv) of paragraph (e) of this subdivision shall not apply, and (i) the board may afford the parties an opportunity to explain their positions with respect to the report of the fact-finding board at a meeting at which the legislative body, or a duly authorized committee thereof, may be present; (ii) thereafter, the legislative body may take such action as is necessary and appropriate to reach an agreement. The board may provide such assistance as may be appropriate.

4. On request of either party or upon its own motion, as provided in subdivision two of this section, and in the event the board determines that an impasse exists in collective negotiations between such employee organization and a public employer as to the conditions of employment of officers or members of any organized fire department, or any other unit of the public employer which previously was a part

of an organized fire department whose primary mission includes the prevention and control of aircraft fires, police force or police department of any county, city, town, village or fire or police district, and detective-investigators, criminal investigators or rackets investigators employed in the office of a district attorney, or as to the conditions of employment of members of any organized unit of troopers, commissioned or noncommissioned officers of the division of state police or as to the conditions of employment of members of any organized unit of investigators, senior investigators and investigator specialists of the division of state police, or as to the terms and conditions of employment of members of collective negotiating units designated as security services and security supervisors, who are police officers, who are forest ranger captains or who are employed by the state department of correctional services and are designated as peace officers pursuant to subdivision twenty-five of section 2.10 of the criminal procedure law, or in regard to members of the collective negotiating unit designated as the agency law enforcement services unit who are police officers pursuant to subdivision thirty-four of section 1.20 of the criminal procedure law or who are forest rangers, or as to the conditions of employment of any organized unit of deputy sheriffs who are engaged directly in criminal law enforcement activities that aggregate more than fifty per centum of their service as certified by the county sheriff and are police officers pursuant to subdivision thirty-four of section 1.20 of the criminal procedure law as certified by the municipal police training council or Suffolk county correction officers or Suffolk county park police, the board shall render assistance as follows:

(a) to assist the parties to effect a voluntary resolution of the dispute, the board shall appoint a mediator from a list of qualified persons maintained by the board;

(b) if the mediator is unable to effect settlement of the controversy within fifteen days after his appointment, either party may petition the board to refer the dispute to a public arbitration panel;

(c) (i) upon petition of either party, the board shall refer the dispute to a public arbitration panel as hereinafter provided;

(ii) the public arbitration panel shall consist of one member appointed by the public employer, one member appointed by the employee organization and one public member appointed jointly by the public employer and employee organization who shall be selected within ten days after receipt by the board of a petition for creation of the arbitration panel. If either party fails to designate its member to the public arbitration panel, the board shall promptly, upon receipt of a request by either party, designate a member associated in interest with the public employer or employee organization he is to represent. Each of the respective parties is to bear the cost of its member appointed or designated to the arbitration panel and each of the respective parties is to share equally the cost of the public member. If, within seven days after the mailing date, the parties are unable to agree upon the one public member, the board shall submit to the parties a list of qualified, disinterested persons for the selection of the public member. Each party shall alternately strike from the list one of the names with the order of striking determined by lot, until the remaining one person shall be designated as public member. This process shall be completed within five days of receipt of this list. The parties shall notify the board of the designated public member. The public member shall be chosen as chairman;

(iii) the public arbitration panel shall hold hearings on all matters related to the dispute. The parties may be heard either in person, by counsel, or by other representatives, as they may respectively designate. The panel may grant more than one adjournment each for each party; provided, however, that a second request of either party and any subsequent adjournment may be granted on request of either party, provided that the party which requests the adjournment shall pay the arbitrator's fee. The parties may present, either orally or in writing, or both, statements of fact, supporting witnesses and other evidence, and argument of their respective positions with respect to each case. The panel shall have authority to require the production of such additional evidence, either oral or written as it may desire from the parties and shall provide at the request of either party that a full and complete record be kept of any such hearings, the cost of such record to be shared equally by the parties;

(iv) all matters presented to the public arbitration panel for its determination shall be decided by a majority vote of the members of the panel. The panel, prior to a vote on any issue in dispute before it, shall, upon the joint request of its two members representing the public employer and the employee organization respectively, refer the issues back to the parties for further negotiations;

(v) the public arbitration panel shall make a just and reasonable determination of the matters in dispute. In arriving at such determination, the panel shall specify the basis for its findings, taking into consideration, in addition to any other relevant factors, the following:

a. comparison of the wages, hours and conditions of employment of the employees involved in the arbitration proceeding with the wages, hours, and conditions of employment of other employees performing similar services or requiring similar skills under similar working conditions and with other employees generally in public and private employment in comparable communities;

b.   the interests and welfare of the public and the financial ability of the public employer to pay;

c.   comparison of peculiarities in regard to other trades or professions, including specifically, (1) hazards of employment; (2) physical qualifications; (3) educational qualifications; (4) mental qualifications; (5) job training and skills;

d.   the terms of collective agreements negotiated between the parties in the past providing for compensation and fringe benefits, including, but not limited to, the provisions for salary, insurance and retirement benefits, medical and hospitalization benefits, paid time off and job security.

(vi)  the determination of the public arbitration panel shall be final and binding upon the parties for the period prescribed by the panel, but in no event shall such period exceed two years from the termination date of any previous collective bargaining agreement or if there is no previous collective bargaining agreement then for a period not to exceed two years from the date of determination by the panel. Such determination shall not be subject to the approval of any local legislative body or other municipal authority. Notwithstanding the provisions of this subparagraph to the contrary, where the parties to a public arbitration are those anticipated by the provisions of paragraphs (e) and (f) of this subdivision the state and such parties may agree to confer authority to the public arbitration panel to issue a final and binding determination for a period up to and including four years.

(vii) the determination of the public arbitration panel shall be subject to review by a court of competent jurisdiction in the manner prescribed by law.

(d)  The provisions of this subdivision shall expire thirty-six years from July first, nineteen hundred seventy-seven.

(e)  With regard to members of any organized unit of troopers, investigators, senior investigators, investigator specialists and commissioned or non-commissioned officers of the division of state police, the provisions of this section shall not apply to issues relating to disciplinary procedures and investigations or eligibility and assignment to details and positions, which shall be governed by other provisions prescribed by law.

(f)  With regard to any members of collective negotiating units designated as security services or security supervisors, who are police officers, who are forest ranger captains or who are employed by the state department of correctional services and are designated as peace officers pursuant to subdivision twenty-five of section 2.10 of the criminal procedure law, or in regard to members of the collective negotiating unit designated as the agency law enforcement services unit who are police officers pursuant to subdivision thirty-four of section 1.20 of the criminal procedure law or who are forest rangers, the provisions of this section shall only apply to the terms of collective bargaining agreements directly relating to compensation, including, but not limited to, salary, stipends, location pay, insurance, medical and hospitalization benefits; and shall not apply to non-compensatory issues including, but not limited to, job security, disciplinary procedures and actions, deployment or scheduling, or issues relating to eligibility for overtime compensation which shall be governed by other provisions proscribed by law.

(g)  With regard to members of any organized unit of deputy sheriffs who are engaged directly in criminal law enforcement activities that aggregate more than fifty per centum of their service as certified by the county sheriff and are police officers pursuant to subdivision thirty-four of section 1.20 of the criminal procedure law as certified by the municipal police training council, the provisions of this section shall only apply to the terms of collective bargaining agreements directly relating to compensation, including, but not limited to, salary, stipends, location pay, insurance, medical and hospitalization benefits; and shall not apply to non-compensatory issues including, but not limited to, job security, disciplinary procedures and actions, deployment or scheduling, or issues relating to eligibility for overtime compensation which shall be governed by other provisions proscribed by law. Provided, further, that with regard to any organized unit of deputy sheriffs who are engaged directly in criminal law enforcement activities that aggregate more than fifty per centum of their service and are police officers pursuant to subdivision thirty-four of section 1.20 of the criminal procedure law as certified by the municipal police training council, the provisions of this subdivision pertaining to interest arbitration shall only apply in the event that the collective bargaining agreement between the public employer and the public employee organization has been expired for a period of not less than twelve months and the parties have fully utilized all other impasse resolution procedures available under this subdivision.

(h)  With regard to Suffolk county correction officers the provisions of this section shall not apply to issues relating to disciplinary procedures and investigations or eligibility and assignment to details and positions, which shall be governed by other provisions prescribed by law.

(i)    With regard to Suffolk county park police officers the provisions of this section shall not apply to issues relating to disciplinary procedures and investigations or eligibility and assignment to details and positions, which shall be governed by other provisions prescribed by law.

5.    (a) In the event that the board certifies that a voluntary resolution of the contract negotiations between either (i) the New York city transit authority (hereinafter referred to as TA-public employer) and the public employee organization certified or recognized to represent the majority of employees of such TA-public employer, or (ii) the metropolitan transportation authority, including its subsidiaries, the New York city transit authority, including its subsidiary, and the Triborough bridge and tunnel authority (all hereinafter referred to as MTA-public employer) and a public employee organization certified or recognized to represent employees of such MTA-public employer not subject to the jurisdiction of the Federal Railway Labor Act 1 and not subject to the provisions of subparagraph (i) hereof, which has made an election pursuant to paragraph (f) of this subdivision, cannot be effected, or upon the joint request of the TA-public employer or the MTA-public employer (hereinafter jointly referred to as public employer) and any such affected employee organization, such board shall refer the dispute to a public arbitration panel, consisting of one member appointed by the public employer, one member appointed by the employee organization and one public member appointed jointly by the public employer and employee organization who shall be selected within ten days after receipt by the board of a petition for creation of the arbitration panel. If either party fails to designate its member to the public arbitration panel, the board shall promptly, upon receipt of a request by either party, designate a member associated in interest with the public employer or employee organization he is to represent. Each of the respective parties is to bear the cost of its member appointed or designated to the arbitration panel and each of the respective parties is to share equally the cost of the public member. If, within seven days after the mailing date, the parties are unable to agree upon the one public member, the board shall submit to the parties a list of qualified, disinterested persons for the selection of the public member. Each party shall alternately strike from the list one of the names with the order of striking determined by lot, until the remaining one person shall be designated as public member. This process shall be completed within five days of receipt of the list. The parties shall notify the board of the designated public member. The public member shall be chosen as chairman.

(b)  The arbitration panel shall hold hearings on all matters within the scope of negotiations related to the dispute for which the panel was appointed. The parties may be heard either in person, by counsel or by other representatives as they may respectively designate. The parties may present, either orally or in writing or both, statement [sic] of fact, supporting witnesses and other evidence and argument of their respective position [sic] with respect to each case. The panel shall have authority to require the production of such additional evidence, either oral or written, as it may desire from the parties and shall provide at the request of either party that a full and complete record be kept of any such hearings, the cost of such record to be shared equally by the parties.

(c)  All matters presented to such panel for its determination shall be decided by a majority vote of the members of the panel. The panel, prior to a vote on any issue in dispute before it, may refer the issue back to the parties for further negotiations.

(d)  Such panel shall make a just and reasonable determination of matters in dispute. In arriving at such determination, the panel shall specify the basis for its findings, taking into consideration, in addition to any other relevant factors, the following:

(i)  comparison of the wages, hours, fringe benefits, conditions and characteristics of employment of the public employees involved in the impasse proceeding with the wages, hours, fringe benefits, conditions and characteristics of employment of other employees performing similar work and other employees generally in public or private employment in New York city or comparable communities;

(ii)  the overall compensation paid to the employees involved in the impasse proceeding, including direct wage compensation, overtime and premium pay, vacations, holidays and other excused time, insurance, pensions, medical and hospitalization benefits, food and apparel furnished, and all other benefits received;

(iii)  the impact of the panel's award on the financial ability of the public employer to pay, on the present fares and on the continued provision of services to the public;

(iv)  changes in the average consumer prices for goods and services, commonly known as the cost of living;

(v)  the interest and welfare of the public; and

(vi)  such other factors as are normally and customarily considered in the determination of wages, hours, fringe benefits and other working conditions in collective negotiations or impasse panel proceedings.

(e)  The panel shall have full authority to resolve the matters in dispute before it and issue a determination which shall be final and binding upon the parties, notwithstanding any other provision of this article. Except for the purposes of judicial review, any provision of a determination of the arbitration panel, the implementation of which requires an enactment of law, shall not become binding until the appropriate legislative body enacts such law.

(f)  (i) Within sixty days of the enactment of this provision, and only within such time period, any such public employee organization described in subparagraph (ii) of paragraph (a) of this subdivision may elect to be covered by the provisions of this section by filing in writing a notice of participation with the chairman of the board and the chairman of the metropolitan transportation authority.

(ii)  Within sixty days of the enactment of this subparagraph and only within such time period, any such public employee organization certified or recognized to represent employees of an MTA-public employer (described in subparagraph (ii) of paragraph (a) of this subdivision) not subject to the jurisdiction of the Federal Railway Labor Act but which was subject to such jurisdiction during the sixty-day period set forth in subparagraph (i) of this paragraph may elect to be covered by the provisions of this section by filing in writing a notice of participation with the chairman of the board and the chairman of the metropolitan transportation authority.

(iii)  Once such an election is made pursuant to subparagraph (i) or (ii) of this paragraph, any such public employee organization shall thereafter be subject to the provisions of this section unless such organization and the chairman of the metropolitan transportation authority file a joint agreement in writing with the chairman of the board that provides for a rescission of the election made pursuant to this paragraph.

(g)  This subdivision shall not apply to a certified or recognized public employee organization which represents any public employees described in subdivision sixteen of section twelve hundred four of the public authorities law and nothing contained within this section shall be construed to divest the public employment relations board or any court of competent jurisdiction of the full power or authority to enforce any order made by the board or such court prior to the effective date of this subdivision.

## § 209–a. Improper Employer Practices; Improper Employee Organization Practices; Application

1.  Improper employer practices. It shall be an improper practice for public employer or its agents deliberately (a) to interfere with,

restrain or coerce public employees in the exercise of their rights guaranteed in section two hundred two of this article for the purpose of depriving them of such rights; (b) to dominate or interfere with the formation or administration of any employee organization for the purpose of depriving them of such rights; (c) to discriminate against any employee for the purpose of encouraging or discouraging membership in, or participation in the activities of, any employee organization; (d) to refuse to negotiate in good faith with the duly recognized or certified representatives of its public employees; (e) to refuse to continue all the terms of an expired agreement until a new agreement is negotiated, unless the employee organization which is a party to such agreement has, during such negotiations or prior to such resolution of such negotiations, engaged in conduct violative of subdivision one of section two hundred ten of this article; (f) to utilize any state funds appropriated for any purpose to train managers, supervisors, or other administrative personnel regarding methods to discourage union organization or to discourage an employee from participating in a union organizing drive; or (g) to fail to permit or refuse to afford a public employee the right, upon the employee's demand, to representation by a representative of the employee organization, or the designee of such organization, which has been certified or recognized under this article when at the time of questioning by the employer of such employee it reasonably appears that he or she may be the subject of a potential disciplinary action. If representation is requested, and the employee is a potential target of disciplinary action at the time of questioning, a reasonable period of time shall be afforded to the employee to obtain such representation. It shall be an affirmative defense to any improper practice charge under paragraph (g) of this subdivision that the employee has the right, pursuant to statute, interest arbitration award, collectively negotiated agreement, policy or practice, to present to a hearing officer or arbitrator evidence of the employer's failure to provide representation and to obtain exclusion of the resulting evidence upon demonstration of such failure. Nothing in this section shall grant an employee any right to representation by the representative of an employee organization in any criminal investigation.

2.  Improper employee organization practices. It shall be an improper practice for an employee organization or its agents deliberately (a) to interfere with, restrain or coerce public employees in the exercise of the rights granted in section two hundred two, or to cause, or attempt to cause, a public employer to do so; (b) to refuse to negotiate collectively in good faith with a public employer, provided it is the duly recognized or certified representative of the employees of such employer; or (c) to breach its duty of fair representation to public employees under this article.

3. The public employer shall be made a party to any charge filed under subdivision two of this section which alleges that the duly recognized or certified employee organization breached its duty of fair representation in the processing of or failure to process a claim that the public employer has breached its agreement with such employee organization.

## § 210.  Prohibition of Strikes

1. No public employee or employee organization shall engage in a strike, and no public employee or employee organization shall cause, instigate, encourage, or condone a strike.

2. Violations and penalties; presumption; prohibition against consent to strike; determination; notice; probation; payroll deductions; objections; and restoration.

(a) Violations and penalties. A public employee shall violate this subdivision by engaging in a strike or violating paragraph (c) of this subdivision and shall be liable as provided in this subdivision pursuant to the procedures contained herein. In addition, any public employee who violates subdivision one of this section may be subject to removal or other disciplinary action provided by law for misconduct.

(b) Presumption. For purposes of this subdivision an employee who is absent from work without permission, or who abstains wholly or in part from the full performance of his duties in his normal manner without permission, on the date or dates when a strike occurs, shall be presumed to have engaged in such strike on such date or dates.

(c) Prohibition against consent to strike. No person exercising on behalf of any public employer any authority, supervision or direction over any public employee shall have the power to authorize, approve, condone or consent to a strike, or the engaging in a strike, by one or more public employees, and such person shall not authorize, approve, condone or consent to such strike or engagement.

(d) Determination. In the event that it appears that a violation of this subdivision may have occurred, the chief executive officer of the government involved shall, on the basis of such investigation and affidavits as he may deem appropriate, determine whether or not such violation has occurred and the date or dates of such violation. If the chief executive officer determines that such violation has occurred, he shall further determine, on the basis of such further investigation and affidavits as he may deem appropriate, the names of employees who committed such violation and the date or dates thereof. Such determination shall not be deemed to be final until the completion of the procedures provided for in this subdivision.

(e) Notice. The chief executive officer shall forthwith notify each employee that he has been found to have committed such violation, the date or dates thereof and of his right to object to such determination pursuant to paragraph (g) of this subdivision; he shall also notify the chief fiscal officer of the names of all such employees and of the total number of days, or part thereof, on which it has been determined that such violation occurred. Notice to each employee shall be by personal service or by certified mail to his last address filed by him with his employer.

(f) Payroll deductions. Not earlier than thirty nor later than ninety days following the date of such determination, the chief fiscal officer of the government involved shall deduct from the compensation of each such public employee an amount equal to twice his daily rate of pay for each day or part thereof that it was determined that he had violated this subdivision; such rate of pay to be computed as of the time of such violation. In computing such deduction, credit shall be allowed for amounts already withheld from such employee's compensation on account of his absence from work or other withholding of services on such day or days. In computing the aforesaid thirty to ninety day period of time following the determination of a violation pursuant to subdivision (d) of paragraph two of this section and where the employee's annual compensation is paid over a period of time which is less than fifty-two weeks, that period of time between the last day of the last payroll period of the employment term in which the violation occurred and the first day of the first payroll period of the next succeeding employment term shall be disregarded and not counted.

(g) Objections and restoration. Any employee determined to have violated this subdivision may object to such determination by filing with the chief executive officer, (within twenty days of the date on which notice was served or mailed to him pursuant to paragraph (e) of this subdivision) his sworn affidavit, supported by available documentary proof, containing a short and plain statement of the facts upon which he relies to show that such determination was incorrect. Such affidavit shall be subject to the penalties of perjury. If the chief executive officer shall determine that the affidavit and supporting proof establishes that the employee did not violate this subdivision, he shall sustain the objection. If the chief executive officer shall determine that the affidavit and supporting proof fails to establish that the employee did not violate this subdivision, he shall dismiss the objection and so notify the employee. If the chief executive officer shall determine that the affidavit and supporting proof raises a question of fact which, if resolved in favor of the employee, would establish that the employee did not violate this subdivision, he shall appoint a hearing officer to determine whether in fact the employee did violate this subdivision after a hearing at which such employee shall bear the burden of proof. If the hearing officer shall determine that the employee failed to establish that he did not violate this subdivision, the chief executive officer shall so notify the employee. If the chief executive officer sustains an objection or the hearing officer determines on a preponderance of the evidence that such employee did not violate this subdivision, the chief executive officer shall forthwith notify the chief fiscal officer who shall thereupon cease all further deductions and refund any deductions previously made pursuant to this subdivision. The determinations provided in this paragraph shall be reviewable pursuant to article seventy-eight of the civil practice law and rules.

3.    (a) An employee organization which is determined by the board to have violated the provisions of subdivision one of this section shall, in accordance with the provisions of this section, lose the rights granted pursuant to the provisions of paragraph (b) of subdivision one of section two hundred eight of this chapter.

(b)    In the event that it appears that a violation of subdivision one of this section may have occurred, it shall be the duty of the chief executive officer of the public employer involved (i) forthwith to so notify the board and the chief legal officer of the government involved, and (ii) to provide the board and such chief legal officer with such facilities, assistance and data as will enable the board and such chief legal officer to carry out their duties under this section.

(c)    In the event that it appears that a violation of subdivision one of this section may have occurred, the chief legal officer of the government involved, or the board on its own motion, shall forthwith institute proceedings before the board to determine whether such employee organization has violated the provisions of subdivision one of this section.

(d)    Proceedings against an employee organization under this section shall be commenced by service upon it of a written notice, together with a copy of the charges. A copy of such notice and charges shall also be served, for their information, upon the appropriate government officials who recognize such employee organization and grant to it the rights accompanying such recognition. The employee organization shall have eight days within which to serve its written answer to such charges. The board's hearing shall be held promptly thereafter and at such hearing, the parties shall be permitted to be represented by counsel and to summon witnesses in their behalf. Compliance with the technical rules of evidence shall not be required.

(e) In determining whether an employee organization has violated subdivision one of this section, the board shall consider (i) whether the employee organization called the strike or tried prevent it, and (ii) whether the employee organization made or was making good faith efforts to terminate the strike.

(f) If the board determines that an employee organization has violated the provisions of subdivision one of this section, the board shall order forfeiture of the rights granted pursuant to the provisions of paragraph (b) of subdivision one, and subdivision three of section two hundred eight of this chapter, for such specified period of time as the board shall determine, or, in the discretion of the board, for an indefinite period of time subject to restoration upon application, with notice to all interested parties, supported by proof of good faith compliance with the requirements of subdivision one of this section since the date of such violation, such proof to include, for example, the successful negotiation, without a violation of subdivision one of this section, of a contract covering the employees in the unit affected by such violation; provided, however, that where a fine imposed on an employee organization pursuant to subdivision two of section seven hundred fifty-one of the judiciary law remains wholly or partly unpaid, after the exhaustion of the cash and securities of the employee organization, the board shall direct that, notwithstanding such forfeiture, such membership dues deduction shall be continued to the extent necessary to pay such fine and such public employer shall transmit such moneys to the court. In fixing the duration of the forfeiture, the board shall consider all the relevant facts and circumstances, including but not limited to: (i) the extent of any willful defiance of subdivision one of this section (ii) the impact of the strike on the public health, safety, and welfare of the community and (iii) the financial resources of the employee organization; and the board may consider (i) the refusal of the employee organization or the appropriate public employer or the representative thereof, to submit to the mediation and fact-finding procedures provided in section two hundred nine and (ii) whether, if so alleged by the employee organization, the appropriate public employer or its representatives engaged in such acts of extreme provocation as to detract from the responsibility of the employee organization for the strike. In determining the financial resources of the employee organization, the board shall consider both the income and the assets of such employee organization. In the event membership dues are collected by the public employer as provided in paragraph (b) of subdivision one of section two hundred eight of this chapter, the books and records of such public employer shall be prima facie evidence of the amount so collected.

(g)  An employee organization whose rights granted pursuant to the provisions of paragraph (b) of subdivision one, and subdivision three of section two hundred eight of this article have been order [sic] forfeited pursuant to this section may be granted such rights after the termination of such forfeiture only after complying with the provisions of clause (b) of subdivision three of section two hundred seven of this article.

(h)  No compensation shall be paid by a public employer to a public employee with respect to any day or part thereof when such employee is engaged in a strike against such employer. The chief fiscal officer of the government involved shall withhold such compensation upon receipt of the notice provided by paragraph (e) of subdivision two of section two hundred ten; notwithstanding the failure to have received such notice, no public employee or officer having knowledge that such employee has so engaged in such a strike shall deliver or caused [sic] to be delivered to such employee any cash, check or payment which, in whole or in part, represents such compensation.

4.  Within sixty days of the termination of a strike, the chief executive officer of the government involved shall prepare and make public a report in writing, which shall contain the following information: (a) the circumstances surrounding the commencement of the strike, (b) the efforts used to terminate the strike, (c) the names of those public employees whom the public officer or body had reason to believe were responsible for causing, instigating or encouraging the strike and (d) related to the varying degrees of individual responsibility, the sanctions imposed or proceedings pending against each such individual public employee.

## § 211.  Application for Injunctive Relief

Notwithstanding the provisions of section eight hundred seven of the labor law, where it appears that public employees or an employee organization threaten or are about to do, or are doing, an act in violation of section two hundred ten of this article, the chief executive officer of the government involved shall (a) forthwith notify the chief legal officer of the government involved, and (b) provide such chief legal officer with such facilities, assistance and data as will enable the chief legal officer to carry out his duties under this section, and, notwithstanding the failure or refusal of the chief executive officer to act as aforesaid, the chief legal officer of the government involved shall forthwith apply to the supreme court for an injunction against such violation. If an order of the court enjoining or restraining such violation does not receive compliance, such chief legal officer shall forthwith apply to the supreme court to punish such violation under section seven hundred fifty of the judiciary law.

## § 214.   Management and Confidential Employees; Membership and Office in Employee Organizations

No managerial or confidential employee, as determined pursuant to subdivision seven of section two hundred one of this article, shall hold office in or be a member of any employee organization which is or seeks to become pursuant to this article the certified or recognized representative of the public employees employed by the public employer of such managerial or confidential employee.

# WISCONSIN MUNICIPAL EMPLOYMENT RELATIONS ACT

■ ■ ■

Wis. Stat. §§ 111.70 & 111.77
(selections)

## SUBCHAPTER IV. MUNICIPAL EMPLOYMENT RELATIONS

**111.70 Municipal employment. (1)** DEFINITIONS. As used in this subchapter:

(a) "Collective bargaining" means the performance of the mutual obligation of a municipal employer, through its officers and agents, and the representative of its municipal employees in a collective bargaining unit, to meet and confer at reasonable times, in good faith, with the intention of reaching an agreement, or to resolve questions arising under such an agreement, with respect to wages, hours, and conditions of employment for public safety employees or transit employees and with respect to wages for general municipal employees, and with respect to a requirement of the municipal employer for a municipal employee to perform law enforcement and fire fighting services under s. 60.553, 61.66, or 62.13 (2e), except as provided in sub. (4) (mb) and (mc) and s. 40.81 (3) and except that a municipal employer shall not meet and confer with respect to any proposal to diminish or abridge the rights guaranteed to any public safety employees under ch. 164. Collective bargaining includes the reduction of any agreement reached to a written and signed document.

(b) "Collective bargaining unit" means a unit consisting of municipal employees that is determined by the commission under sub. (4) (d) 2. a. to be appropriate for the purpose of collective bargaining.

(c) "Commission" means the employment relations commission.

(cm) "Consumer price index change" means the average annual percentage change in the consumer price index for all urban consumers, U.S. city average, as determined by the federal department of labor, for the 12 months immediately preceding the current date.

(d) "Craft employee" means a skilled journeyman craftsman, including the skilled journeyman craftsman's apprentices and helpers, but shall not include employees not in direct line of progression in the craft.

(e)  "Election" means a proceeding conducted by the commission in which the employees in a collective bargaining unit cast a secret ballot for collective bargaining representatives, or for any other purpose specified in this subchapter.

(f)  "Fair-share agreement" means an agreement between a municipal employer and a labor organization that represents public safety employees or transit employees under which all or any of the public safety employees or transit employees in the collective bargaining unit are required to pay their proportionate share of the cost of the collective bargaining process and contract administration measured by the amount of dues uniformly required of all members.

(fm)  "General municipal employee" means a municipal employee who is not a public safety employee or a transit employee.

(g)  "Labor dispute" means any controversy concerning wages, hours and conditions of employment, or concerning the representation of persons in negotiating, maintaining, changing or seeking to arrange wages, hours and conditions of employment.

(h)  "Labor organization" means any employee organization in which employees participate and which exists for the purpose, in whole or in part, of engaging in collective bargaining with municipal employers concerning grievances, labor disputes, wages, hours or conditions of employment.

(i)  "Municipal employee" means any individual employed by a municipal employer other than an independent contractor, supervisor, or confidential, managerial or executive employee.

(j)  "Municipal employer" means any city, county, village, town, metropolitan sewerage district, school district, long–term care district, transit authority under s. 59.58 (7) or 66.1039, local cultural arts district created under subch. V of ch. 229, or any other political subdivision of the state, or instrumentality of one or more political subdivisions of the state, that engages the services of an employee and includes any person acting on behalf of a municipal employer within the scope of the person's authority, express or implied.

(k)  "Person" means one or more individuals, labor organizations, associations, corporations or legal representatives.

(L)  "Professional employee" means:

1.  Any employee engaged in work:

a.  Predominantly intellectual and varied in character as opposed to routine mental, manual, mechanical or physical work;

b.  Involving the consistent exercise of discretion and judgment in its performance;

c.    Of such a character that the output produced or the result accomplished cannot be standardized in relation to a given period of time;

d.    Requiring knowledge of an advanced type in a field of science or learning customarily acquired by a prolonged course of specialized intellectual instruction and study in an institution of higher education or a hospital, as distinguished from a general academic education or from an apprenticeship or from training in the performance of routine mental, manual or physical process; or

2.    Any employee who:

a.    Has completed the courses of specialized intellectual instruction and study described in subd. 1. d.;

b.    Is performing related work under the supervision of a professional person to qualify to become a professional employee as defined in subd. 1.

(m) "Prohibited practice" means any practice prohibited under this subchapter.

(mm) "Public safety employee" means any municipal employee who is employed in a position that, on July 1, 2011, is one of the following:

1. Classified as a protective occupation participant under any of the following:

a.    Section 40.02 (48) (am) 9., 10., 13., 15., or 22.

b.    A provision that is comparable to a provision under subd.

1.    a. that is in a county or city retirement system.

2.    An emergency medical service provider for emergency medical services departments.

(n)  "Referendum" means a proceeding conducted by the commission in which public safety employees or transit employees in a collective bargaining unit may cast a secret ballot on the question of authorizing a labor organization and the employer to continue a fair-share agreement.

(ne) "School district employee" means a municipal employee who is employed to perform services for a school district.

(nm)    "Strike" includes any strike or other concerted stoppage of work by municipal employees, and any concerted slowdown or other concerted interruption of operations or services by municipal employees, or any concerted refusal to work or perform their usual duties as municipal employees, for the purpose of enforcing demands upon a municipal employer.

(o)  "Supervisor" means:

1.   As to other than municipal and county fire fighters, any individual who has authority, in the interest of the municipal employer, to hire, transfer, suspend, lay off, recall, promote, discharge, assign, reward or discipline other employees, or to adjust their grievances or effectively to recommend such action, if in connection with the foregoing the exercise of such authority is not of a merely routine or clerical nature, but requires the use of independent judgment.

2.   As to fire fighters employed by municipalities with more than one fire station, the term "supervisor" shall include all officers above the rank of the highest ranking officer at each single station. In municipalities where there is but one fire station, the term "supervisor" shall include only the chief and the officer in rank immediately below the chief. No other fire fighter shall be included under the term "supervisor" for the purposes of this subchapter.

(p)   "Transit employee" means a municipal employee who is determined to be a transit employee under sub. (4) (bm).

**(1p)** COUNTY EMPLOYEES IN A COUNTY WITH A POPULATION OF 750,000 OR MORE

With respect to municipal employees who are employed by a county with a population of 750,000 or more, the county executive is responsible for the municipal employer functions under this subchapter.

**(2)**  RIGHTS OF MUNICIPAL EMPLOYEES. Municipal employees have the right of self–organization, and the right to form, join, or assist labor organizations, to bargain collectively through representatives of their own choosing, and to engage in lawful, concerted activities for the purpose of collective bargaining or other mutual aid or protection. Municipal employees have the right to refrain from any and all such activities. A general municipal employee has the right to refrain from paying dues while remaining a member of a collective bargaining unit. A public safety employee or a transit employee, however, may be required to pay dues in the manner provided in a fair-share agreement; a fair– share agreement covering a public safety employee or a transit employee must contain a provision requiring the municipal employer to deduct the amount of dues as certified by the labor organization from the earnings of the employee affected by the fair-share agreement and to pay the amount deducted to the labor organization. A fair-share agreement covering a public safety employee or transit employee is subject to the right of the municipal employer or a labor organization to petition the commission to conduct a referendum. Such petition must be supported by proof that at least 30% of the employees in the collective bargaining unit desire that the fair-share agreement be terminated. Upon so finding, the commission shall conduct a referendum. If the continuation of the agreement is not supported by at least the majority of the eligible employees, it shall terminate. The commission shall declare any fair-share agreement suspended upon such conditions and for such time as the commission decides whenever it finds that the labor organization involved has refused on the basis of race, color, sexual orientation, creed, or sex to receive as a member any public safety employee or transit employee of the municipal employer in the bargaining unit involved, and such agreement is subject to this duty of the commission. Any of the parties to such agreement or any public safety employee or transit employee covered by the agreement may come before the commission, as provided in s. 111.07, and ask the performance of this duty.

**(3)** PROHIBITED PRACTICES AND THEIR PREVENTION. (a) It is a prohibited practice for a municipal employer individually or in concert with others:

1. To interfere with, restrain or coerce municipal employees in the exercise of their rights guaranteed in sub. (2).

2. To initiate, create, dominate or interfere with the formation or administration of any labor organization or contribute financial support to it, but the municipal employer is not prohibited from reimbursing its employees at their prevailing wage rate for the time spent conferring with the employees, officers or agents.

3. To encourage or discourage a membership in any labor organization by discrimination in regard to hiring, tenure, or other terms or conditions of employment; but the prohibition shall not apply to a fair-share agreement that covers public safety employees or transit employees.

4. To refuse to bargain collectively with a representative of a majority of its employees in an appropriate collective bargaining unit. Such refusal includes action by the employer to issue or seek to obtain contracts, including those provided for by statute, with individuals in the collective bargaining unit while collective bargaining, mediation, or fact-finding concerning the terms and conditions of a new collective bargaining agreement is in progress, unless such individual contracts contain express language providing that the contract is subject to amendment by a subsequent collective bargaining agreement. Where the employer has a good faith doubt as to whether a labor organization claiming the support of a majority of its employees in an appropriate bargaining unit does in fact have that support, it may file with the commission a petition requesting an election to that claim. An employer shall not be deemed to have refused to bargain until an election has been held and the results thereof certified to the employer by the commission. The violation shall include, though not be limited thereby, to the refusal to execute a collective bargaining agreement previously agreed upon.

5.   To violate any collective bargaining agreement previously agreed upon by the parties with respect to wages, hours and conditions of employment affecting public safety employees or transit employees, including an agreement to arbitrate questions arising as to the meaning or application of the terms of a collective bargaining agreement or to accept the terms of such arbitration award, where previously the parties have agreed to accept such award as final and binding upon them or to violate any collective bargaining agreement affecting general municipal employees, that was previously agreed upon by the parties with respect to wages.

6.   To deduct labor organization dues from the earnings of a public safety employee or a transit employee, unless the municipal employer has been presented with an individual order therefor, signed by the employee personally, and terminable by at least the end of any year of its life or earlier by the public safety employee or transit employee giving at least 30 days' written notice of such termination to the municipal employer and to the representative organization, except when a fair-share agreement is in effect.

7m. To refuse or otherwise fail to implement an arbitration decision lawfully made under sub. (4) (cg).

8.   After a collective bargaining agreement expires and before another collective bargaining agreement takes effect, to fail to follow any grievance arbitration agreement in the expired collective bargaining agreement.

9.   If the collective bargaining unit contains a public safety employee or transit employee, after a collective bargaining agreement expires and before another collective bargaining agreement takes effect, to fail to follow any fair-share agreement in the expired collective bargaining agreement.

(b)   It is a prohibited practice for a municipal employee, individually or in concert with others:

1.   To coerce or intimidate a municipal employee in the enjoyment of the employee's legal rights, including those guaranteed in sub. (2).

2.   To coerce, intimidate or induce any officer or agent of a municipal employer to interfere with any of its employees in the enjoyment of their legal rights, including those guaranteed in sub. (2), or to engage in any practice with regard to its employees which would constitute a prohibited practice if undertaken by the officer or agent on the officer's or agent's own initiative.

3.   To refuse to bargain collectively with the duly authorized officer or agent of a municipal employer, provided it is the recognized or certified exclusive collective bargaining representative of employees in an

appropriate collective bargaining unit. Such refusal to bargain shall include, but not be limited to, the refusal to execute a collective bargaining agreement previously agreed upon.

4.  To violate any collective bargaining agreement previously agreed upon by the parties with respect to wages, hours and conditions of employment affecting municipal employees, including an agreement to arbitrate questions arising as to the meaning or application of the terms of a collective bargaining agreement or to accept the terms of such arbitration award, where previously the parties have agreed to accept such awards as final and binding upon them.

5.  To coerce or intimidate an independent contractor, supervisor, confidential, managerial or executive employee, officer or agent of the municipal employer, to induce the person to become a member of the labor organization of which employees are members.

6m. To refuse or otherwise fail to implement an arbitration decision lawfully made under sub. (4) (cg).

7. After a collective bargaining agreement expires and before another collective bargaining agreement takes effect, to fail to follow any grievance arbitration agreement in the expired collective bargaining agreement.

(c)  It is a prohibited practice for any person to do or cause to be done on behalf of or in the interest of municipal employers or municipal employees, or in connection with or to influence the outcome of any controversy as to employment relations, any act prohibited by par. (a) or (b).

(d)  The duty to bargain does not compel either party to agree to a proposal or require the making of a concession.

**(3g)** WAGE DEDUCTION PROHIBITION. A municipal employer may not deduct labor organization dues from the earnings of a general municipal employee or supervisor.

**(4)** POWERS OF THE COMMISSION. The commission shall conduct any election under this subsection by secret ballot and shall adhere to the following provisions relating to bargaining in municipal employment in addition to other powers and duties provided in this subchapter:

(a)  *Prevention of prohibited practices.* Section 111.07 shall govern procedure in all cases involving prohibited practices under this subchapter except that wherever the term "unfair labor practices" appears in s. 111.07 the term "prohibited practices" shall be substituted.

(b)  *Failure to bargain.* Whenever a dispute arises between a municipal employer and a union of its employees concerning the duty to bargain on any subject, the dispute shall be resolved by the commission on petition for a declaratory ruling. The decision of the commission shall be issued within 15 days of submission and shall have the effect of an order issued under s. 111.07. The filing of a petition under this paragraph shall not prevent the inclusion of the same allegations in a complaint involving prohibited practices in which it is alleged that the failure to bargain on the subjects of the declaratory ruling is part of a series of acts or pattern of conduct prohibited by this subchapter.

(bm) *Transit employee determination.* The commission shall determine that any municipal employee is a transit employee if the commission determines that the municipal employer who employs the municipal employee would lose federal funding under 49 USC 5333 (b) if the municipal employee is not a transit employee.

(c) *Methods for peaceful settlement of disputes; public safety employees.* 1. 'Mediation.' The commission may function as a mediator in labor disputes involving a collective bargaining unit containing a public safety employee. Such mediation may be carried on by a person designated to act by the commission upon request of one or both of the parties or upon initiation of the commission. The function of the mediator is to encourage voluntary settlement by the parties but no mediator has the power of compulsion.

2. 'Arbitration.' Parties to a dispute pertaining to the meaning or application of the terms of a written collective bargaining agreement involving a collective bargaining unit containing a public safety employee may agree in writing to have the commission or any other appropriate agency serve as arbitrator or may designate any other competent, impartial and disinterested person to so serve.

3. 'Fact-finding.' Unless s. 111.77 applies, if a dispute involving a collective bargaining unit containing a public safety employee has not been settled after a reasonable period of negotiation and after the settlement procedures, if any, established by the parties have been exhausted, and the parties are deadlocked with respect to any dispute between them arising in the collective bargaining process, either party, or the parties jointly, may petition the commission, in writing, to initiate fact-finding, and to make recommendations to resolve the deadlock, as follows:

a. Upon receipt of the petition to initiate fact-finding, the commission shall make an investigation with or without a formal hearing, to determine whether a deadlock in fact exists. After its investigation the commission shall certify the results thereof. If the commission decides that fact-finding should be initiated, it shall appoint a qualified, disinterested person or 3–member panel, when jointly requested by the parties, to function as a fact finder.

b.   The fact finder appointed under subd. 3. a. may establish dates and place of hearings which shall be where feasible, and shall conduct the hearings pursuant to rules established by the commission. Upon request, the commission shall issue subpoenas for hearings conducted by the fact finder. The fact finder may administer oaths. Upon completion of the hearing, the fact finder shall make written findings of fact and recommendations for solution of the dispute and shall cause the same to be served on the parties and the commission. Cost of fact-finding proceedings shall be divided equally between the parties. At the time the fact finder submits a statement of his or her costs to the parties, the fact finder shall submit a copy of the statement to the commission at its Madison office.

c.   Nothing in this subdivision prohibits any fact finder appointed under subd. 3. a. from endeavoring to mediate the dispute, in which the fact finder is involved, at any time prior to the issuance of the fact finder's recommendations.

d.   Within 30 days of the receipt of the fact finder's recommendations under subd. 3. b., or within the time mutually agreed upon by the parties, each party shall give notice to the other party, in writing as to its acceptance or rejection, in whole or in part, of the fact finder's recommendations and transmit a copy of the notice to the commission at its Madison office.

(cg) *Methods for peaceful settlement of disputes; transit employees.* 1. 'Notice of commencement of contract negotiations.' To advise the commission of the commencement of contract negotiations involving a collective bargaining unit containing transit employees, whenever either party requests the other to reopen negotiations under a binding collective bargaining agreement, or the parties otherwise commence negotiations if no collective bargaining agreement exists, the party requesting negotiations shall immediately notify the commission in writing. Upon failure of the requesting party to provide notice, the other party may provide notice to the commission. The notice shall specify the expiration date of the existing collective bargaining agreement, if any, and shall provide any additional information the commission may require on a form provided by the commission.

2.   'Presentation of initial proposals; open meetings.' The meetings between parties to a collective bargaining agreement or proposed collective bargaining agreement under this subchapter that involve a collective bargaining unit containing a transit employee and that are held to present initial bargaining proposals, along with supporting rationale, are open to the public. Each party shall submit its initial bargaining proposals to the other party in writing. Failure to comply with this

subdivision does not invalidate a collective bargaining agreement under this subchapter.

3. 'Mediation.' The commission or its designee shall function as mediator in labor disputes involving transit employees upon request of one or both of the parties, or upon initiation of the commission. The function of the mediator is to encourage voluntary settlement by the parties. No mediator has the power of compulsion.

4. 'Grievance arbitration.' Parties to a dispute pertaining to the meaning or application of the terms of a written collective bargaining agreement involving a collective bargaining unit containing a transit employee may agree in writing to have the commission or any other appropriate agency serve as arbitrator or may designate any other competent, impartial, and disinterested person to serve as an arbitrator.

5. 'Voluntary impasse resolution procedures.' In addition to the other impasse resolution procedures provided in this paragraph, a municipal employer that employs a transit employee and labor organization may at any time, as a permissive subject of bargaining, agree in writing to a dispute settlement procedure, including binding interest arbitration, which is acceptable to the parties for resolving an impasse over terms of any collective bargaining agreement under this subchapter. The parties shall file a copy of the agreement with the commission. If the parties agree to any form of binding interest arbitration, the arbitrator shall give weight to the factors enumerated under subds. 7. and 7g.

6. 'Interest arbitration.' a. If in any collective bargaining unit containing transit employees a dispute has not been settled after a reasonable period of negotiation and after mediation by the commission under subd. 3. and other settlement procedures, if any, established by the parties have been exhausted, and the parties are deadlocked with respect to any dispute between them over wages, hours, or conditions of employment to be included in a new collective bargaining agreement, either party, or the parties jointly, may petition the commission, in writing, to initiate compulsory, final, and binding arbitration, as provided in this paragraph. At the time the petition is filed, the petitioning party shall submit in writing to the other party and the commission its preliminary final offer containing its latest proposals on all issues in dispute. Within 14 calendar days after the date of that submission, the other party shall submit in writing its preliminary final offer on all disputed issues to the petitioning party and the commission. If a petition is filed jointly, both parties shall exchange their preliminary final offers in writing and submit copies to the commission when the petition is filed.

am. Upon receipt of a petition under subd. 6. a. to initiate arbitration, the commission shall determine, with or without a formal hearing, whether arbitration should be commenced. If in determining whether an impasse exists the commission finds that the procedures under this paragraph have not been complied with and compliance would tend to result in a settlement, it may order compliance before ordering arbitration. The validity of any arbitration award or collective bargaining agreement is not affected by failure to comply with the procedures. Prior to the close of the investigation each party shall submit in writing to the commission its single final offer containing its final proposals on all issues in dispute that are subject to interest arbitration under this subdivision. If a party fails to submit a single, ultimate final offer, the commission shall use the last written position of the party. Such final offers may include only mandatory subjects of bargaining, except that a permissive subject of bargaining may be included by a party if the other party does not object and is then treated as a mandatory subject. At that time, the parties shall submit to the commission a stipulation, in writing, with respect to all matters that they agree to include in the new or amended collective bargaining agreement. The commission, after determining that arbitration should be commenced, shall issue an order requiring arbitration and immediately submit to the parties a list of 7 arbitrators. The parties shall alternately strike names from the list until one name is left [and] that person shall be appointed arbitrator. The petitioning party shall notify the commission in writing of the identity of the arbitrator. The commission shall then formally appoint the arbitrator and submit to him or her the final offers of the parties. The final offers are public documents and the commission shall make them available. In lieu of a single arbitrator and upon request of both parties, the commission shall appoint a tripartite arbitration panel consisting of one member selected by each of the parties and a neutral person designated by the commission who shall serve as a chairperson. An arbitration panel has the same powers and duties provided in this section as any other appointed arbitrator, and all arbitration decisions by a panel shall be determined by majority vote. In lieu of selection of the arbitrator by the parties and upon request of both parties, the commission shall establish a procedure for randomly selecting names of arbitrators. Under the procedure, the commission shall submit a list of 7 arbitrators to the parties. Each party shall strike one name from the list. From the remaining 5 names, the commission shall randomly appoint an arbitrator. Unless both parties to an arbitration proceeding otherwise agree in writing, every individual whose name is submitted by the commission for appointment as an arbitrator must be a resident of this state at the time of submission and every individual who is designated as an arbitration panel chairperson must be a resident of this state at the time of designation.

b.    The arbitrator shall, within 10 days of his or her appointment under subd. 6. am., establish a date and place for the arbitration hearing. Upon petition of at least 5 citizens of the jurisdiction served by the municipal employer, filed within 10 days after the date on which the arbitrator is appointed, the arbitrator shall hold a public hearing in the jurisdiction to provide both parties the opportunity to present supporting arguments for their positions and to provide to members of the public the opportunity to offer their comments. The final offers of the parties, as transmitted by the commission to the arbitrator, are the basis for continued negotiations, if any, between the parties with respect to the issues in dispute. At any time prior to the arbitration hearing, either party, with the consent of the other party, may modify its final offer in writing.

c.    Before issuing his or her arbitration decision, the arbitrator shall, on his or her own motion or at the request of either party, conduct a meeting open to the public to provide the opportunity to both parties to present supporting arguments for their complete offer on all matters to be covered by the proposed agreement. The arbitrator shall adopt without further modification the final offer of one of the parties on all disputed issues submitted under subd. 6. am., except those items that the commission determines not to be mandatory subjects of bargaining and those items that have not been treated as mandatory subjects by the parties, and including any prior modifications of the offer mutually agreed upon by the parties under subd. 6. b. The decision shall be final and binding on both parties and shall be incorporated into a written collective bargaining agreement. The arbitrator shall serve a copy of his or her decision on both parties and the commission.

e.    Arbitration proceedings may not be interrupted or terminated by reason of any prohibited practice complaint filed by either party at any time.

f.    The parties shall divide the costs of arbitration equally. The arbitrator shall submit a statement of his or her costs to both parties and to the commission.

g.    If a question arises as to whether any proposal made in negotiations by either party is a mandatory, permissive, or prohibited subject of bargaining, the commission shall determine the issue under par. (b). If either party to the dispute petitions the commission for a declaratory ruling under par. (b), the proceedings under subd. 6. c. shall be delayed until the commission renders a decision in the matter, but not during any appeal of the commission order. The arbitrator's award shall be made in accordance with the commission's ruling, subject to automatic amendment by any subsequent court reversal.

7.    'Factor given greatest weight.' In making any decision under the arbitration procedures under this paragraph, the arbitrator or arbitration panel shall consider and shall give the greatest weight to the economic conditions in the jurisdiction of the municipal employer. The arbitrator or

arbitration panel shall give an accounting of the consideration of this factor in the arbitrator's or panel's decision.

7g. 'Factor given greater weight.' In making any decision under the arbitration procedures under this paragraph, the arbitrator or arbitration panel shall consider and shall give greater weight to any state law or directive lawfully issued by a state legislative or administrative officer, body, or agency that places limitations on expenditures that may be made or revenues that may be collected by a municipal employer than to any of the factors specified in subd. 7r.

7r. 'Other factors considered.' In making any decision under the arbitration procedures under this paragraph, the arbitrator or arbitration panel shall give weight to the following factors:

a.    The lawful authority of the municipal employer.

b.    Stipulations of the parties.

c.    The interests and welfare of the public and the financial ability of the unit of government to meet the costs of any proposed settlement.

d.    Comparison of wages, hours and conditions of employment of the transit employees involved in the arbitration proceedings with the wages, hours, and conditions of employment of other employees performing similar services.

e.    Comparison of the wages, hours and conditions of employment of the transit employees involved in the arbitration proceedings with the wages, hours, and conditions of employment of other employees generally in public employment in the same community and in comparable communities.

f.    Comparison of the wages, hours and conditions of employment of the transit employees involved in the arbitration proceedings with the wages, hours, and conditions of employment of other employees in private employment in the same community and in comparable communities.

g.    The average consumer prices for goods and services, commonly known as the cost of living.

h.    The overall compensation presently received by the transit employees, including direct wage compensation, vacation, holidays, and excused time, insurance and pensions, medical and hospitalization benefits, the continuity and stability of employment, and all other benefits received.

i.    Changes in any of the foregoing circumstances during the pendency of the arbitration proceedings.

j.    Such other factors, not confined to the foregoing, which are normally or traditionally taken into consideration in the determination of wages, hours and conditions of employment through voluntary collective bargaining, mediation, fact-finding, arbitration or otherwise between the parties, in the public service or in private employment.

8. 'Rule making.' The commission shall adopt rules for the conduct of all arbitration proceedings under subd. 6., including, but not limited to, rules for:

a. The appointment of tripartite arbitration panels when requested by the parties.

b. The expeditious rendering of arbitration decisions, such as waivers of briefs and transcripts.

c. The removal of individuals who have repeatedly failed to issue timely decisions from the commission's list of qualified arbitrators.

d. Proceedings for the enforcement of arbitration decisions. 8m. 'Term of agreement; reopening of negotiations.' Except for the initial collective bargaining agreement between the parties and except as the parties otherwise agree, every collective bargaining agreement covering transit employees shall be for a term of 2 years, but in no case may a collective bargaining agreement for any collective bargaining unit consisting of transit employees subject to this paragraph be for a term exceeding 3 years. No arbitration award involving transit employees may contain a provision for reopening of negotiations during the term of a collective bargaining agreement, unless both parties agree to such a provision. The requirement for agreement by both parties does not apply to a provision for reopening of negotiations with respect to any portion of an agreement that is declared invalid by a court or administrative agency or rendered invalid by the enactment of a law or promulgation of a federal regulation.

9. 'Application.' Chapter 788 does not apply to arbitration proceedings under this paragraph.

(cm) *Methods for peaceful settlement of disputes; general municipal employees.* 1. 'Notice of commencement of contract negotiations.' For the purpose of advising the commission of the commencement of contract negotiations involving a collective bargaining unit containing general municipal employees, whenever either party requests the other to reopen negotiations under a binding collective bargaining agreement, or the parties otherwise commence negotiations if no such agreement exists, the party requesting negotiations shall immediately notify the commission in writing. Upon failure of the requesting party to provide such notice, the other party may so notify the commission. The notice shall specify the expiration date of the existing collective bargaining agreement, if any, and shall set forth any additional information the commission may require on a form provided by the commission.

2.   'Presentation of initial proposals; open meetings.' The meetings between parties to a collective bargaining agreement or proposed collective bargaining agreement under this subchapter that involve a collective bargaining unit containing a general municipal employee and that are held for the purpose of presenting initial bargaining proposals, along with supporting rationale, shall be open to the public. Each party shall submit its initial bargaining proposals to the other party in writing. Failure to comply with this subdivision is not cause to invalidate a collective bargaining agreement under this subchapter.

3.   'Mediation.' The commission or its designee shall function as mediator in labor disputes involving general municipal employees upon request of one or both of the parties, or upon initiation of the commission. The function of the mediator shall be to encourage voluntary settlement by the parties. No mediator has the power of compulsion.

4.   'Grievance arbitration.' Parties to a dispute pertaining to the meaning or application of the terms of a written collective bargaining agreement involving a collective bargaining unit containing a general municipal employee may agree in writing to have the commission or any other appropriate agency serve as arbitrator or may designate any other competent, impartial and disinterested person to so serve.

8m. 'Term of agreement; reopening of negotiations.' Except for the initial collective bargaining agreement between the parties, every collective bargaining agreement covering general municipal employees shall be for a term of one year and may not be extended. No collective bargaining agreement covering general municipal employees may be reopened for negotiations unless both parties agree to reopen the collective bargaining agreement. The requirement for agreement by both parties does not apply to a provision for reopening of negotiations with respect to any portion of an agreement that is declared invalid by a court or administrative agency or rendered invalid by the enactment of a law or promulgation of a federal regulation.

(d) *Selection of representatives and determination of appropriate units for collective bargaining.* 1. A representative chosen for the purposes of collective bargaining by a majority of the municipal employees voting in a collective bargaining unit shall be the exclusive representative of all employees in the unit for the purpose of collective bargaining. Any individual employee, or any minority group of employees in any collective bargaining unit, shall have the right to present grievances to the municipal employer in person or through representatives of their own choosing, and the municipal employer shall confer with said employee in relation thereto, if the majority representative has been afforded the opportunity to be present at the conferences. Any adjustment resulting from these conferences shall not be inconsistent with the conditions of employment established by the majority representative and the municipal employer.

2. a. The commission shall determine the appropriate collective bargaining unit for the purpose of collective bargaining and shall whenever possible avoid fragmentation by maintaining as few collective bargaining units as practicable in keeping with the size of the total municipal workforce. The commission may decide whether, in a particular case, the municipal employees in the same or several departments, divisions, institutions, crafts, professions, or other occupational groupings constitute a collective bargaining unit. Before making its determination, the commission may provide an opportunity for the municipal employees concerned to determine, by secret ballot, whether they desire to be established as a separate collective bargaining unit. The commission may not decide, however, that any group of municipal employees constitutes an appropriate collective bargaining unit if the group includes both professional employees and nonprofessional employees, unless a majority of the professional employees vote for inclusion in the unit. The commission may not decide that any group of municipal employees constitutes an appropriate collective bargaining unit if the group includes both school district employees and general municipal employees who are not school district employees. The commission may not decide that any group of municipal employees constitutes an appropriate collective bargaining unit if the group includes both public safety employees and general municipal employees, if the group include includes both transit employees and general municipal employees, or if the group includes both transit employees and public safety employees. The commission may not decide that any group of municipal employees constitutes an appropriate collective bargaining unit if the group includes both craft employees and noncraft employees unless a majority of the craft employees vote for inclusion in the unit. The commission shall place the professional employees who are assigned to perform any services at a charter school, as defined in s. 115.001 (1), in a separate collective bargaining unit from a unit that includes any other professional employees whenever at least 30% of those professional employees request an election to be held to determine that issue and a majority of the professional employees at the charter school who cast votes in the election decide to be represented in a separate collective bargaining unit.

b. Any election held under subd. 2. a. shall be conducted by secret ballot taken in such a manner as to show separately the wishes of the employees voting as to the unit they prefer.

c. A collective bargaining unit shall be subject to termination or modification as provided in this subchapter.

d.   Nothing in this section shall be construed as prohibiting 2 or more collective bargaining units from bargaining collectively through the same representative.

3.   a. Whenever, in a particular case, a question arises concerning representation or appropriate unit, calling for a vote, the commission shall certify the results in writing to the municipal employer and the labor organization involved and to any other interested parties.

b.   Annually, the commission shall conduct an election to certify the representative of the collective bargaining unit that contains a general municipal employee. The election shall occur no later than December 1 for a collective bargaining unit containing school district employees and no later than May 1 for a collective bargaining unit containing general municipal employees who are not school district employees. The commission shall certify any representative that receives at least 51 percent of the votes of all of the general municipal employees in the collective bargaining unit. If no representative receives at least 51 percent of the votes of all of the general municipal employees in the collective bargaining unit, at the expiration of the collective bargaining agreement, the commission shall decertify the current representative and the general municipal employees shall be nonrepresented. Notwithstanding sub. (2), if a representative is decertified under this subd. 3. b., the affected general municipal employees may not be included in a substantially similar collective bargaining unit for 12 months from the date of decertification. The commission shall assess and collect a certification fee for each election conducted under this subd. 3. b. Fees collected under this subd. 3. b. shall be credited to the appropriation account under s. 20.425 (1) (i).

c.   Any ballot used in a representation proceeding under this subdivision shall include the names of all persons having an interest in representing or the results. The ballot should be so designed as to permit a vote against representation by any candidate named on the ballot. The findings of the commission, on which a certification is based, shall be conclusive unless reviewed as provided by s. 111.07 (8).

4.   Whenever the result of an election conducted pursuant to subd. 3. is inconclusive, the commission, on request of any party to the proceeding, may conduct a runoff election. Any such request must be made within 30 days from the date of certification. In a runoff election the commission may drop from the ballot the name of the candidate or choice receiving the least number of votes.

5.   Questions as to representation may be raised by petition of the municipal employer or any municipal employee or any representative thereof. Where it appears by the petition that a situation exists requiring prompt action so as to prevent or terminate an emergency, the

commission shall act upon the petition forthwith. The fact that an election has been held shall not prevent the holding of another election among the same group of employees, if it appears to the commission that sufficient reason for another election exists.

(jm) *Binding arbitration, first class cities.* This paragraph shall apply only to members of a police department employed by cities of the 1st class. If the representative of members of the police department, as determined under par. (d), and representatives of the city reach an impasse on the terms of the agreement, the dispute shall be resolved in the following manner:

1. Either the representative of the members of the police department or the representative of the city may petition the commission for appointment of an arbitrator to determine the terms of the agreement relating to the wages, hours and working conditions of the members of the police department and other matters subject to arbitration under subd. 4.

2. The commission shall conduct a hearing on the petition, and upon a determination that the parties have reached an impasse on matters relating to wages, hours and conditions of employment or other matters subject to arbitration under subd. 4. on which there is no mutual agreement, the commission shall appoint an arbitrator to determine those terms of the agreement on which there is no mutual agreement. The commission may appoint any person it deems qualified, except that the arbitrator may not be a resident of the city which is party to the dispute.

3. Within 14 days of the arbitrator's appointment, the arbitrator shall conduct a hearing to determine the terms of the agreement relating to wages, hours and working conditions and other matters subject to arbitration under subd. 4. The arbitrator may subpoena witnesses at the request of either party or on the arbitrator's own motion. All testimony shall be given under oath. The arbitrator shall take judicial notice of all economic and social data presented by the parties which is relevant to the wages, hours and working conditions of the police department members or other matters subject to arbitration under subd. 4. The other party shall have an opportunity to examine and respond to such data. The rules of evidence applicable to a contested case, as defined in s. 227.01 (3), shall apply to the hearing before the arbitrator.

4. In determining those terms of the agreement on which there is no mutual agreement and on which the parties have negotiated to impasse, as determined by the commission, the arbitrator, without restriction because of enumeration, shall have the power to:

a. Set all items of compensation, including base wages, longevity pay, health, accident and disability insurance programs, pension programs, including amount of pension, relative contributions, and all eligibility conditions, the terms and conditions of overtime compensation and compensatory time, vacation pay, and vacation eligibility, sickness pay amounts, and sickness pay eligibility, life insurance, uniform allowances and any other similar item of compensation.

b.    Determine regular hours of work, what activities shall constitute overtime work and all standards and criteria for the assignment and scheduling of work.

c.    Determine a seniority system, and how seniority shall affect wages, hours and working conditions.

d.    Determine a promotional program.

e.    Determine criteria for merit increases in compensation and the procedures for applying such criteria.

f.    Determine all work rules affecting the members of the police department, except those work rules created by law.

g.    Establish any educational program for the members of the police department deemed appropriate, together with a mechanism for financing the program.

h.    Establish a system for resolving all disputes under the agreement, including final and binding 3rd-party arbitration.

i.    Determine the duration of the agreement and the members of the department to which it shall apply.

j.    Establish a system for administration of the collective bargaining agreement between the parties by an employee of the police department who is not directly accountable to the chief of police or the board of fire and police commissioners in matters relating to that administration.

k.    Establish a system for conducting interrogations of members of the police department that is limited to the hours between 7 a.m. and 5 p.m. on working days, as defined in s. 227.01 (14), if the interrogations could lead to disciplinary action, demotion, or dismissal, but one that does not apply if the interrogation is part of a criminal investigation.

4w.  In determining the proper compensation to be received by members of the police department under subd. 4., the arbitrator shall give greater weight to the economic conditions in the 1st class city than the arbitrator gives to the factors under subd. 5. The arbitrator shall give an accounting of the consideration of this factor in the arbitrator's decision.

5.    In determining the proper compensation to be received by members of the police department under subd. 4., in addition to the factor under subd. 4w., the arbitrator shall utilize:

a.    The most recently published U.S. bureau of labor statistics "Standards of Living Budgets for Urban Families, Moderate and Higher

Level", as a guideline to determine the compensation necessary for members to enjoy a standard of living commensurate with their needs, abilities and responsibilities; and

b.    Increases in the cost of living as measured by the average annual increases in the U.S. bureau of labor statistics "Consumer Price Index" since the last adjustment in compensation for those members.

6.    In determining all noncompensatory working conditions and relationships under subd. 4., including methods for resolving disputes under the labor agreement, the arbitrator shall consider the patterns of employee–employer relationships generally prevailing between technical and professional employees and their employers in both the private and public sectors of the economy where those relationships have been established by a labor agreement between the representative of those employees and their employer.

7.    All subjects described in subd. 4. shall be negotiable between the representative of the members of the police department and the city.

8.    Within 30 days after the close of the hearing, the arbitrator shall issue a written decision determining the terms of the agreement between the parties which were not the subject of mutual agreement and on which the parties negotiated in good faith to impasse, as determined by the commission, and which were the subject of the hearing under this paragraph. The arbitrator shall state reasons for each determination. Each proposition or fact accepted by the arbitrator must be established by a preponderance of the evidence.

9.    Subject to subds. 11. and 12., within 14 days of the arbitrator's decision, the parties shall reduce to writing the total agreement composed of those items mutually agreed to between the parties and the determinations of the arbitrator. The document shall be signed by the arbitrator and the parties, unless either party seeks judicial review of the determination pursuant to subd. 11.

10.    All costs of the arbitration hearing, including the arbitrator's fee, shall be borne equally by the parties.

11.    Within 60 days of the arbitrator's decision, either party may petition the circuit court for Milwaukee County to set aside or enforce the arbitrator's decision. If the decision was within the subject matter jurisdiction of the arbitrator as set forth in subd. 4., the court must enforce the decision, unless the court finds by a clear preponderance of the evidence that the decision was procured by fraud, bribery or collusion. The court may not review the sufficiency of the evidence supporting the arbitrator's determination of the terms of the agreement.

12. Within 30 days of a final court judgment, the parties shall reduce the agreement to writing and with the arbitrator execute the agreement pursuant to subd. 9.

13. Subsequent to the filing of a petition before the commission pursuant to subd. 1. and prior to the execution of an agreement pursuant to subd. 9., neither party may unilaterally alter any term of the wages, hours and working conditions of the members of the police department or any other matter subject to arbitration under subd. 4.

(L) *Strikes prohibited.* Nothing contained in this subchapter constitutes a grant of the right to strike by any municipal employee or labor organization, and such strikes are hereby expressly prohibited.

(mb) *Prohibited subjects of bargaining; general municipal employees.* The municipal employer is prohibited from bargaining collectively with a collective bargaining unit containing a general municipal employee with respect to any of the following:

1. Any factor or condition of employment except wages, which includes only total base wages and excludes any other compensation, which includes, but is not limited to, overtime, premium pay, merit pay, performance pay, supplemental compensation, pay schedules, and automatic pay progressions.

2. Except as provided in s. 66.0506 or 118.245, whichever is applicable, any proposal that does any of the following:

a. If there is an increase in the consumer price index change, provides for total base wages for authorized positions in the proposed collective bargaining agreement that exceeds the total base wages for authorized positions 180 days before the expiration of the previous collective bargaining agreement by a greater percentage than the consumer price index change.

b. If there is a decrease or no change in the consumer price index change, provides for any change in total base wages for authorized positions in the proposed collective bargaining agreement from the total base wages for authorized positions 180 days before the expiration of the previous collective bargaining agreement.

(mbb) For purposes of determining compliance with par. (mb), the commission shall provide, upon request, to a municipal employer or to any representative of a collective bargaining unit containing a general municipal employee, the consumer price index change during any 12–month period. The commission may get the information from the department of revenue.

(mc) *Prohibited subjects of bargaining; public safety employees.* The municipal employer is prohibited from bargaining collectively with a collective bargaining unit containing a public safety employee with respect to any of the following:

5. If the collective bargaining unit contains a public safety employee who is initially employed on or after July 1, 2011, the requirement under ss. 40.05 (1) (b), 59.875, and 62.623 that the municipal employer may not pay, on behalf of that public safety employee any employee required contributions or the employee share of required contributions, and the impact of this requirement on the wages, hours, and conditions of employment of that public safety employee. If a public safety employee is initially employed by a municipal employer before July 1, 2011, this subdivision does not apply to that public safety employee if he or she is employed as a public safety employee by a successor municipal employer in the event of a combined department that is created on or after that date.

6. Except for the employee premium contribution, all costs and payments associated with health care coverage plans and the design and selection of health care coverage plans by the municipal employer for public safety employees, and the impact of such costs and payments and the design and selection of the health care coverage plans on the wages, hours, and conditions of employment of the public safety employee.

(p) *Permissive subjects of collective bargaining; public safety and transit employees.* A municipal employer is not required to bargain with public safety employees or transit employees on subjects reserved to management and direction of the governmental unit except insofar as the manner of exercise of such functions affects the wages, hours, and conditions of employment of the public safety employees or of the transit employees in a collective bargaining unit.

**(5)** PROCEDURES.

Municipal employers, jointly or individually, may employ a qualified person to discharge the duties of labor negotiator and to represent such municipal employers, jointly or individually, in conferences and negotiations under this section. In cities of the 1st, 2nd or 3rd class any member of the city council, including the mayor, who resigns therefrom may, during the term for which the member is elected, be eligible to the position of labor negotiator under this subsection, which position during said term has been created by or the selection to which is vested in such city council, and s. 66.0501 (2) shall be deemed inapplicable thereto.

**(7m)** INJUNCTIVE RELIEF; PENALTIES; CIVIL LIABILITY. (a)

*Injunction; prohibited strike.* At any time after the commencement of a strike which is prohibited under sub. (4) (*l* ), the municipal employer or any citizen directly affected by such strike may petition the circuit court for an injunction to immediately terminate the strike. If the court determines that the strike is prohibited under sub. (4) (*l* ), it shall issue an order immediately enjoining the strike, and in addition shall impose the penalties provided in par. (c).

(c) *Penalties.* 1. 'Labor organizations.' a. Any labor organization that represents public safety employees or transit employees which violates sub. (4) (*l* ) may not collect any dues under a collective bargaining agreement or under a fair-share agreement from any employee covered by either agreement for a period of one year. At the end of the period of suspension, any such agreement shall be reinstated unless the labor organization is no longer authorized to represent the public safety employees or transit employees covered by the collective bargaining agreement or fair-share agreement or the agreement is no longer in effect.

b. Any labor organization which violates sub. (4) (*l* ) after an injunction has been issued shall be required to forfeit $2 per member per day, but not more than $10,000 per day. Each day of continued violation constitutes a separate offense.

2. 'Individuals.' Any individual who violates sub. (4) (*l* ) after an injunction against a strike has been issued shall be fined $10. Each day of continued violation constitutes a separate offense. After the injunction has been issued, any municipal employee who is absent from work because of purported illness is presumed to be on strike unless the illness is verified by a written report from a physician to the municipal employer. The court shall order that any fine imposed under this subdivision be paid by means of a salary deduction at a rate to be determined by the court.

4. 'Contempt of court.' The penalties provided in this paragraph do not preclude the imposition by the court of any penalty for contempt provided by law.

(d) *Compensation forfeited.* No municipal employee may be paid wages or salaries by the municipal employer for the period during which he or she engages in any strike.

**(8)** SUPERVISORY UNITS. (a) This section, except sub. (4) (cg) and (cm), applies to law enforcement supervisors employed by a 1st class city. This section, except sub. (4) (cm) and (jm), applies to law enforcement supervisors employed by a county having a population of 500,000 or more. For purposes of such application, the terms "municipal employee" and "public safety employee" include such a supervisor.

(b) This subchapter does not preclude law enforcement supervisors employed by municipal employers other than 1st class cities and counties having a population of 500,000 or more or fire fighting supervisors from organizing in separate units of supervisors for the purpose of negotiating with their municipal employers.

(c) The commission shall by rule establish procedures for certification of such units of supervisors and the levels of supervisors to be included in the units. Supervisors may not be members of the same bargaining unit of which their subordinates are members. The commission may require that the representative of any supervisory unit shall be an organization that is a separate local entity from the representative of the nonsupervisory municipal employees, but such requirement does not prevent affiliation by a supervisory representative with the same parent state or national organization as the nonsupervisory municipal employee representative.

**(9)** POWERS OF CHIEF OF POLICE. Nothing in s. 62.50 grants the chief of police in cities of the 1st class any authority which diminishes or in any other manner affects the rights of municipal employees who are members of a police department employed by a city of the 1st class under this section or under any collective bargaining agreement which is entered into between a city of the 1st class and a labor organization representing the members of its police department.

**111.71  General provisions. (1)** The commission may adopt reasonable rules relative to the exercise of its powers and authority and proper rules to govern its proceedings and to regulate the conduct of all elections and hearings. The commission shall, upon request, provide a transcript of a proceeding to any party to the proceeding for a fee, established by rule, by the commission at a uniform rate per page. All transcript fees shall be credited to the appropriation account under s. 20.425 (1) (i).

**(2)** The commission shall assess and collect a filing fee for filing a complaint alleging that a prohibited practice has been committed under s. 111.70 (3). The commission shall assess and collect a filing fee for filing a request that the commission act as an arbitrator to resolve a dispute involving the interpretation or application of a collective bargaining agreement under s. 111.70 (4) (c) 2., (cg) 4., or (cm) 4. The commission shall assess and collect a filing fee for filing a request that the commission initiate fact-finding under s. 111.70 (4) (c) 3. The commission shall assess and collect a filing fee for filing a request that the commission act as a mediator under s. 111.70 (4) (c) 1., (cg) 3., or (cm) 3. The commission shall assess and collect a filing fee for filing a request that the commission initiate compulsory, final and binding arbitration under s. 111.70 (4) (cg) 6. or (jm) or 111.77 (3). For the performance of commission actions under ss. 111.70 (4) (c) 1., 2. and 3., (cg) 3., 4., and 6., (cm) 3. and 4., and (jm) and 111.77 (3), the commission shall require that the parties to the dispute equally share in the payment of the fee and, for the performance of commission actions involving a complaint alleging that a prohibited practice has been committed under s. 111.70 (3), the commission shall require that the party filing the complaint pay the entire fee. If any party has paid a filing fee requesting the commission to act as a mediator for a labor dispute and the parties do not enter into a voluntary settlement of the dispute, the commission may not subsequently assess or collect a filing fee to initiate fact-finding or arbitration to resolve the same labor dispute. If any request for the performance of commission actions concerns issues arising as a result of more than one unrelated event or occurrence, each such separate event or occurrence shall be treated as a separate request. The commission shall promulgate rules establishing a schedule of filing fees to be paid under this subsection. Fees required to be paid under this subsection shall be paid at the time of filing the complaint or the request for fact-finding, mediation or arbitration. A complaint or request for fact-finding, mediation or arbitration is not filed until the date such fee or fees are paid, except that the failure of the respondent party to pay the filing fee for having the commission initiate compulsory, final and binding arbitration under s. 111.70 (4) (cg) 6. or (jm) or 111.77 (3) may not prohibit the commission from initiating such arbitration. The commission may initiate collection proceedings against the respondent party for the payment of the filing fee. Fees collected under this subsection shall be credited to the appropriation account under s. 20.425 (1) (i).

**(4m)** The commission shall collect on a systematic basis information on the operation of the arbitration law under s. 111.70 (4) (cg). The commission shall report on the operation of the law to the legislature on an annual basis. The report shall be submitted to the chief clerk of each house of the legislature for distribution to the legislature under s. 13.172 (2).

**(5m)** The commission shall, on a regular basis, provide training programs to prepare individuals for service as arbitrators or arbitration panel members under s. 111.70 (4) (cg). The commission shall engage in appropriate promotional and recruitment efforts to encourage participation in the training programs by individuals throughout the state, including at least 10 residents of each congressional district. The commission may also provide training programs to individuals and organizations on other aspects of collective bargaining, including on areas of management and labor cooperation directly or indirectly affecting collective bargaining. The commission may charge a reasonable fee for participation in the programs.

**(6)** This subchapter may be cited as "Municipal Employment Relations Act".

**111.77 Settlement of disputes.** Municipal employers and public safety employees, as provided in sub. (8), have the duty to bargain collectively in good faith including the duty to refrain from strikes or lockouts and to comply with the following:

**(1)** If a contract is in effect, the duty to bargain collectively means that a party to such contract shall not terminate or modify such contract unless the party desiring such termination or modification:

(a) Serves written notice upon the other party to the contract of the proposed termination or modification 180 days prior to the expiration date thereof or, if the contract contains no expiration date, 60 days prior to the time it is proposed to make such termination or modification. This paragraph shall not apply to negotiations initiated or occurring in 1971.

(b) Offers to meet and confer with the other party for the purpose of negotiating a new contract or a contract containing the proposed modifications.

(c) Notifies the commission within 90 days after the notice provided for in par. (a) of the existence of a dispute.

(d) Continues in full force and effect without resorting to strike or lockout all terms and conditions of the existing contract for a period of 60 days after such notice is given or until the expiration date of the contract, whichever occurs later.

(e) Participates in mediation sessions by the commission or its representatives if specifically requested to do so by the commission.

(f) Participates in procedures, including binding arbitration, agreed to between the parties.

**(2)** If there has never been a contract in effect, the union shall notify the commission within 30 days after the first demand upon the employer of the existence of a dispute provided no agreement is reached by that time, and in such case sub. (1) (b), (e) and (f) shall apply.

**(3)** Where the parties have no procedures for disposition of a dispute and an impasse has been reached, either party may petition the commission to initiate compulsory, final and binding arbitration of the dispute. If in determining whether an impasse has been reached the commission finds that any of the procedures set forth in sub. (1) have not been complied with and that compliance would tend to result in a settlement, it may require such compliance as a prerequisite to ordering arbitration. If after such procedures have been complied with or the commission has determined that compliance would not be productive of a settlement and the commission determines that an impasse has been reached, it shall issue an order requiring arbitration. The commission shall in connection with the order for arbitration submit a panel of 5 arbitrators from which the parties may alternately strike names until a single name is left, who shall be appointed by the commission as arbitrator, whose expenses shall be shared equally between the parties. Arbitration proceedings under this section shall not be interrupted or terminated by reason of any prohibited practice charge filed by either party at any time.

**(4)** There shall be 2 alternative forms of arbitration:

(a) *Form 1.* The arbitrator shall have the power to determine all issues in dispute involving wages, hours and conditions of employment.

(b) *Form 2.* The commission shall appoint an investigator to determine the nature of the impasse. The commission's investigator shall advise the commission in writing, transmitting copies of such advice to the parties of each issue which is known to be in dispute. Such advice shall also set forth the final offer of each party as it is known to the investigator at the time that the investigation is closed. Neither party may amend its final offer thereafter, except with the written agreement of the other party. The arbitrator shall select the final offer of one of the parties and shall issue an award incorporating that offer without modification.

**(5)** The proceedings shall be pursuant to form 2 unless the parties shall agree prior to the hearing that form 1 shall control.

**(6)** (am) In reaching a decision, the arbitrator shall give greater weight to the economic conditions in the jurisdiction of the municipal employer than the arbitrator gives to the factors under par. (bm). The arbitrator shall give an accounting of the consideration of this factor in the arbitrator's decision.

(bm) In reaching a decision, in addition to the factors under par. (am), the arbitrator shall give weight to the following factors:

1.   The lawful authority of the employer.

2.   Stipulations of the parties.

3.   The interests and welfare of the public and the financial ability of the unit of government to meet these costs.

4.   Comparison of the wages, hours and conditions of employment of the employees involved in the arbitration proceeding with the wages, hours and conditions of employment of other employees performing similar services and with other employees generally:

a.   In public employment in comparable communities.

b.   In private employment in comparable communities.

5.   The average consumer prices for goods and services, commonly known as the cost of living.

6.   The overall compensation presently received by the employees, including direct wage compensation, vacation, holidays and excused time,

insurance and pensions, medical and hospitalization benefits, the continuity and stability of employment, and all other benefits received.

7. Changes in any of the foregoing circumstances during the pendency of the arbitration proceedings.

8. Such other factors, not confined to the foregoing, which are normally or traditionally taken into consideration in the determination of wages, hours and conditions of employment through voluntary collective bargaining, mediation, fact-finding, arbitration or otherwise between the parties, in the public service or in private employment.

**(7)** Proceedings, except as specifically provided in this section, shall be governed by ch. 788.

**(8)** (a) This section applies to public safety employees who are supervisors employed by a county having a population of 500,000 or more. For purposes of such application, the term "municipal employee" includes such a supervisor.

(b) This section shall not apply to members of a police department employed by a 1st class city nor to any city, village or town having a population of less than 2,500.

**(9)** Section 111.70 (4) (c) 3., (cg), and (cm) does not apply to employments covered by this section.

# INDIANA CODE PROVISIONS CRIMINALIZING COLLECTIVE BARGAINING BY PUBLIC EMPLOYEES

## (ENACTED AS PART OF THE 2011 STATE BUDGET)

■ ■ ■

Indiana Code Title 4 Article 15 Chapter 17 §§ 1–10

IC 4-15-17-1 to IC 4-15-17-10
(Effective: July 1, 2011)

### Employee Organizations

### § 1 Applicability of Chapter

Sec. 1. (a) Except as provided in subsection (b), this chapter does not apply to the following:

    (1)  The state police department.

    (2)  A state educational institution (as defined in IC 21-7-13-32).

    (3)  A political subdivision (as defined in IC 3-5-2-38).

    (b) Sections 8, 9, and 10 of this chapter apply to the state police department.

### § 2 "Employee Organization" Defined

Sec. 2. As used in this chapter, "employee organization" means an entity that works in whole or in part for the common interest of employees.

### § 3 "State" Defined

Sec. 3. (a) As used in this chapter, "state" means any of the following:

    (1)  A department, commission, division, authority, board, bureau, or office of state government that exercises any executive powers.

### § 4 Illegal Activities

Sec. 4. Collective bargaining between the state and employee organizations and strikes by state employees are illegal.

## § 5 Prohibited Activities by State

Sec. 5. The state shall not:

(1)  recognize a union or any other employee organization as a representative of the employees of the state;

(2)  bargain collectively with an employee organization;

(3)  enter into a collectively bargained agreement; or

(4)  require an employee to join or financially support an employee organization.

## § 6 Allowable aActivities by Employees

Sec. 6. An employee of the state is entitled to do any of the following in a manner that does not interfere with the performance of the duties of the employee or of another employee of the state or adversely affect the conduct of state business:

(1)  Be a member of or otherwise associate with an employee organization.

(2)  Consult with others for the common good of employees.

(3)  Financially support an employee organization.

(4)  Petition for the redress of grievances.

## § 7 Devices Contrary to Public Policy

Sec. 7.   Any contract, agreement, settlement, conditions of cooperation, or any other device resulting from negotiations between:

(1)  the state; and

(2)  an employee organization;

is contrary to public policy and is illegal, unenforceable, void, and of no effect.

## § 8 Prohibition Against Strike by Public Employees

Sec. 8.   (a) As used in this section, "strike" means any of the following:

(1)  A work stoppage or partial cessation of work.

(2)  The abstinence, in whole or in part, from the full, faithful, and proper performance of the employee's duties of employment.

(3)  Any other interruption or interference with the activities of the state.

(4)  The threat or encouragement of the activities described in subdivisions (1) through

(b)  An employee of the state shall not strike.

(c)  An approved leave of absence or the unconditional resignation of an employee from employment is not a strike.

## § 9  Violations of Chapter

Sec. 9.    A person who violates this chapter commits a Class C infraction. A court may assess damages against a person who violates this chapter, in addition to any civil penalties that are imposed.

## § 10    Relationship Between State Police Department and State Police Alliance

Sec. 10. This chapter does not alter, impair, or negate the existing relationship between the state police department and the Indiana state police alliance.

# WORKER ADJUSTMENT AND RETRAINING NOTIFICATION ACT OF 1988

■ ■ ■

102 Stat. 890 (1988), 29 U.S.C. §§ 2101–2109

## § 2101. Definitions; Exclusions From Definition of Loss of Employment

Definitions

As used in this chapter—

(1) the term "employer" means any business enterprise that employs—

(A) 100 or more employees, excluding part-time employees; or

(B) 100 or more employees who in the aggregate work at least 4,000 hours per week (exclusive of hours of overtime);

(2) the term "plant closing" means the permanent or temporary shutdown of a single site of employment, or one or more facilities or operating units within a single site of employment, if the shutdown results in an employment loss at the single site of employment during any 30-day period for 50 or more employees excluding any part-time employees

(3) the term "mass layoff" means a reduction in force which—

(A) is not the result of a plant closing; and

(B) results in an employment loss at the single site of employment during any 30 day period for—(i)(I) at least 33 percent of the employees (excluding any part-time employees); and

(II) at least 50 employees (excluding any part-time employees); or

(ii) at least 500 employees (excluding any part-time employees);

(4) the term "representative" means an exclusive representative of employees within the meaning of section 159(a) or 158(f) of this title or section 152 of Title 45;

(5) the term "affected employees" means employees who may reasonably be expected to experience an employment loss as a consequence of a proposed plant closing or mass layoff by their employer;

229

(6) subject to subsection (b) of this section, the term "employment loss" means (A) an employment termination, other than a discharge for cause, voluntary departure, or retirement, (B) a layoff exceeding 6 months, or (C) a reduction in hours of work of more than 50 percent during each month of any 6 month period;

(7) the term "unit of local government" means any general purpose political subdivision of a State which has the power to levy taxes and spend funds, as well as general corporate and police powers; and

(8) the term "part-time employee" means an employee who is employed for an average of fewer than 20 hours per week or who has been employed for fewer than 6 of the 12 months preceding the date on which notice is required.

(b) Exclusions from definition of employment loss

(1) In the case of a sale of part or all of an employer's business, the seller shall be responsible for providing notice for any plant closing or mass layoff in accordance with section 2102 of this title, up to and including the effective date of the sale. After the effective date of the sale of part or all of an employer's business, the purchaser shall be responsible for providing notice for any plant closing or mass layoff in accordance with section 2102 of this title. Notwithstanding any other provision of this chapter, any person who is an employee of the seller (other than a part-time employee) as of the effective date of the sale shall be considered an employee of the purchaser immediately after the effective date of the sale.

(2) Notwithstanding subsection (a)(6) of this section, an employee may not be considered to have experienced an employment loss if the closing or layoff is the result of the relocation or consolidation of part or all of the employer's business and, prior to the closing or layoff—

(A) the employer offers to transfer the employee to a different site of employment within a reasonable commuting distance with no more than a 6–month break in employment; or

(B) the employer offers to transfer the employee to any other site of employment regardless of distance with no more than a 6–month break in employment, and the employee accepts within 30 days of the offer or of the closing or layoff, whichever is later.

## § 2102. Notice Required Before Plant Closings and Mass Layoffs

(a) Notice to employees, State dislocated worker units, and local governments

An employer shall not order a plant closing or mass layoff until the end of a 60-day period after the employer serves written notice of such an order—

(1) to each representative of the affected employees as of the time of the notice or, if there is no such representative at that time, to each affected employee; and

(2) to the State or entity designated by the State to carry out rapid response activities under section 2864(a)(2)(A) of this title, and the chief elected official of the unit of local government within which such closing or layoff is to occur.

If there is more than one such unit, the unit of local government which the employer shall notify is the unit of local government to which the employer pays the highest taxes for the year preceding the year for which the determination is made.

(b) Reduction of notification period

(1) An employer may order the shutdown of a single site of employment before the conclusion of the 60-day period if as of the time that notice would have been required the employer was actively seeking capital or business which, if obtained, would have enabled the employer to avoid or postpone the shutdown and the employer reasonably and in good faith believed that giving the notice required would have precluded the employer from obtaining the needed capital or business.

(2)(A) An employer may order a plant closing or mass layoff before the conclusion of the 60-day period if the closing or mass layoff is caused by business circumstances that were not reasonably foreseeable as of the time that notice would have been required.

(B) No notice under this chapter shall be required if the plant closing or mass layoff is due to any form of natural disaster, such as a flood, earthquake, or the drought currently ravaging the farmlands of the United States.

(3) An employer relying on this subsection shall give as much notice as is practicable and at that time shall give a brief statement of the basis for reducing the notification period.

(c) Extension of layoff period

A layoff of more than 6 months which, at its outset, was announced to be a layoff of 6 months or less, shall be treated as an employment loss under this chapter unless—

(1) the extension beyond 6 months is caused by business circumstances (including unforeseeable changes in price or cost) not reasonably foreseeable at the time of the initial layoff; and

(2) notice is given at the time it becomes reasonably foreseeable that the extension beyond 6 months will be required.

(d) Determinations with respect to employment loss

For purposes of this section, in determining whether a plant closing or mass layoff has occurred or will occur, employment losses for 2 or more groups at a single site of employment, each of which is less than the minimum number of employees specified in section 2101(a)(2) or (3) of this title but which in the aggregate exceed that minimum number, and which occur within any 90-day period shall be considered to be a plant closing or mass layoff unless the employer demonstrates that the employment losses are the result of separate and distinct actions and causes and are not an attempt by the employer to evade the requirements of this chapter.

## § 2103. Exemptions

This chapter shall not apply to a plant closing or mass layoff if—

(1) the closing is of a temporary facility or the closing or layoff is the result of the completion of a particular project or undertaking, and the affected employees were hired with the understanding that their employment was limited to the duration of the facility or the project or undertaking; or

(2) the closing or layoff constitutes a strike or constitutes a lockout not intended to evade the requirements of this chapter. Nothing in this chapter shall require an employer to serve written notice pursuant to section 2102(a) of this title when permanently replacing a person who is deemed to be an economic striker under the National Labor Relations Act [29 U.S.C. §§ 151 et seq.]: Provided, That nothing in this chapter shall be deemed to validate or invalidate any judicial or administrative ruling relating to the hiring of permanent replacements for economic strikers under the National Labor Relations Act.

## § 2104. Administration and Enforcement of Requirements

(a) Civil actions against employers

(1) Any employer who orders a plant closing or mass layoff in violation of section 2102 of this title shall be liable to each aggrieved employee who suffers an employment loss as a result of such closing or layoff for—

(A) back pay for each day of violation at a rate of compensation not less than the higher of—

(i) the average regular rate received by such employee during the last 3 years of the employee's employment; or

(ii) the final regular rate received by such employee; and

(B) benefits under an employee benefit plan described in section 1002(3) of this title, including the cost of medical expenses incurred during the employment loss which would have been covered under an employee benefit plan if the employment loss had not occurred.

Such liability shall be calculated for the period of the violation, up to a maximum of 60 days, but in no event for more than one-half the number of days the employee was employed by the employer.

(2) The amount for which an employer is liable under paragraph (1) shall be reduced by—

(A) any wages paid by the employer to the employee for the period of the violation;

(B) any voluntary and unconditional payment by the employer to the employee that is not required by any legal obligation; and

(C) any payment by the employer to a third party or trustee (such as premiums for health benefits or payments to a defined contribution pension plan) on behalf of and attributable to the employee for the period of the violation.

In addition, any liability incurred under paragraph (1) with respect to a defined benefit pension plan may be reduced by crediting the employee with service for all purposes under such a plan for the period of the violation.

(3) Any employer who violates the provisions of section 2102 of this title with respect to a unit of local government shall be subject to a civil penalty of not more than $500 for each day of such violation, except that such penalty shall not apply if the employer pays to each aggrieved employee the amount for which the employer is liable to that employee within 3 weeks from the date the employer orders the shutdown or layoff.

(4) If an employer which has violated this chapter proves to the satisfaction of the court that the act or omission that violated this chapter was in good faith and that he employer had reasonable grounds for believing that the act or omission was not a violation of this chapter the court may, in its discretion, reduce the amount of the liability or penalty provided for in this section.

(5) A person seeking to enforce such liability, including a representative of employees or a unit of local government aggrieved under paragraph (1) or (3), may sue either for such person or for other persons similarly situated, or both, in any district court of the United States for any district in which the violation is alleged to have occurred, or in which the employer transacts business.

(6) In any such suit, the court, in its discretion, may allow the prevailing party a reasonable attorney's fee as part of the costs.

(7) For purposes of this subsection, the term, "aggrieved employee" means an employee who has worked for the employer ordering the

plant closing or mass layoff and who, as a result of the failure by the employer to comply with section 2102 of this title, did not receive timely notice either directly or through his or her representative as required by section 2102 of this title.

(b) Exclusivity of remedies

The remedies provided for in this section shall be the exclusive remedies for any violation of this chapter. Under this chapter, a Federal court shall not have authority to enjoin a plant closing or mass layoff.

## § 2105. Procedures in Addition to Other Rights of Employees

The rights and remedies provided to employees by this chapter are in addition to, and not in lieu of, any other contractual or statutory rights and remedies of the employees, and are not intended to alter or affect such rights and remedies, except that the period of notification required by this chapter shall run concurrently with any period of notification required by contract or by any other statute.

## § 2106. Procedures Encouraged Where Not Required

It is the sense of Congress that an employer who is not required to comply with the notice requirements of section 2102 of this title should, to the extent possible, provide notice to its employees about a proposal to close a plant or permanently reduce its workforce.

## § 2107. Authority to Prescribe Regulations

(a) The Secretary of Labor shall prescribe such regulations as may be necessary to carry out this chapter. Such regulations shall, at a minimum, include interpretative regulations describing the methods by which employers may provide for appropriate service of notice as required by this chapter.

(b) The mailing of notice to an employee's last known address or inclusion of notice in the employee's paycheck will be considered acceptable methods for fulfillment of the employer's obligation to give notice to each affected employee under this chapter.

## § 2108. Effect on Other Laws

The giving of notice pursuant to this chapter, if done in good faith compliance with this chapter, shall not constitute a violation of the National Labor Relations Act [29 U.S.C. §§ 151 et seq.] or the Railway Labor Act [45 U.S.C. §§ 151 et seq.].

## § 2109. Report    on    Employment    and    International Competitiveness

Two years after August 4, 1988, the Comptroller General shall submit to the Committee on Small Business of both the House and Senate, the Committee on Labor and Human Resources, and the Committee on Education and Labor a report containing a detailed and objective analysis of the effect of this chapter on employers (especially small and medium-sized businesses), the economy (international competitiveness), and employees (in terms of levels and conditions of employment). The Comptroller General shall assess both costs and benefits, including the effect on productivity, competitiveness, unemployment rates and compensation, and worker retraining and readjustment.

# SELECTED STATISTICS ON UNION DENSITY AND BOARD PROCESSES

■ ■ ■

Figure 1. Union Density in the Private Sector and Public Sector, Average Percentage for Each Four Year Period, Fiscal Years 1929-2007

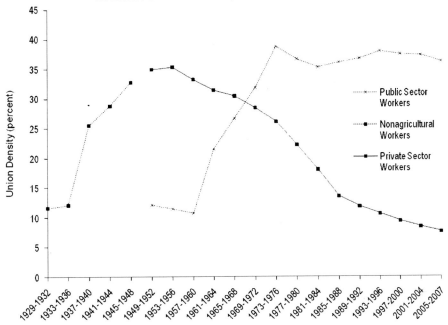

*Sources*: Richard B. Freeman, *Spurts in Union Growth: Defining Moments and Social Processes* (Nat'l Bureau of Econ. Research, Working Paper No. 6012, 1997); Leo Troy & Neil Sheflin, Union Sourcebook: Membership, Finances, Structure, Directory (1985); Barry T. Hirsch & David A. Macpherson, *Union Membership, Coverage, Density, and Employment*, http://www.unionstats.com.
*Note*: The figures for nonagricultural workers are from Freeman, *supra*; the figures for 1949-1983 are from Troy & Sheflin, *supra*; the figures for 1984-2007 are from Hirsch & Macpherson, *supra*.
Prepared by Dae Hwan Kim for use in LABOR LAW IN THE CONTEMPORARY WORKPLACE.

Figure 2. NLRB Union Representation Elections and Eligible Voters, Average Number for Each Four Year Period, Fiscal Years 1937-2006

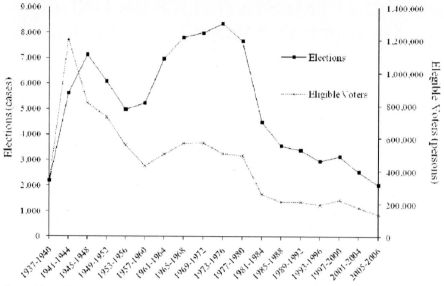

*Source*: National Labor Relations Board, Annual Reports (various years).
Prepared by Dae Hwan Kim for use in LABOR LAW IN THE CONTEMPORARY WORKPLACE.

Figure 3. NLRB Union Representation Elections: Union Win Rate and Proportion of Eligible Voters in Newly Certified Units, Average Percentage for Each Four Year Period, Fiscal Years 1937-2006

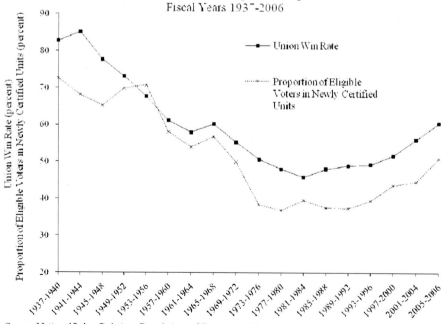

*Source*: National Labor Relations Board, Annual Reports (various years).
Prepared by Dae Hwan Kim for use in LABOR LAW IN THE CONTEMPORARY WORKPLACE.

Figure 4a  Discriminatory Discharge During NLRB Union Representation Elections. Ave
Number for Each Four Year Period, Fiscal Years 1937-2006

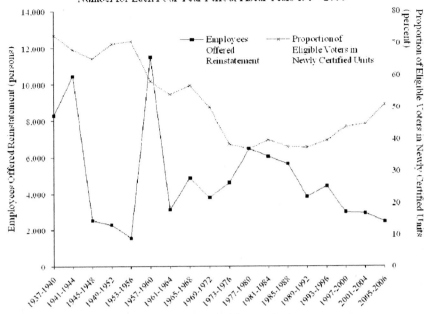

*Source*: National Labor Relations Board, Annual Reports (various years).
Prepared by Dae Hwan Kim for use in LABOR LAW IN THE CONTEMPORARY WORKPLACE.

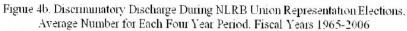

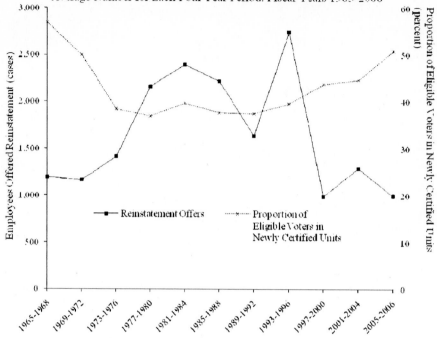

Figure 4b. Discriminatory Discharge During NLRB Union Representation Elections, Average Number for Each Four Year Period. Fiscal Years 1965-2006

*Source*: National Labor Relations Board, Annual Reports (various years).
Prepared by Dae Hwan Kim for use in LABOR LAW IN THE CONTEMPORARY WORKPLACE.

Figure 5. Average Amount of Backpay Awards, Average Number for Each Four Year
Period, Fiscal Years 1937-2006

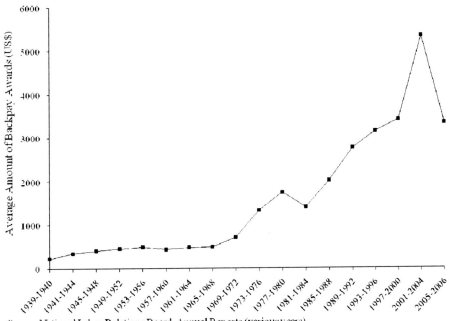

*Source*: National Labor Relations Board, Annual Reports (various years).
Prepared by Dae Hwan Kim for use in LABOR LAW IN THE CONTEMPORARY WORKPLACE.

Figure 6. Unfair Labor Practice Charges Alleged, Average Number for Each Four Year
Period, Fiscal Years 1937-2006

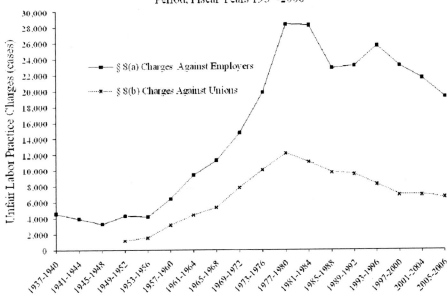

*Source*. National Labor Relations Board, Annual Reports (various years).
Prepared by Dae Hwan Kim for use in LABOR LAW IN THE CONTEMPORARY WORKPLACE.

Figure 7. Unfair Labor Practice Charges Against Employers Per NLRB Union Representation Elections, Average Number for Each Four Year Period, Fiscal Years 1937-2006

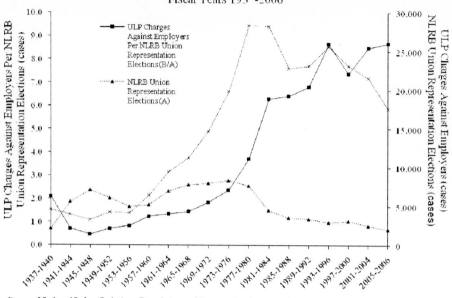

Source: National Labor Relations Board, Annual Reports (various years).
Prepared by Dae Hwan Kim for use in LABOR LAW IN THE CONTEMPORARY WORKPLACE.